Family Constellation

Its Effects on Personality and Social Behavior

Third Edition

WALTER TOMAN, Ph.D.

SPRINGER PUBLISHING COMPANY • New York

First Edition, 1961
Second Edition, 1969

German language edition published in 1974
by Verlag C. H. Beck, Munich

Springer Publishing Company, Inc.
200 Park Avenue South
New York, N.Y. 10003

79 80 / 10 9 8 7 6 5 4 3

Library of Congress Catalog Card Number: 68-57349
International Standard Book Numbers: 0-8261-0494-0 (cloth edition)
0-8261-0495-9 (paper edition)

Printed in the United States of America

PREFACE

This book, in its third completely revised edition, reports on the results of many years of research in the area of family development and family relations. Theoretical assumptions that are implicit in psychoanalytic and learning models of behavior were gradually extracted from clinical-psychological and psychotherapeutic data encountered in the author's practical work. These theoretical assumptions provided the guidelines for the systematic research that followed. They have been tested and proven valid in systematic studies of more than 3000 families. Financial support for this large systematic study came from the Deutsche Forschungsgemeinschaft. Many studies by the author's coworkers and by researchers in Europe and in the United States confirmed and supplemented the findings.

The first part, "Theory and Research," introduces the basic types of relationships that prevail between siblings, between spouses, and between children and their parents. It offers guidelines for the description and better comprehension of more complicated family situations and of losses of family members. In this context we will report on critical field experiments, some of which have been previously published in psychological journals.

The second part of the book deals with "Application and Practice." It presents detailed descriptions of the social behavior of the eight basic types of sibling positions and of the only child. It also presents the sixteen basic types of relationships between spouses and between parents and children. These descriptions demonstrate how the reader might characterize any family constellation that he knows or comes across, how he might analyze the relationships between family members and how he might interpret them, using simple rules that have been empirically tested. A few concrete examples of such analyses and interpretations are given. A chapter on quantification of characteristics of family constellations, on related theories, and on related research concludes the book.

Ever since my first publication of *Family Constellation* in 1962, interest in the topic has grown steadily. Psychologists, psychiatrists, social workers, ministers, and teachers, and many other persons have been utilizing our descriptions of family context and the individual's life situations. Professional journals have reflected a growing interest in the subject. Popular journals in Central Europe, among them *Constanze, Brigitte, Stern, Eltern, Schule, Vital,* and popular English language publications including the *London Times,* the *Sunday Express,* and in the United States, *Psychology Today, Redbook,* and *Woman's Day,* as well as radio and television stations on both sides of the Atlantic, have repeatedly reported on the subject and on our research.

Walter Toman

CONTENTS

I. Theory and Research

1.   Introduction

Every person is born into a family. This family, however, might be incomplete or become incomplete in the course of a person's life. The father, the mother, or siblings may be lost as a consequence of death, of divorce, or of other forms of separation.

On the average, in western European industrial societies man grows up in a two- or three-child family, in the United States in a three-child family, and both father and mother stay in the family. At the time of marriage, the father is approximately 27 years of age (about 26 in the U.S.), the mother is 24 years of age (23 in the U.S.). The average age difference between them is 3 years. It generally takes one to two years before the first child is born, the last child born about 7 (to 8) years after marriage. The average age difference between children is 3 to 4 years.

Parents who have more than three children tend to have married somewhat earlier. They may be married more than 7 years before they have their last child, and the age difference between their children may be 2 to 3 years.

The spouses' average age at marriage has varied somewhat not only during different periods of history, but also in different social strata. The average age difference among spouses, however, seems to have remained the same, with the husband about three years older than the wife.

In 9 out of 10 cases the family remains complete at least until the youngest child reaches adolescence. In 10% of all families with children one parent is lost through separation, divorce, or death before the child is 15 years old, in 5% even before the child has completed his 6th year of life; this includes cases where one parent is absent from the birth of the child onward. In 8 out of 10 cases the lost or missing parent is the father, in 2 out of 10 cases it is the mother.

Each parent tends to come from a family of 4 children. Generally, 2 of the 3 siblings of the parent are married. In 8 out of 10 cases they also have children.

Deviations from these averages may imply different psychological consequences. The typical ways in which parents and siblings influence each other will be described. If parents are many more than 3 years apart in age, if they have their first child at a much greater age than average parents, if the age difference between siblings is considerably more or considerably less than 3 to 4 years, if a parent or a child is lost, if such a loss occurs quite early or rather late in a person's life, the family situation is permanently altered in important aspects in comparison with the average family. It may be assumed—and it has been demonstrated in many ways (e.g. Bowlby 1951; Toman 1962a, 1965a)—that such changed family situations have different effects upon a person's social behavior both within the family and in extra-familial social contexts.

According to Hull (1943) and Freud (1916/17; also Toman 1960a, c, 1968), a person transfers or generalizes his experiences within the family to social situations outside the family, for instance to the playground, to kindergarten or school, to acquaintances he might have and to friends he might make, to groups and clubs that he joins, to his chosen work and to professional situations that he is partly in a position to choose to be a part of, and which he attends, at any rate, day after day, often for many years.

Apart from the effect of people on the individual,

residences and changes of residence as well as illnesses involving temporary separations from the family may play a part. On the average, a youth experiences one or two changes of residence before his fifteenth year. During that time, he has usually suffered about three illnesses or accidents that did not require hospitalization, and one illness or accident that did. Hospitalization lasted an average of four weeks.

Deviations from these averages, such as a larger number of changes of residence or of hospitalizations, may (adversely) affect a person's social behavior (Toman & Preiser 1973). On the other hand, no changes of residence and few or no illnesses may affect a person's social behavior more favorably.

The purpose of this book is to describe the most important and most easily distinguishable effects of various different social and family environments. We proceed from the assumption that a person's family represents the most influential context of his life, and that it exerts its influence more regularly, more exclusively, and earlier in a person's life than do any other life contexts. Playground, school, college, organizations and clubs, employment, and so on become effective only much later in a person's life, only for part of the day, and often only for limited periods of time. The family context usually persists even at those times. Generally speaking, the individual remains a physical member of the family far into adulthood, although admittedly for increasingly shorter and more irregular periods of time.

One may assume that it is the early and more pervasive life contexts rather than contexts emerging relatively late and more sporadically that serve as a basis for generalizations of past experiences to new contexts. The family's influence on a person's behavior in school is usually greater than the school's influence on his behavior in the family. A person's experiences at home and in school are more likely to be transferred to his job situation than are his experiences at work to his experiences in school or at home.

This is not to say that events occurring later in a person's life can exert any influence whatsoever on events that had taken place earlier. The past can no longer be changed. Only a person's interpretation of the past can be changed. From his experiences at school and at work a person may be able to reevaluate retrospectively some of his experiences at home. Even his relationships to members of his family may be considerably modified. We should expect, however, that these modified relationships will exert weaker influences on that person's future life in his family and on his behavior in contexts outside the family than would his original early relationships to family members. This does not mean to imply an inescapable determinism, but recent and contemporary influences should not be overestimated in view of the early influences that have been having their effect for much longer. The effects of the latter are often covert. They appear in sentiments and attitudes, in basic wishes and interests of which the person may be partly unaware. They do affect his social behavior, and, to be sure, they often do so more strongly, the less conscious they are.

2.   Persons Comprising a Family

As outlined before, most families are composed of a father, a mother, and several children. Most often the father is the bread-winner and the mother takes care of the house and the children, at least until the youngest child has started to go to school. In the long run and under the given circumstances, this seems to be the most popular and possibly the optimal solution in most nations. There is nothing intrinsically abnormal in a father taking care of the house and of the children while the mother holds a job, although this seems to be the exception. Such a couple must be prepared, at any rate, to be viewed as odd by other families or by other children; they should be aware that such evaluations by the environment may create some problems for their own children.

If both parents are working, they will have to entrust their children to the care of somebody else, and thereby they will lose a portion of their parental role. Those persons who take care of the children are likely to become their psychological parents. They and their life and family situations may exert a greater influence on the children than do the actual parents and their life and family situations.

An average and intact family with several children may differ significantly from another average intact family in the age sequence and sex distribution of their children. Let us briefly consider families with only two children. They may have two boys, two girls, or a boy and a girl. In the latter case, either the boy or the girl may be the elder child. A family with three children may have three boys, two boys and a girl, a boy and two girls, or three girls, whereby sibling configurations of both boys and girls can come in several varieties. With two boys and a girl, for instance, the girl can be the eldest, the middle, or the youngest child. Analogously, with a boy and two girls, the boy can be the oldest, the middle, or the youngest among the siblings. In other words, when we consider the age rank and the sex of a child alone, three children can come in 8 different combinations. Generally speaking, a given configuration of siblings is one of 2^n possible configurations of siblings, where n is the number of children.

A given child in a two-child family can be a boy or a girl. If it is a boy, he can be the older or the younger of the two children, and he may have a brother or a sister for a sibling. The same holds for a girl. She can be the older or the younger sister either of a brother or of another sister. In short: in a family with two children, a given child can assume one of four possible positions.

If a child—let us say a boy—comes from a three-child family, he may be the oldest, the middle, or the youngest child, and he may have two brothers, two sisters, a brother and a sister, or a sister and a brother. Thus the given boy can assume one of three possible age-rank positions and he can have one of four possible configurations of siblings. In other words, he is holding one of 12 possible positions. The same would be true of a girl. More generally speaking, a given person holds one of $n \cdot 2^{n-1}$ possible positions in his sibling configuration, where n is again the number of children in that configuration.

The number of possible sibling positions increases with an increasing number of children. A child with four siblings, such as a child in a configuration of five children, holds one of $5 \cdot 2^4$ possible positions. That makes one of 80 possibilities.

In the course of a description of all the possibilities we may easily lose perspective. We shall therefore choose the two-child family as a paradigm in examining all its possible sibling positions.

Two Brothers

Let us look first at the older and the younger brother of two brothers.

The older brother of a brother has to get used to life with a child of his own sex when his new sibling is born. Under ordinary circumstances, he is about three years old at the time this happens. By the time he is six years old, he has shared three years of life with his brother, or half of his own life, and his younger brother has shared all three years of his. It would be strange if the two did not somehow learn to get along with each other. It is also likely, however, that they will approach new relationships outside the family, say with playmates or other peers, according to the expectations they have developed at home with each other.

Under ordinary circumstances the older brother of a brother learns, among other things, to assume responsibility and leadership vis-à-vis his brother. The parents demand that he heed the little one's interests, that he protect him, and that he give him things even if he gets nothing in return, or, at best, only a little praise from his parents. He must renounce certain things in the younger brother's favor without, at first, understanding why. He does not like this, but through identification with his parents he gets used to the idea. As he gets older, it becomes progressively easier for him to extract favors in return from the little one and even to win the parents' support in this. He enjoys the fact that his little brother accepts his leadership and his responsible role.

The little one may even consider him his idol. In some matters and at some times, however, the younger brother will challenge the older brother, reject his leads and his care, and begin to compete with him. This the older brother will not like very well.

The power conflicts between the two will be milder and their personalities will develop into greater mutual independence if the two brothers are four or five years apart in age. In this case, however, the older brother is particularly aware from the start that they have only one woman to share among three men and that they will have to be satisfied with only a portion of the mother's attention and time. If, on the other hand, the two brothers are only one or two years apart in age, their conflicts become particularly intense, although they are only vaguely conscious of them. In this case the two do not fight as much for a fair give-and-take nor for who will show the greater achievement, but for which one will get the most.

The younger brother of a brother has lived with an older, taller, smarter, stronger, more perfect boy than himself as far back as he can remember. This may not dawn on him during his first year of life, when his mother is around most of his waking hours, but in his second and third year his father and his "big brother" enter significantly into his life. The younger brother will of course notice that he is under the protection of his big brother outside the house, but at home and in the family, where he spends more of his time at first than anywhere else, he does not need all that protection. On the contrary, the two get into each other's way. As long as the younger brother does not find ways to play by himself, the older brother forces his will upon him. He also urges him unconsciously to do things as well as or even better than he can, and to become as big and smart and strong as he is as quickly as possible.

The younger brother succeeds only superficially in the beginning. He may even be ridiculed for his efforts. The need, however, to catch up with his brother, even to overtake him, or at least to oppose or resist him at times, may stay with him and carry over to his future interactions with peers outside the family.

The parents themselves are inclined to present the older brother as an example and idol to the younger brother; at the same time, they also tend to be more tolerant and ready to take the younger son's part than that of the older one. Since the mother is the only female in the house, there is more rivalry among the brothers for her favor than there is in other families. In comparison to other family constellations, actual contact with their mother, as well as the possibilities of practicing "contact with females" with each other by means of role playing, are reduced. To them a woman seems harder to reach and to understand than she does to children in other sibling positions.

In summary we can say that, through their experiences in the family, the older and the younger brother of brothers are well prepared for contacts with peers of the same sex, but not with peers of the opposite sex. The older brother has learned to lead and to assume responsibility for peers of the same sex; the younger one has learned to imitate, to follow his brother and boys in general, and to compete with and to oppose them as well.

Brother and Sister

A brother and a sister arrange their life with each other differently.

The older brother of a sister has also been around for about three years before his sibling appears. About this time or soon thereafter he realizes that there are two sexes in his family and elsewhere. He may therefore soon feel happy about the sex of his sibling. He and his sister are, after all, something like father and mother. A little girl seems to deserve the abundant care her mother offers her. Father, too, usually treats mother with tenderness and consideration. He, the older brother of a sister, does not have to compete with his little sister. What he learns to do for her will be repaid by her love and affection. She will love him as his mother loves his father.

These are rather common ideas among older brothers of sisters in their early lives. He is not only being groomed for a role of caring and helping, but also for leading and taking charge vis-à-vis a girl.

He can more easily accept his little sister if he is four or five years older than she, even if he does experience conflicts more consciously and more clearly than a boy who is closer to his sister in age. If, on the other hand, he is merely one or two years older than she, the sex of his sibling escapes his notice at first. The baby is a competitor for the favor and affection of the parents, even a rival for sheer food. Under this frightening situation, it may take longer than usual (that is, some time up to his fifth year) to lose his fear that his parents favor his sister, that she receives more than he ever did, and that she is called upon far less to work and apply herself.

The younger sister of a brother tends to develop into a particularly feminine person. She learns to look up to her brother and to accept not only his protection and care, but also his leadership. She seems to know that he likes her and that she can depend on him. There are things she need not do, such as hard physical work or tasks where she may get dirty. She need not fend for herself, for instance with other children at home or on the playground. Her brother takes care of that.

Her father and mother are usually content with the role she plays. She is the little darling of the family. Her father is kind, helpful, and forgiving, and her mother also does not object to her daughter's special treatment. All family members seem to recognize that they can practice relationships with the other sex in various ways: brother and sister can play father and mother with each other. The brother can also play father vis-à-vis mother, the sister mother via-à-vis father. The brother can usually identify easily with his father, the sister with her mother.

In summary we may say that both siblings, the older brother of a sister and the younger sister of a brother, get used to life with a peer of the opposite sex. The brother also tends to assume a role of leadership and responsibility with girls other than his sister. The younger sister of a brother, in turn, is likely to let other boys lead and spoil her. Outside the family both siblings remain more interested in contacts with peers of the opposite sex than with those of the same sex.

Sister and Brother

A sister and a brother arrange their lives with each other in still another way.

The older sister of a brother will generally be three years old when her sibling arrives, and it soon dawns on her that his sex has its advantages. She can play mother for her little brother, just as mother does with both of them and with father. She has to take care of the little one, has to guard and protect him and will be held responsible for him by the parents, but she also gets a little in return: he looks up to her. He appreciates and loves her and before long learns to do her courtesies and favors too, however slight and shallow they may be. The older sister seems to realize that her younger brother, being the first and only boy in the family, tends to be taken more seriously and to be valued somewhat higher than herself. If she wants to be sure of her parents' affection, she must take care of him.

If she is four or five years older than her brother, she becomes accustomed to the situation even more quickly than if the age difference is only three years, but this does not mean that there are no fights and quarrels. In fact, the two siblings speak their minds in no uncertain terms at times. If the age difference between the sister and the brother is merely one or two years, then the sister feels more threatened by his arrival and has trouble expressing her feelings. She may take up to her fifth year of life to get used to her little brother before she is able to adopt a nurturing attitude toward him. In each case, the role of maternal care and responsibility as well as an awareness of her somewhat lesser importance in the family stays with her far into adulthood. She can handle boys well anywhere. She senses their interests, may even adopt those interests herself and subordinate her own. She can identify more readily than other girls with "her boys' " successes, especially when they accept her nurturance and care. She can give them comfort and consolation, and does it with a certain satisfaction. When other people are in trouble, they come to her, and she likes that.

The younger brother of a sister is usually allowed to pursue his own wishes and interests in a rather carefree and sometimes even in a selfish or incoherent manner. He is treated more tolerantly and more generously than his big sister, and frequently more so than, say, a younger brother of a brother. The younger brother of a sister increasingly learns to understand his sister better, but he does so ultimately for his own purposes. He tends to take her help and motherly care as a matter of course. If he cannot get what he wants, he finds ways to lure his sister or other girls into acting as mother on his behalf. A little pretense of helplessness or a minor compliment may already do the trick.

There are also good possibilities for identification and interaction with the parents in this configuration. The older sister can play mother for her brother or her father; the brother, in turn, could play father for his sister and his mother. The sister does this, but the brother tends not to, and may encounter some disapproval over his reluctance or tardiness. He is accused of selfishness and indifference. He does not think of others enough. He does whatever he pleases. He lets them help and wait on him.

In conclusion, we can say that the younger brother of a sister and the older sister of a brother both remain more interested in contacts with peers of the opposite sex than of the same sex. Even outside the family the sister tends to wish to direct and care for boys and young men, whereas the brother is likely to entice girls and women to mother and spoil him while he continues to do what he wants without much regard for others.

Parents, incidentally, tend to approve of such a course of development, since the brother is the younger and smaller one. Some parents are initially disturbed by the fact that the relationship between their children is the converse of roles assumed in conventional families in that the daughter becomes the leader and assumes responsibilities, whereas the son appears to be volatile, carefree, and reliant on others in everyday life situations. However, eventually they become used to the idea. Their response depends on their own experiences with siblings (see chapter 8). At worst, the children's identification with their parents will be hampered, in comparison to other two-child family configurations. The parents' relationship with each other does not become the model for the relationship between their children. The two pairs regard each other with some surprise, but they do not substitute for each other. If, however, the parents themselves can accept the reversal of authority that they observe between their children, possibly because they themselves have this kind of relationship with each other, then all those options for identification and interaction between parents and children are open that prevail in the relationship described above between an older brother and his younger sister. The son can play father—although not a very authoritative father—for his sister and his mother and the daughter can play mother for her brother and her father.

Two Sisters

Two sisters are in yet another different situation.

The older sister of a sister has also been around for an average of three years before the younger sister is born. She has an advantage of height, strength, and intelligence over the little one that diminishes only in the course of years. Like other oldest siblings, however, she must cope with the shock of having a competitor for her parents' time and attention. Depending on the age difference between her and her sister, she may feel cheated of her parents' affection and loving care (when the difference is one or two years), shaken in her control over her parents and in her "negotiating position" (when the difference is two or three years), or she may feel her relationship to her father threatened by yet another rival for his love in addition to her mother (when the two sisters are four or five years apart). She notices long before her little sister does that the three of them, mother, sister and herself, will have to share the father's affection and attention.

The larger the age gap is between the two sisters, the more conscious will the older girl be of her experiences of conflict with her younger sister and with her parents; at the same time, it is that much easier for her to accept and handle these conflicts. Sooner or later she learns to overcome her jealousy and to assume responsibility for her little sister. She has to play a parental role for her, mostly that of the mother. She may also become an idol for her little sister in the process, may order her around, and the little one will have to obey. This is how the parents want it. Since the older sister also identifies with the father, she is likely to treat her little sister a bit harshly at times. The older sister deals with her younger sister the way she has observed her father deal with her mother or with herself. She notices with astonishment, envy, and sorrow that her father is milder and more tolerant in his contacts with her little sister than he is with her mother or with herself. She suspects him of favoritism: she believes he loves the little sister more dearly than her mother or herself.

The younger sister of a sister grows up in an atmosphere of greater freedom than did the older sister, but she is also dependent upon her. At first she accepts the authority of her big sister; she wants to emulate her; she has no qualms about being helped by her. As time goes on, however, she tries to assert herself, to do things as well or even better than she sees her sister do them, and to oppose her sister. The younger sister of a sister learns how to resist and to oppose others, but she remains largely dependent upon their suggestions and ideas. Her own plans are made in response to plans of her sister and other members of the family. Often she has to know what her big sister wants before she can tell what she wants herself.

The younger sister is more likely than the older one to become the parents' darling, particularly her father's. The older sister is expected to obey the parents, to identify with them, to renounce her wishes in favor of the younger child. The parents remain more tolerant vis-à-vis the younger one even after she has grown up. They do not insist as adamantly on obedience to them and to their example as they do with their older daughter. They seem to have an unconscious feeling that the younger one is permitted to do what she likes; thus, they may even encourage their younger daughter to become impulsive, ambitious, and obstinate.

One can say, in summary, that both sisters learn about the relationship between man and woman only indirectly, that is, only by observing their parents. Both sisters are better prepared for contacts with peers of the same sex than with those of the opposite sex. Having been her father's favorite, however, the younger sister has a certain advantage in her dealings with boys and men. On the other hand, her ambition and competitiveness may undo her advantage. She seems to want too much. She wants too many boys to like her, and at the same time she cannot resist competing with them.

A Person with Several Siblings of the Same Type

The sibling positions and their psychological and behavior characteristics also apply if a person has not one, but two or three siblings of the same type. The *oldest brother of two or three sisters* develops similar social preferences as does the older brother of just one sister. The same is true for the *youngest brother of several sisters*. In both instances, though, the brother's position may be considered more pronounced than in a two-child family. He becomes more "precious" to the family because he is the only boy, while there are several girls.

Both the oldest brother of several sisters and the youngest brother of several sisters obviously learn from several siblings what role they are to take. They come to know more facets of the relationship between girls and boys. They may even learn how to play one girl against another. This generally makes the characteristics of their sibling positions clearer than those of a brother of but one sister, yet they are similar.

The oldest brother of several brothers and the *youngest brother of several brothers* may also vary in their relationships to their siblings. The oldest brother is the oldest for all of them. Each brother has to establish some relationship with him. Each of them had for a time been the youngest, and for each of them he was and is the biggest among the brothers. Generally, his bigness becomes more impressive for a younger brother, the later his entry into the sibling configuration occurs. Similarly, the youngest brother is the youngest for all of them, although the oldest brother usually gets used to his existence more easily than, say, the second youngest. Here, too, we may expect that the oldest brother of several brothers is more distinct in his characteristics than the oldest brother of a family with just two boys. Similarly, the youngest brother of brothers will often appear to be more typical than the youngest brother of just one older brother.

The same holds true for girls. The *oldest sister of several brothers* is usually more caring, more responsible and ready for leadership vis-à-vis men than is the oldest sister of but one brother. The *youngest sister of several brothers* often shows a greater need for dependence, but also seems to be more feminine and spoiled than the younger sister of only one brother. *The oldest sister of several sisters* is more strongly identified with her parents or with her father and makes an even more domineering appearance than does the older sister of just one sister. The *youngest sister of several sisters* tends to be even more ambitious, more in need of guidance and more ready to take opposition than is the younger sister of one sister. Both the oldest and the youngest sister of several sisters are better used to dealing with persons of the same sex and less accustomed to contacts with males than are the older or the younger sister of just one sister.

In all these cases subgroups may form among the siblings. In a configuration of four children, for example, the oldest child may focus on one of his siblings, perhaps on the youngest or on the second youngest. The other two siblings may form a secondary group. A youngest sibling may lean heavily on one of his older siblings and ignore the others. All this depends on aspects that will be discussed in a later section of this chapter. One aspect, however, must be taken up at once.

Just as the oldest child—who, after all, started out as a single child—may have been upset by the arrival of a sibling and may develop conflicts with him, the second child is upset by, and in conflict over, the arrival of the third, and the n-th child by the arrival of the (n + 1)th child. He (or she) recognizes that his part as the youngest is over, even if he does try to hold on to it for a while longer. This is no longer much of a problem for the older siblings. The more siblings they see arrive, the less they suffer from the arrival of each new one.

It seems obvious that a child can accept his second-youngest or third-youngest sibling more easily than the sibling immediately succeeding him. This is true at least if all successive siblings are of the same sex as the next youngest. In their affinities and affections among each other, siblings are sometimes inclined to skip the closest in age among the younger ones. Among five siblings, for example, the first and the third may form one subgroup, the second and the fifth another, and the fourth child may remain an isolated or merely tolerated hanger-on of one of the subgroups.

Multiple Sibling Positions

We have come to know eight types of sibling position: the oldest brother of brothers, the youngest brother of brothers, the oldest brother of sisters, the youngest brother of sisters, the oldest sister of sisters, the youngest sister of sisters, the oldest sister of brothers, and the youngest sister of brothers. If there are more than two children in the family, the sibling configuration must be made up of one or more of these eight basic types. A given person in a sibling configuration may simultaneously have several sibling relationships, not only of the same type, but of different types as well. Let us call them multiple sibling positions. We may expect that the sibling relationships described for the eight basic types of sibling positions will combine in some fashion in multiple sibling positions. A person holding such a multiple position may show characteristics and preferences of social behavior that correspond to two or more of the basic types of sibling relationships.

Multiple distal sibling positions are the multiple positions held by the oldest or by the youngest siblings. Within the family situation, the oldest brother of both brothers and sisters can obviously learn how to play the senior, how to lead and to assume responsibility for boys as well as for girls. The youngest brother of brothers and sisters gets used to being carefree and unconcerned vis-à-vis peers of both sexes. The oldest sister of brothers and sisters can act motherly, responsibly, and as a leader with both boys and girls alike, and the youngest sister of brothers and sisters will be not only submissive and dependent, but also ambitious and opposing toward peers of both sexes.

Multiple nondistal or *middle sibling positions* comprising two types of sibling relationships include the middle brother of brothers, the middle brother of an older brother and a younger sister, the middle brother of an older sister and a younger brother, and the middle brother of two sisters.

I am sure the reader can visualize for himself what combinations of characteristics and behavior preferences can be expected with each of the middle positions listed. The same would hold for a middle sister, who may have sisters only, older brothers and younger sisters, older sisters and younger brothers, or brothers only.

Middle sibling positions comprising three types of relationships are all those just mentioned, with the addition of one of the two missing types of siblings. For example, a middle brother of older and younger brothers may also have older sisters, or a middle sister of older brothers and younger sisters may also have younger brothers, etc. An observer may find it difficult to distinguish the characteristics and preferences attributable to each of these roles or sibling relationships when there are so many that a middle sibling may assume among his brothers and/or sisters. The roles mingle, and the person in question does not hold a distinct position among his siblings. The more pronounced roles, such as those of the oldest girl, the oldest boy, the youngest girl, or the youngest boy, have been taken by other siblings.

This becomes most apparent with a person who has older and younger brothers as well as older and younger sisters. He is absolutely in the middle. He is prepared for all types of relationships: for those with older and with younger peers, male and female alike. It can be expected that he will not feel unhappy with any type of relationship he may enter later in his life, but he will not be exuberantly happy either. In any single given relationship to another person he might be missing all those respective relationships that remain unrealized. A middle brother of older and younger brothers as well as sisters who befriends an older sister of brothers, for example, may miss being able to behave and respond the way he did to his younger sisters, and he may also miss the company of boys and men.

These middle siblings may feel overlooked or excluded even while they are still in the family. They think they notice that they matter the least among their siblings. Hence they may long to leave the family earlier in life than their siblings would. They may move out, move far away, or opt for a professional career quite different from that of the rest of the family.

Families with many children naturally have more middle siblings than do families with fewer children. In this case it is important to note their position relative to the rest of the siblings. A person may have not only an older brother and an older sister, but also three younger brothers and four younger sisters. By definition he holds a middle sibling position, but he is near the upper end in the age sequence of his siblings. We can assume that he, more than other middle siblings such as the third or fourth youngest in his sibling configuration, may also become an identification figure for the younger ones, may assume roles of leadership and responsibility and identify with the parents himself. On the other hand, the third or fourth youngest, who are also middle siblings by definition, but who are surrounded by a larger number of older than of younger siblings, may sooner learn to behave like younger siblings.

In large sibling configurations, therefore, middle siblings may differ from other middle siblings. They may either be older middle siblings or younger middle siblings.

The Size of a Sibling Configuration

Sibling configurations range from the single child, who will be discussed later and may be said to have no sibling position at all, to some fifteen children. Configurations of five or more children, however, occur only in 10% of the families with children. In urban Central Europe, the average family has two or three children; the average family in the U.S. has three.

In larger families, that is, those with five and more children, the number of middle siblings necessarily increases. With three children, there is one middle sibling, with four children there are two, with n children, there are n-2 middle siblings. The probability of multiple distal sibling positions increases at the same time. The oldest child of four siblings may have four brothers, three brothers and a sister, two brothers and two sisters, one brother and three sisters, or four sisters. There are a total of 2^4 different possibilities of arranging four children each of whom may be either a boy or a girl. Apart from sibling groups of four boys or of four girls, there are 14 other configurations containing both sexes. Thus, the probability of an oldest sibling having brothers as well as sisters among four siblings is 14/16, or 87%. In contrast, if an oldest child has only two siblings, these may be two brothers, a brother and a sister, a sister and a brother, or two sisters. Two of these four sets contain siblings of only one sex, and two of them contain both sexes. The probability that the oldest of three siblings has brothers as well as sisters is therefore 2/4 or 50%, in other words, much smaller than with the oldest of four other siblings.

If each sibling can develop a relationship to every other sibling in his configuration, there is still only one relationship between two siblings. There are three relationships between three siblings, six between four, ten between five, or, generally speaking, $\binom{n}{2}$ possible relationships between siblings. Among four siblings, say two brothers and two sisters, the oldest brother has a relationship to his younger brother and to each of his two sisters, the younger brother to his older brother and also to each of his sisters, and so on. Thus there are twelve relationships but since each of these relationships comes up twice, the number must be divided in half.

One may gather from this how much more complicated and variegated family life would have to be in families with many children as compared to those with few. Moreover, every child also develops a relationship to his father and his mother, and all of these relationships may differ from one another.

It has been pointed out that families with many children have more middle siblings and those children, especially those absolutely in the middle, are in danger of being ignored and isolated. Their position seems to be too ambiguous. They represent something different for each type of sibling they have. The siblings with the more prominent positions seem to feel that the middle siblings are there for all of them and therefore actually for none of them.

This need not always be so. Rather larger sibling configurations tend to split into subgroups. Six siblings may form two groups of three children each. The fourth oldest could thus become a kind of oldest sibling himself: the oldest of the little ones.

This type of splitting into subgroups depends among other things upon the age difference between siblings. The larger the age difference is between two successive (adjacent) siblings in comparison with the age differences between the other siblings the more likely will it effect a split in the sibling configuration, a separation into subgroups, at precisely this point. If the age difference between the first three of six siblings were two years respectively, and if the fourth child were five years younger than the third, with the fifth and sixth again each two years younger than the next oldest, then the first three siblings would probably form one subgroup and the next three another.

There may be other reasons for subdivision in larger sibling configurations, such as physical characteristics, intelligence, vitality, looks, and likenesses with other family members. These characteristics are generally independent of the characteristics of sibling positions. This point will be taken up later (page 67).

Parents, too, may effect subdivisions. Their own preferences of social behavior may result in different amounts of time, attention, and favors that they give to different children. Parents may get along better with some of their children than with others. They may be able to identify easily with some, and poorly with others. If, however, the child happens to be unconsciously preferred by one or both parents, he or she may also have greater authority over the siblings, may attract some and ignore others. The ways in which parents may exert influences upon their children will be dealt with separately in chapter 8.

From what we have said so far it might seem as if smaller or larger configurations of children simply existed and exercised their effects or were themselves being affected in a relatively constant manner. This may be so, once the parents have decided to have no more children. Until then, however, or, in other words, while the configuration of children is still changing, the parents determine what will happen not only by interacting with their children, but also by deciding to have another child either now or at a later date.

The fact that the sex of the already existing children plays a role in the parents' decision to have more children has been clearly demonstrated in the actual birth sequences.

In a sample of family constellations taken in Nürnberg and Zürich (see also chapter 10), all those families whose child configurations started with a boy were singled out, as were all those families whose child configurations started with a girl. We then tested how many more children these families had. Those parents whose oldest child was a boy had an average of 1.51 more children, those whose oldest child was a girl had an average of 1.38 more children. Next, we singled out those families whose configurations of children started with two boys or with two girls in succession. Two boys in succession were followed by an average of 1.07 children, whereas two girls in succession at the start were followed by only 0.71 children. Finally we singled out those families who had three boys initially and those who first had three girls. Three boys were followed by an average of 1.06 additional children, three girls by an average of only 0.50 additional children.

According to appropriate statistical frequency tests, these differences in number of subsequent children were highly significant (Toman 1971, Toman & Preiser 1973). Sibling configurations starting with boys clearly tended to be larger than those beginning with girls. Whether this means that parents whose first children are girls tend to stop having children sooner than other parents because they want a son but do not believe they will have one, or whether parents whose first children are boys continue to have more children because they also want a daughter is still not known. It could also be that more "vital" parents, i.e., those who want to have more children to begin with, happen to have more boys.

Only Children

An only child has no sibling position. Oldest siblings have been single children for a while but were dethroned when their first sibling arrived. The only child, however, retains his privileged position. His main contacts are his parents. They devote more time, more attention, more affection to him than parents do to a given child in a larger sibling configuration, even if these latter parents spend a larger total of time, attention, and affection on their children. An individual child has to share all that with others and thus gets less for himself.

In his family, the only child is not or is only indirectly prepared for contacts with peers. He learns how a man and a woman relate to each other by observing his parents, but he has little opportunity to practice it with other children. Nursery school and kindergarten usually give him his first opportunity. It is here that only children experience the shock for the first time that they are not the only ones vying for the adults' (the teachers') attention. However, they are only exposed to this disturbing situation for a few hours a day and not even every day of the week. At home they command their parents' entire attention. Children with siblings, on the other hand, have had their shock right in the family and can accept the presence of other children, even of many other children such as in kindergarten or in school, more easily than only children can.

Of course, single children too can get accustomed to a new social environment, but they do so by establishing relatively stronger contacts with the teacher than with other children. Only children frequently know better than other children how to handle adults, or how to involve them for their own purposes. Thus they often impress other children as being do-gooders, egotists, or the favorites of the adults.

More than other children of their age, only children look and act like little adults themselves. This is not only because they have usually spent more time with their parents than children who have siblings, but also because they can learn how to behave toward a parent as the other parent would and not as another child does. There are no other children to identify with. An only child behaves toward his father the way his mother does, and vice versa. He can also make his parents help and protect him and do things for him more readily than other children can make their parents. Only children are the focus of their parents' attention anyway. They don't have to share their parents with other children. Cousins and other children may come to their house, to be sure, but they don't stay for long, and the only child clearly recognizes that he does not have to compete with these other children for his parents' favor.

Outside the family, only children often continue to get special treatment. As at home, they want to be in the limelight, under the guidance and protection of older people or people in positions of authority. They strive to find recognition for what they want or do not want to do. They can attract "followers" and take on leadership roles for their peers to the degree to which they identify with adults, with authority figures, or with subject matters. Even then, they unconsciously value the understanding of their superiors more than that of those in their charge.

An only child may differ from another only child. This depends, among other things, upon the sibling position of his same-sex parent. If the father of a male only child is an oldest brother of brothers, through identification with his father the son may assume features, attitudes, and preferences of an oldest brother of brothers. If the mother of a female only child is the youngest sister of brothers, the daughter will become a mixture of an only child and a youngest sister of brothers. She may be less egotistical and moody than other female single children. If the same-sex parent of an only child was an only child himself, then the child tends to show the characteristics and social behavior of an only child to a marked degree.

There may be not only medical and economic, but also psychological reasons behind the parents' choice to have but one child. Conflicts among the parents, losses suffered by one or both of them in their early lives, or other traumatic conditions seem to discourage parents from having more children. In these cases one might view the family with an only child as a mild form of a disturbed family.

On the average, we can say that only children have been more poorly prepared for contacts with peers than children with any other sibling position; they prefer contacts with older persons or people in high positions, or with peers who are willing to play the role of father or mother for them.

Twins

About 1 percent of all children born are twins. In other words, they are rare. Triplets, quadruplets, or quintuplets are even rarer. Animals, however, frequently have twins, quintuplets, or even litters of ten or twelve. Very few animals bear one young at a time. But even if they do, the second-born does not become a sibling of the first-born the way it happens in a human family. We will come back to this subject in chapter 5 (p.72).

As a rule, twins live with each other from birth on. They have experiences that are different from those of other siblings. Siblings with an age difference can avoid each other to some extent. Depending on the size of that age difference, the older of two siblings is more-or-less established when the younger one is born. The younger one diverts a lot of his parents' attention to himself, but there are areas, such as the general use of the house or the apartment, where the younger one cannot interfere at first. He sleeps more and at different times than the oldest sibling and the parents, he is fed at different times, he cannot yet run around the house, etc. At dinner, on walks, on the playground, on the way to and from kindergarten or school the younger one is usually not present.

This is different with twins. They are always a twosome. They are born practically at the same time, even if the family tends to "force" one of them to be the older and the other the younger one. Two ordinary siblings are also a twosome, but the older one has had several years of experience as a single child. He knows what he has lost and what he dislikes about his sibling. He can wish him (or her) "to get lost," since he has known a time when he was "lost," that is, nonexistent. In contrast, the youngest sibling has considerable difficulties imagining life without his older sibling. He may get an inkling of it through identifying with his older sibling, by vicarious action or imitation. In that case, he may even adopt the ways in which the older sibling tries to solve his conflicts with him.

Twins cannot do that. Developmentally they are on the same level. Neither has the advantage of greater physical or mental power, or experience. They can learn little from each other in their dealings with their physical and social environment that they would not learn all by themselves. What they can do, however, is to resist control by others, and even to manipulate others themselves by acting alike and "in collusion." They are two, and that helps. Other children have to do it alone.

We have already indicated that the environment tries to handle twins as if they were ordinary siblings. The family appoints one of the twins to be the older and the other to be the younger sibling, even if they are identical twins. In cases of nonidentical twins, the age difference (of perhaps half an hour) or likenesses with certain family members, differences in physical height, intelligence, or vitality may play a part. If the twins are a boy and a girl (which means that they are definitely nonidentical twins), the authority-preferences of the parents tend to determine what age ranks the twins will be given. If the father was the oldest and the mother the youngest among their siblings, they are likely to make the boy the senior and the girl the junior sibling even if their actual birth order was the reverse.

In such a way twins who have no other siblings may assume characteristics of the basic types of sibling positions. Yet more frequently they meet the world as a pair, especially if they are identical twins. They have always been a pair, and they find it hard to imagine life without the other. Therefore they take longer than other siblings to separate in their youth or adulthood. More than do others, they seek out siblings or even twins for friends as well as for lovers and spouses.

Twins may have other siblings. In that case, both of

them take on the characteristics of the social behavior that a single person would in their sibling position. When the twins are, say, the oldest boys and have two younger sisters and a younger brother, they learn to take the roles of oldest brothers of brothers and of sisters. When the twins are girls and have come after an oldest sister, both of them are likely to assume the features of younger sisters of sisters.

What has been said of twins applies for triplets and quadruplets as well. Their relationships to each other, however, are more complex and variegated. They also remain more detached from other siblings, if they have any, than do twins. They mean more work for the parents, to be sure. They really do take their parents away from their siblings to a greater extent than twins do. The other siblings notice this and try to put up a common front against the triplets or quadruplets.

Triplets and quadruplets are so rare that it is difficult to recognize and confirm common trends. The environment responds to quadruplets—and especially to quintuplets—with greater interest than to twins or individual children. The rare event mobilizes agencies, the mass media, and donors with or without ulterior motives, all of whom may bring about a drastic change in the life of the family concerned. Therefore we will say no more about triplets, quadruplets, or quintuplets.

In their relationship with each other, twins should be viewed as siblings. One should try to determine by observation and inquiry which one plays the part of the senior, of the sibling in charge, and which one plays the part of the junior, of the impulsive and dependent one. Beyond that one also has to find out the position the twins might have among their other siblings. Both twins are likely to adopt the social behavior and interaction preferences that correspond to their overall sibling position.

Age Differences

We have already discussed age differences between siblings (p. 11ff and p. 24f). The conflicts arising between successive siblings vary according to the age difference between them.

When the youngest sibling is born only one or two years after the oldest, the latter sees his sibling as a rival for the care, attention, and affection of his parents as well as for their free gifts and favors, even for food.

When the difference in age is three or four years, the older of two siblings feels threatened in his power and control over his parents. Greed for food and the need for affection and help are less important now. The older sibling is irked by the fact that the parents set up tasks for him (or her), but not for the younger one. He must offer returns for parental favors, whereas the younger one gets them for free. The older sibling recognizes, however, that he can also get returns from his parents, among other things, for helping and protecting the younger sibling.

If two siblings are four or five years apart, the older one has usually learned to respond sex-specifically to his parents and to other people by the time the younger one arrives. An atmosphere of competition and power continues to prevail in dealings with persons of the same sex, albeit in a more civilized form than before, but there is now more of an atmosphere of tenderness, courtship, or waiting for such attention in contacts with persons of the opposite sex. A boy or a man should treat a girl or a woman nicely. A girl should appear pretty and gentle and may pass out favors or withhold them as she pleases. A boy may not. Men and women seem to come in pairs. Father and mother are also such a pair. The child himself might form such a pair with one of his parents, even better with another child, say, his sibling. This is how children of four and five begin to see things.

If this is really the case, it seems possible that the older sibling may recognize the sex of his younger sibling in its consequences right from his birth, and not merely a few years later, as do siblings with smaller age differences. The family situation can improve or worsen depending on the sex of the second-born. The child's family changes to either one with three persons of one sex and one person of the other whose attention and affection will be sought even more vehemently, or to a family of two persons of one sex and two persons of the other sex. The latter case may smooth things out.

If the age difference between successive siblings is six or more years, the two tend to become something less than full-fledged siblings for each other. The older one is hardly affected by the younger child. He (or she) has started to go to kindergarten or school and has already set up his domain or territory at home. Not only can he do without his parents for the time he spends in classes; even at home he has no insatiable need for parental attention. It takes perhaps another two years before the younger sibling can seriously get in his way. At that time, though, the older child is engaged in activities and concerned about "property" and possessions of a kind that do not automatically attract the younger sibling's spontaneous interest and wants.

At any rate, siblings who are six or more years apart tend to become quasi-only children, unless one or both of them happen to be surrounded by other siblings that are closer in age. If three children, each of whom is two years apart from his nearest sibling, were to get another sibling who, for example, was eight years younger than the youngest of them, this child would become a quasi-only child. It is unlikely that the other three will be influenced in their sibling position as much by the newcomer as they were by each other. If a boy has turned ten years old before getting two sisters in quick succession, he is likely to be a quasi-only child, even though also bearing some features of an oldest brother of sisters.

Generally speaking, small age distances tend to bind siblings more strongly to each other. This is true even when they cannot resolve some of their conflicts with each other and suffer from them, perhaps unconsciously. The larger the age distance is, the less the siblings will affect each other, but they will usually be that much more aware of, and articulate about, their conflicts. These conflicts are resolvable, as a rule. The fact that such siblings express their conflicts may make it seem as if they were more severe than those between siblings of smaller age differences. This impression is often wrong. The actual and effective conflicts between siblings of smaller age differences are usually deeper and harder to reconcile.

An older sibling tends to determine the character of his sibling relationship to a greater extent than does a younger sibling. The younger one creates a new situation and a considerable problem for the older sibling by his mere arrival, but the older sibling decides more or less in unison with his parents how to interpret the new family situation and how to continue shaping it. The greater the number of older siblings the newborn encounters, the less can he (or she) do himself in terms of interpreting and shaping the family situation. The older siblings rearrange their relationships with each other and decide among themselves how their new sibling is to be incorporated and who may or should devote more time to him than the rest. A newborn is ignorant at first of all these "negotiations" and usually has no other choice but to accept the role imposed upon him, at least for the time being. If the newcomer is the only one of his sex, though, or if, because of looks, special talents, or an exceptionally happy disposition, he or she has become particularly dear to the parents, he or she may exert a greater influence than usual over his older siblings and take a more active role in shaping their family life. Of course even then it takes the parents' support to become all that influential.

Small age differences result in stronger ties among siblings than large age differences both in large sibling configurations and in smaller ones. This implies that immediate siblings, that is, those adjacent in age, are likely to influence each other more strongly than nonadjacent siblings, that is, those who are farther apart from each other in their sibling configuration. This is true even when a sibling seems to skip the next oldest or the next youngest in his affection and turns to the second-next oldest or second-next youngest instead. This skipping may happen for good psychological reasons, but the nonspontaneous or reactive character of such a sibling preference often does not escape a careful observer's notice. If three brothers have a sister and still another brother, the shock of the arrival of another sibling could be particularly severe for the third-oldest, because everybody else in the family will be delighted about the birth of a girl. For the two older brothers this is not the first experience of a shock over a newcomer; they can probably handle it with greater ease than the third-oldest and respond positively to their little sister. The third-oldest, because of his mixed feelings, may have had no chance to hit it off with her. In contrast, he may have much less of a problem with the fifth child, the youngest brother. He has fewer reservations about him, can turn to him with more composure and, as a consequence, the two may form a stronger attachment to each other than to the rest of their siblings. We may suspect, though, that the third-oldest brother and perhaps the youngest brother too may be glancing with envy at the happy harmony prevailing among the other three or at least among two of the other three. Their own attachment to each other may appear second-rate compared to theirs. The third brother would rather be attached to his next oldest brother, if that brother had not turned away from him, and to his younger sister, if his older brothers had not snatched her for themselves.

The influence in a sibling configuration of nonadjacent siblings upon one another will be smaller the greater the number of siblings positioned between them in age. It will also be smaller, however, the greater the age difference is between two siblings regardless of how many siblings are between them, if any. The influence of such a distant sibling may be enhanced under two conditions. He can take the father's or the mother's place for the other child. This may be because one parent has been lost or because there are so many children in the family that the oldest may be fifteen or twenty years older than the youngest. Or a sibling may take the position of a child vis-à-vis another sibling. These two conditions are not necessarily mutual.

The fact that small age distances among siblings result in stronger ties than large age distances also implies that, of the two siblings adjacent to a person, the sibling closer in age is likely to be more influential. A middle sister with a brother two years older and another brother six years younger than herself will become more of a youngest sister of brothers than of an older sister of brothers (see also p. 191).

Age differences between children and parents and between the parents themselves are also important. On the average, the oldest child is about 28 or 29 years younger than his father and 25 or 26 years younger than his mother. The youngest child is an average of seven years younger than the oldest. If there are more than three children, these age distances from the parents and from other siblings tend to be smaller (see chapter 1).

If parents are considerably older than this, if there is an age gap of say 40 years and 37 years respectively between them and their oldest child, contacts with the child tend to be less intimate. These parents are inclined to be either stricter and more authoritarian than parents of average ages in relation to their children's ages, or too over-protective and permissive. Often such parents have only one child. They may be more like grandparents to their child than ordinary parents would.

If parents are considerably younger than the average, perhaps 20 and 17 or 20 and 18 years old when their first child is born, they are frequently reluctant to assume their parental roles. Often they let things take their course. They may not concern themselves much with their children but leave them to the care of someone else. Under fortunate circumstances this someone may be their own parents. Even if these very young parents do keep their children themselves, they tend to become big brothers and sisters rather than parents for them. The grandparents of the children, or other people who are taking care of them, tend to become their psychological parents. Grandparents, however, are often less consistent in their dealings with their grandchildren than are the parents. They either spoil them or they are more indifferent and less available to them. In some instances they may literally want their grandchildren to leave them alone.

One of the characteristics of the family backgrounds of young delinquents and criminals as compared to that of the average youth turned out to be the relatively old age and the relatively young age of their parents. Often at least one parent was either over 50 or less than 20 years old when the person in question was born (Toman & Preiser, 1973).

The average age difference between the parents is about three years. In the large majority of cases the husband is older than the wife. Only in 15% of all cases is the wife older than the husband.

If the age difference between spouses is 10 or 15 years, the older spouse (usually the husband) takes a parental rather than a partner's role toward the younger spouse, at least in certain areas and aspects of their family life. The husband behaves somewhat like a father toward his wife. She becomes both his wife and his child, and if they have children of their own, they may be a bit like grandchildren to him. If such a marriage succeeds, the wife has usually had psychological reasons for looking for a father rather than a peer in marriage. She may have lost her own father early in life, or she may have lost her mother and had to take her place in the family.

If the wife is considerably older than the husband, her part in their relationship tends to be that of a mother rather than of a partner or peer, and the husband is likely to want just that. He may have reasons deriving from his own family constellation, and so might she. The children in such a family recognize sooner or later who the head of the family is and to whom they had better turn: to mother. Their father is more of a companion who might get their mother to help them, but who is often not too helpful by himself.

3.   Changes in Family Constellations

Family constellations change during the course of time. The family members grow older. In an objective sense, this occurs uniformly: everyone ages by the same number of years. Subjectively, however, the rates of growing older vary for different family members. In two years a child 4 years of age grows older by 50 per cent of his original age, a child of 8 years by 25 per cent, a young adult of 20 years by 10 percent. The subjective rate of aging (a), which may also reflect physical and psychological growth processes, can be viewed as a function of the difference between the new age (t_2) and the original age (t_1) on the one hand and the original age (t_1) on the other: $a = (t_2 - t_1)/t_1$. In other words, young family members change faster in the course of time than do older family members, particularly parents. Even the influences that a newborn member of the family may exert on the relationships between the other family members are likely to be greatest in the beginning and tend to dwindle as he grows into the family. The "establishment" of individuals with much slower subjective growth rates and a much longer span of their relationships to each other than to the newcomer tends to prevail.

Changes within family constellations during the course of time are basically similar for different families. The addition of a new family member through birth or the fact that the family has reached its final configuration affects all families in comparable ways.

There are, however, special cases of changes in the family that require attention. Families may not only increase their membership by begetting and bearing still another child. They may also take in a foster-child or adopt a child. Moreover, parents may separate and marry others, single persons as well as individuals who had been married before. Thus the children may not only get a new parent, but also new siblings who could be either half-brothers and half-sisters or step-brothers and step-sisters. Finally, family members may leave for periods of time or for good, either because of long travels or business relocations, or because of legal separation, divorce, or death. These changes will be dealt with in the next section.

Loss of Family Members

In an average of 10 per cent of all families, a person is likely to permanently lose a parent during his childhood or youth. The parent may die or separate himself from the family for good either by divorce or without legal formalities, or he may have been missing since birth. In 8 out of 10 instances the person lost is the father, in 2 out of 10 cases it is the mother.

Siblings may also be lost through death or separation. Loss of a sibling during a person's childhood or youth occurs in 10 percent of the families with children.

Regardless of whether such losses of family members occur through death, or chronic illness and hospitalization, separation, or abandonment of a family member, they represent significant changes in a person's family constellation. They affect the life experiences of all members of the family, not so much by the occurrence of the event of loss itself as by the lost person's permanent absence.

Psychologists are inclined to argue that nothing can be said about the effect of the loss of a person until those who suffered the loss have been questioned. This is only partly true. For example, one can maintain without questioning anyone that life will go on for all members of the family without the person who has been lost. There can be no more direct interactions with the lost person. No further immediate experiences with the lost person are possible, although during the course of mourning the lost person may be talked about a lot and facets and aspects of that person may be discussed that were unknown to some members of the family. No family member can speak to the lost person any more; no one can get a response from him

This state of the permanent absence of a family member starting from a certain point in time can strike one family sooner than another. A given loss may be suffered by one family member at an early age and by another member at an older age. A sibling may be 2 years old at the time of loss, another 16. The person lost may be an 8-year-old sister or the 46-year-old father. The sibling lost may be one of two or one of ten children. If a parent has been lost, the remaining parent may soon form a new tie, may not do so for a long time, or may never do so. The substitute parent that he or she recruits may be a familiar person or a perfect stranger. He or she may be like or unlike the person lost. The substitute parent may enter the family alone or bring with him a retinue of children. If a sibling has been lost, the parents may beget another child or adopt one.

Without asking the individuals concerned, we may assume that these and other varieties of losses of family members are likely to have different effects. They change the life situation of a family in a specific way. The changed life situation, in turn, gives rise to specific experiences.

We may anticipate, moreover, that two families with

similar compositions of people and exposed to similar losses of family members would subsequently find themselves in life situations that also bear resemblances. At least some of the experiences of the changed life situation will be similar in those two families. If both families had lost their father, the family members are not likely to behave as if they had lost their mother, a sibling, or no one. In both families a 5-year-old daughter will have a different experience of loss than a 12-year-old son. The similarity of their experience of loss may be greater for the 5-year-old daughters in these two families even though each of them has actually lost a different person, than the similarity of the experience of loss suffered by the 5-year-old daughter and the 12-year-old son in one and the same family, even though they have lost the identical person. Folklore, too, seems to indicate that a substitute parent, such as a stepfather or a stepmother, has certain things in common with other stepparents regardless of the circumstances, the time, and the kind of family into which they enter.

We should remind ourselves that we have been implying all along that oldest brothers of brothers have common characteristics with other oldest brothers of brothers, that youngest sisters of brothers have common characteristics with other youngest sisters of brothers—characteristics that they may not share with their respective siblings in spite of the fact that they are all related and live in the same family context. Of course, there are other characteristics that they might sooner share with their siblings than with unrelated persons who happen to have the same sibling position. Such characteristics include the family idiom, physical likenesses, similarities in intelligence, vitality, etc. (see p. 66f).

Apart from permanent losses of persons, there are also temporary and partial losses.

Temporary losses are absences of family members for a certain period of time. The absence is terminated by the lost person's ultimate return to the family. This may be a matter of days, weeks, months, or years. Temporary losses may be treated like permanent losses while they last. The earlier in a child's life such a temporary loss occurs, the harder it is for a child to distinguish such a temporary loss from a permanent loss, although older family members might know from the start how long the person's absence is going to be. In his immediate experience the temporary loss and the permanent loss are about the same for the child.

Partial losses are losses of certain (positive) characteristics or aspects of a person in the family. A child may learn that his father can also throw a tantrum, that he drinks, or that he was once in jail, or that his mother had been married before. The child loses the belief that his father is always kind and controlled, that he is a sober person or that he is a man without a criminal record, or that his mother has loved no other man than his father. We may call such losses *qualitative partial losses*. One can also speak of partial losses when a family member, say the father or a sibling who used to be around every day, happens to be home only on weekends—perhaps because of the father's extended business trips or the sibling's transfer to a boarding school—or when a family member falls ill and no longer helps in the house, but rather needs help himself. These losses are actually changed forms of the presence of family members. They will concern us more at a later point. We might call these losses *temporal partial losses*.

Partial losses are harder to evaluate than are permanent losses. They may require additional information and interpretations. This is particularly true of qualitative partial losses. Permanent or temporary losses, on the other hand, can be described and distinguished rather well by a few objective characteristics.

The most general effect of the loss of family members is probably the insecurity that the person suffering the loss displays thereafter in his relations to other people. The graver the loss, the greater the insecurity of the bereaved in his present and future social relationships. Losses of persons are more severe, in turn:

a. the more recently they have occurred,
b. The earlier in a person's life they have occurred,
c. the older the person lost is (in relation to the oldest family member),
d. the longer a person has lived together with the lost person,
e. the smaller the family,
f. the greater the imbalance of sexes in the family resulting from the loss,
g. the longer it takes the family to find a replacement for a lost person,
h. the greater the number of losses, and the graver the losses, that have occurred before.

These rules apply for permanent as well as temporary losses of persons. When losses are temporary, rule g must be modified accordingly. It is not the time that elapses before a subsitute for the lost person can be found, but the time before the lost person himself returns, that must be considered (see Toman 1962 a; Toman & Preiser 1973).

Rule c implies that the loss of a parent is considerably graver than the loss of a sibling, the loss of a much older sibling is graver than the loss of a slightly older sibling. This corresponds well to clinicial-psychological observations of losses and their effects.

Rule d implies, among other things, that is is easier for a person to get over the loss of a considerably younger sibling than over that of a slightly younger one. But it also implies that the loss of a sibling older than oneself is psychologically harder to take than the loss of any sibling younger than oneself.

This is plausible in view of the fact that one has usually lived with a sibling older than oneself all of one's life but with a sibling younger than oneself only for as long as that sibling has lived. Besides, an oldest sibling has always known a time when the younger sibling was not yet around. If he is irked by the arrival of his younger sibling, which is true in most cases, he also has an idea of how this situation could be remedied: namely, by restoring the original state of affairs or, in other words, by transporting the newcomer to where he was before he was born. Having experienced the desired state of affairs in reality, the oldest sibling is better able to cope with his wish to get rid of the other. The youngest sibling as a rule has never lived without the older one. He cannot organize his feelings of rivalry and annoyance with his older sibling into a wish to be rid of him, and then suppress that wish, as well as the older sibling can. The younger sibling has never seen such a state of affairs in reality. He has never been without the other. Hence, if he loses the other, the younger sibling is often at an utter loss and more agitated than an older sibling would be.

The validity of rule d is supported by Freud's concept of mourning over losses (Freud 1916; also Toman 1968). The longer one has lived with a person, the more one has learned about him, the more one has got used to his presence, and the harder it is, therefore, to forget him and one's experiences with him and to get used to his (future) absence. The severity of a loss can be estimated by the length of mourning that a person needs in order to get over it. While still mourning, one is distracted from other tasks and concerns in one's life and thus appears insecure. Even so, it is frequently difficult for an outside observer to tell when the period of mourning is over.

The insecurity of a person who has suffered the loss of a family member is more clearly noticeable in the difficulties that the person encounters when entering new social relationships. A person who has suffered a loss knows, not merely theoretically but from bitter and painful experience, that losses are possible. Losses may occur again. As a result, the bereaved person who has suffered such losses unconsciously clings to the old or enters into new ties with other individuals more anxiously, more hastily and less critically than other people do. He also more frequently than not chooses friends from among those persons who have suffered losses themselves—also persons by whom he can be more easily left than other people or whom he himself can more easily leave than he can others (Toman 1962).

If we view neurotic symptoms and delinquent behavior among children and youths as indicators of disturbances in their social development, and if we assume, moreover, that such disturbances are among the possible consequences of losses of family members, then we would expect children or youths who are demonstrably neurotic or delinquent to have experienced early losses of family members more frequently than has the average child or youth. This can be demonstrated. Less than one per cent of the children and youths in the general population have lost their mother before they themselves turn 6 years of age. In contrast, 4 percent of those children and youths who had consulted psychological counseling centers, and 8 percent of those youths who were in jail or in reformatories at the time of the investigation had suffered such losses. Losses of their mothers in early youth—between their 6th and their 14th year of age—were three times more frequent among neurotic youths and six times more frequent among delinquent youths than in the general population. Losses of their fathers during their first 6 six years of life were also twice as frequent among neurotic youngsters and three times as frequent among youngsters in reformatories or jails than among youngsters in general (who showed a 5 percent frequency of such a loss). Losses of their fathers occurring between their 6th and 14th year of life were twice as frequent among young delinquents than among the average youths (with whom such a loss had an empirical probability of 5 percent). Neurotic youths, however, did not differ.

As for separation from the family, not necessarily as a consequence of the parents' divorce or the death of a parent, the following data were obtained: 90 percent of the average youths had never left their parents. This was true of neurotic and criminal youths in only 30 percent of the cases. Neurotic children and youngsters had had an average of two residences away from home, delinquent youngsters even three (often these residences were in boys' or girls' homes), whereas a youth in the general population had had practically no (more precisely 0.2) residences away from home (Toman & Preiser 1973).

Even early losses of family members that had not been

suffered by the children themselves but by their parents during *their* childhood showed demonstrable effects. Of the mothers of neurotic children, 9 percent had lost a parent during their first 6 years of life. In the population in general, this was true of only 3 percent of the mothers. Only rudimentary evidence was available about the mothers of young delinquents. Often those delinquents knew so little about their mothers and their mothers' parents that it could not be established whether their mothers had or had not suffered early losses of a parent. What may be said, however, is that delinquent youths knew significantly less about their parents than did the average youths.

Furthermore, it could be shown of the population at large that spouses, at least one of whom had suffered the loss of a parent in his or her childhood, tended to have married about a year later than spouses who had suffered no such losses. If a husband had suffered the loss of a parent in his early youth (between 6 and 14 years of age), he was likely to have married two years later than other men. Wives who had suffered this kind of a loss, however, showed no such retarding effect in their marriage dates.

Even children's performances in school proved to be influenced by the loss of family members. It could be demonstrated that grade-school children who had lost a parent had significantly poorer school grades than did the average child. In contrast, children who had suffered no such loss, but one of whose parents had lost a parent in their childhood, had significantly better grades than the average child (Zielinski 1966). This might be interpreted as a result of increases in achievement motivation that parents who had suffered early losses of a parent themselves seem unconsciously to impart to their children.

The best remedy for the loss of a person would be to replace the lost person by a person as similar to him as possible, and to do so as soon as possible. Such "most similar" persons, however, are as a rule hard to find. If such a person who is similar in every respect or practically identical with the person who was lost, say a parent, could be recruited—as might be possible with a sibling or even a twin of the lost parent, then the substitute person could be psychologically acceptable to the bereaved soon after the loss has occurred, perhaps even immediately after it. In most instances, however, the loss of a person requires an extensive period of mourning and waiting. This period is usually more extensive the longer one has lived with the lost person, and the less the person coming up as an eventual substitute resembles the person who has been lost.

In some instances it is hard to tell whether a loss is permanent or not. If a divorced father visits his children once in five years, he is as good as permanently lost. Even if he comes regularly every month, his influence may be practically nil, depending on how the family views him and his visits. He, too, may be like a permanently lost father. If not, he is at least a very different father than he was before the divorce. One may say that the children have suffered a temporal partial loss of their father.

Conversely, a dead father, perhaps one who was killed in the war or in an accident through no fault of his own and who will certainly never return to the family, may maintain a certain presence in the minds of his wife and his children. They may speak about him frequently and stay in contact with the father's parents and siblings. In this way, his (posthumous) effect may be greater than that of a divorced father who comes for visits. Even so, as mentioned before, there is no way of having new direct experiences with a dead father, whereas with a divorced father there is. What might happen, however, is that a brother of the dead father, an uncle, that is, or the father's father, may assume the father's role vis-à-vis the children, at least to a certain extent. In the eyes of the children, however, these people, too, soon tend to become individuals in their own right. All the talk and recollection about their father cannot prevail in the end in the children's minds against the actual and enduring contacts with their uncle or with their grandfather.

We will deal with these and related complications in the next section. There is another important case, however, that we should discuss now. Suppose someone does not merely lose a family member, say a father, but he has never had one. His father had been missing since birth. One might think that such a situation is less painful than the loss of a person with whom one has lived for while, and that the effects of such a situation are milder. The opposite, however, seems to be true.

A child, say a boy who grows up without his father, does not know from his own immediate experience what he is missing. A boy, on the other hand, who has lost his father at the age of 3 experiences sorrow and pain over the loss, is depressed for a while, and can only gradually get used to a life without him. However, since the best remedy for a loss is the replacement of the lost person by another, relatively most similar person (see p. 47), the second boy should have an advantage over the first one. The second boy knows what he has lost and what he must seek to replace. He is therefore more likely to find people who may qualify as a father-substitute. The first boy, however, does not know what he is missing, does not search for a substitute, and goes on living as if there were no need for fathers and father figures.

This is exactly where he errs, at least in a world where father figures hold many key positions and stand at important crossroads for the younger generation. The fatherless boy behaves toward these fatherlike persons as if they did not exist. Above all, he will not let them tell him anything. Even today, most father figures do not like this attitude.

Of course the effect of a loss also depends on the special feelings one had toward the lost person while he or she was alive. The more this person was loved, the greater will be the grief over his or her loss. In this case, however, the "labor" of mourning until the loss has been psychologically overcome is usually more effective. The bereaved has overcome the loss when he no longer needs inwardly or outwardly to bemoan or weep over the absence of a loved one in any of those situations in which that person had formerly been present. The work of mourning is considered more effective, the sooner the mourner gets used to the absence of the lost person and can attend to business as usual.

If the love for the lost person was mixed with fear and hatred, however, the work of mourning generally becomes harder. The bereaved person does not quite dare to seek out all those situations in which the lost person used to be present, because he will not only be reminded of his love for that person, but also of his fear and/or his hatred of him . But how can he hate him, if the worst that can happen to anyone has already happened to that person: namely,death? One may assume that, even with a less intensive love for a person, the ambivalence toward him (or her), i.e.,the concomitant presence of feelings of fear and/or of hatred, would prolong the work of mourning and would not lead in the end to a clear and ultimately satisfactory catharsis (Freud 1916, also Toman 1968).

These considerations, if valid at all, would also apply to losses of parents, of siblings, even of one's own children. However, it seems to take parents longer to overcome the loss of their own child than the rules of loss listed above (p.43f) seem to suggest. According to rules b, c, and d, the parents should not be affected too severely. After all, the loss occurs relatively late in the parents' lives (they are young or middle-aged adults), the lost person is quite young, and their life together has been short.

If, despite all this, parents do suffer more than would be expected over the loss of their own child, this may be connected with the reproaches almost all parents inflict upon themselves. They feel that they had not done enough for their child, they had not loved him enough, that they had not paid enough attention to him. They were neglectful and have thus caused the child's death. Indeed the child was more their own product than anything else in life. They created him themselves. Everything that happened to him could only have occurred with their permission or at their request. Whatever the child was given, be it food, clothing, warmth, or loving tenderness, usually came from them.

Parents who actually bear some guilt—however slight —over the loss of their child tend to mourn less efficiently than other parents and take longer to overcome that loss. But even parents who are at no fault whatsoever, objectively speaking, nevertheless still develop guilt feelings. Consequently, they take longer and struggle harder to get used to the absence of their child in their daily lives than one would anticipate from the parents' age and by the relatively short time they have had the child.

On second glance, however, the effects of the loss of one's own child are after all what one would theoretically expect. The best way to remedy a loss is to find a relatively similar substitute (see p.47). However, this is not merely a matter of finding another child; the parents have it in their command to beget another. Sometimes the very decision itself eases the pain of loss.

If parents cannot or do not want to get a substitute for their lost child, at least their unresolved experience of loss will not harm any further child. The children they do have may suffer from their parents' emotional condition, but they often reap additional attention and affection as a result of the loss. The parents seem to want to give their surviving children all they feel they failed to give the departed one. That, in turn, may help the children to overcome their own sorrow over the loss.

The same holds true for the loss of a spouse. If the surviving spouse can find no substitute, he (or she) will suffer more, but his unhappiness will not be passed on to any new children. In our context the effects of losses are considered grave if the bereaved person was very dependent upon the lost person, if it is hard or impossible to find a substitute for him, and if the bereaved person himself cannot actively contribute to the recruitment of the substitute.

In our context the effects of losses do not so much concern the emotional state of the bereaved as they do his long-term behavior and the influence that he himself exerts on other people or friends, on his spouse or, above all, on his chilren. What concerns us here are not the subjective but rather the social effects of losses. We are attempting to gather from a person's long-term behavior and the lasting effects of his actions rather than from the descriptions of his current inner state just how that person is or was able to cope with the loss of a loved one, or, for that matter, even with the relationship itself, while it lasted. The subjective happiness or unhappiness of a childless couple is less relevant in our context than is the subjective happiness or unhappiness of parents. The inner states of the latter may affect their children permanently. The inner states of the former are unlikely to affect anyone as directly as that. A childless couple may also separate and remarry without great consequences to society. Parents can do so only at a psychological cost to all involved.

Step- and Half Siblings

As a result of losses of family members, half and stepsiblings may enter the family. If a parent has been lost and a substitute, a stepfather or a stepmother, has materialized, he or she may also bring children of his or her own into the family. These children become stepsiblings for the children already there. They are not related, that is, they are not "of the same blood."

The remaining parent and the stepparent may also have children of their own. They become half siblings for the other children, and vice versa. Half siblings are part blood relations. They are more closely related than cousins, but not as closely as brothers and sisters. Regular siblings have both parents in common, half siblings have only one of their parents in common. Usually they are younger than the children already present in the family. Stepsiblings, on the other hand, may also be older than the children who were already there, or even of the same age.

When studying the relationships of stepsiblings or half

siblings with each other, one should consider the given individual's position in his original sibling configuration as
well as the possible effects of the loss of a family member
which must have occurred in the first place. Even if parents
add an adopted child to their own children, the adopted
child, at least, has suffered a loss. He is without one or both
parents, or he loses them upon adoption.

When two sibling configurations join in a single family,
the children involved may assume new sibling positions, including multiple ones. As stated above, the latter become
more probable the larger the number of children. A youngest
sibling may become a second youngest or third youngest, an
oldest may find a still older sibling ahead of him. A middle
sibling may become the guide and helper for his youngest
sibling who may have become a middle sibling himself when
the other sibling-group joined them. A family of boys may
get girls with the other sibling-group and the girls may get
boys. There may also be increased struggles for the rare sex
turned even rarer when the other sibling group came to the
house, e.g., when two brothers and a sister get two step-
brothers.

Changes in sibling roles are more likely to occur the
younger the two sibling groups are when they join. The older
the siblings are at the time of the merger, the more likely they
are to stay apart in their daily dealings. The real siblings
stick together, but there may be little interaction between the
two sibling groups.

What matters in all of this is, among other things, the
attitude of the remaining parent toward the incoming sibling
group. If such a parent takes a literal stepmother or stepfather
role vis-à-vis the children the new marriage partner brings
along, the two sibling groups may remain hostile or reserved
toward one another. If the new marriage partners understand each other quite well, however, and accept each
other's children with joy, the two sibling groups tend to get
along better with each other.

As a rule, the smaller of the two sibling groups finds it
more difficult to accept the other than vice versa. This ap-

plies particularly for a group of siblings who were split up when the parents separated. In either case, the relationship of the departed parent to a new spouse and to children taken over or newly begotten may complicate matters for the sibling group staying behind. The situation worsens when both parents take some of their own children along into their new marriages and leave others behind, when they have found new partners who are doing likewise, and when both new couples also have more children of their own. Such complications are not too rare in countries with high divorce rates. The children in such families have trouble finding their part and their own identity in that maze. They may cling to what is left of their original families and may even leave their "parental home" prematurely.

If a new parent brings no children of his own with him into the family, the children born to them thereafter are half siblings of the children already there. Depending on the kind of relationships that the new parents have with each other, these half siblings may be incorporated into the family like real siblings, or, in the worst cases, they may remain strangers who have far greater power over the parents, and against whom the original children do not stand much of a chance. The first-born of the half siblings is often the parents' special favorite. He is, after all, the first child they have had together. He may develop into a super-senior, an ambitious leader, a sibling who jealously watches over his later-born siblings' interests and guards them against those of his half-siblings. Incidentally, two historic examples of such oldest brothers stemming from the second marriage of their fathers are Sigmund Freud, the founder of psychoanalysis, and Hermann Gmeiner, the founder of "children's villages."

If a stepparent does not have any more children with the remaining parent, the children's lot is mostly to cope with the loss of the other parent and to get used to the substitute parent. Their appraisal of the loss depends on various objective circumstances related to the loss (see p. 40f). In line with this, one would naturally expect that the oldest siblings would be less affected than the younger siblings. The loss has occurred later in their lives than in the lives of their younger siblings (p. 44, b). The larger the number of siblings however, the larger the number of family members surviving the loss. This ought to soften the effects of the loss (p.44,e). Moreover, the older siblings unconsciously tend to show their younger ones how to cope with the loss. The older siblings gain additional incentives, so it seems, from the fact that their younger siblings need help. They sometimes act as substitute parents for them. They are the go-betweens. They soften their younger siblings' sufferings, so that the younger ones seem to fare relatively well. If all the children, however, were to be sent individually to separate foster-parents after such a loss, the greater vulnerability of the younger siblings would become immediately evident.

Effects of loss are no less, however, where stepsiblings and half siblings come with the substitute parent. To the extent that he brings along children of his own, he is different from the lost parent. He is less available to the original set of children. He is less of a substitute. The separated parent is a temporary or a temporal partial loss. One does not see very much of him (or her) any more. He may come by once a month. If he does not find another spouse he will be viewed differently than if he does remarry and does take on the new spouse's children or have his own. In that case the temporal or temporal partial loss may become a qualitative partial loss as well (see p. 43).

The children or sibling group who have suffered the more severe loss are likely to be at a disadvantage in their relationships with their half and stepsiblings. They are less likely to get their way. They may feel more aggressive, but since this is usually not tolerated, they become more intimidated or depressed than the children of the other group.

It is not merely the relationship of the new spouses to each other that is important for the children. The relationship between the remaining and the separated parent matters too. If they part as friends, the children can maintain contacts with the parent who has left the family without great conflicts. If the parents parted as enemies, however, this is more difficult. In such instances, the children's conflicts are and remain so severe that a temporary or even a permanent loss of the departing parent may be felt to be the lesser of two evils. Everyone involved would fare better, as a rule, if the separating parents would find a more graceful and more tolerant mode of living apart, so that a permanent loss of the parent could be avoided. Generally speaking, a temporal partial loss of a parent, where at least an occasional presence of the departing parent can be maintained, should be easier for the children to bear than a permanent loss.

The relationship of the remaining parent to the lost parent is important even when the loss has occurred through death. At first glance it might not seem so. Dead means gone forever—true enough; but the manner in which one remembers and thinks about the lost person also determines, among other things, how the substitute person may be accepted by the surviving parent and the children.

For those parents who are fortunate enough to have it, love without conflict or reservations is not only conducive to a pleasant life together and with their children, but it also makes the loss of one's spouse, as painful and irreplaceable as it may be at first, somewhat easier for them to cope with than it is for spouses who have lived in conflict. The latter cannot help wishing unconsciously for a liberation from or the departure of their spouses. If their wish becomes reality, some feelings of guilt are inevitable. Such guilt feelings could be resolved or mitigated if one could make up for the death-wish, for example by acting in a particularly kind and considerate way toward the spouse. In order to be a recipient, however, the spouse must be alive. If he is dead, he will take no notice of all the penitence in the world.

Even the children of a parent who has been loved without conflict and reservations by his spouse can cope better with the loss of their parent than can children who have lost a parent who was partly or mostly hated by the spouse. If the children shared that hatred, if they hated the departed parent too, they retain feelings of guilt long after the loss has occurred. Only if the lost parent was absolutely and literally hated, if all the experiences with the parent had been negative, would this not be the case. On the other hand, if the children loved the parent they lose and if they hated the surviving parent, and continue to do so, they tend to retain a mixture of feelings of revenge as well as of fear of the remaining parent. They may express their guilt over those feelings of revenge by suspecting that whoever comes in as a substitute parent will not stay long with them either. This will be the surviving parent's revenge. Hatred and fear of the remaining parent is often extended to the new stepparent. The children long for the lost parent and are afraid that the remaining parent and the stepparent may turn against them. In collusion with the stepparent, the remaining parent may attempt to get rid of the children, as he did of the spouse.

Adopted Children

One of the most important decisions in everyone's life is the decision to have a child. Whatever good or bad lovers can do to each other is more or less their business. Their happiness or lack of it usually ends with their relationship or with their deaths. If they have produced children, however, their happiness or lack of it lives on with their children. Whatever lovers-turned-parents do, there will be consequences for their children that extend beyond their own lives. One may assume that, other things being equal, nothing will ordinarily entice adults to think of the future more than does the existence of children of their own. With great efforts as well as with instinctive and sensual pleasure did they begin to care about the welfare of their children when the latter were still young and helpless and completely dependent upon their parents. This nurturing attitude is not easy to extinguish, even after the children have grown up and no longer do what the parents want them to do.

The decision to have a child is important in another respect: mankind's survival depends on the willingness of men and women to join forces and produce an average of at least two to three children. Otherwise mankind would decline in number, and while this may not be at all bad in the eyes of some of us, man would sooner or later move to arrest the decline or even to reverse it.

In the eyes of the philosophical observer of life, one of the great miracles is man's ability to reproduce and, what is more, to do this even with plan and with reason rather than perfectly ignorantly as animals do it. Philosophers are taken by the fact that an intimate act of love can have as fabulous a consequence as another little human being. Common sense thinks less of it or takes it for granted. If children had not always been produced by the thousands and millions, we would not be around to ponder the fact.

Most people have the ability to beget children of their own, but some do not. A physical injury, an illness, or a stroke of (bad) luck may have incapacitated them in this respect. They usually discover this when they are already married and have been trying to have children. Learning about their condition is a great disappointment to them, and is aggravated by the fact that it is usually only one of the spouses who cannot have children. The other spouse is almost bound to wonder why he (or she) did not marry someone else with whom he could have children.

If both partners can reconcile themselves to their predicament, or if they decide for special reasons to beget no children of their own, they often try to adopt children. They begin to look for a child who has been abandoned by its parents or who has lost them in other ways, perhaps through death. Adoption agencies offer their discreet services. The prospective parents cannot shop for a child as if they were in a supermarket, for instance by moving from crib to crib in the baby nursery and picking out the prettiest or the most lively, but they may indicate their preferences. They may even choose the sex of their child, which ordinary parents cannot do. Moreover, they can select the age, although most adoption agencies in industrial countries have been recommending earliest possible adoption for the past ten to twenty years. Immediately after birth or at least within the first four to six months of life is not too soon.

A child who has been adopted soon after birth cannot distinguish true parents from adoptive parents through his own experience. He grows up like ordinary children do with their true parents. In most cases his emotional and instinctive attachment is no less than it would be with his true parents. Even if his parents should adopt a second child, this need not differ much in his experience from the arrival of a regular sibling. He does not see his mother become pregnant, to be sure, but even where the mother does, the children may not always notice, unless the parents take pains to point it out to them in the process.

Sooner or later adopted children are likely to discover that they have been adopted—that is, that their parents are not their "real parents." In the past, adoptive parents have tried to hide this fact from their children as long as possible. Today things have become more reasonable. Children are being told the truth, at least to the extent that they ask about it. As with questions about sex, they often merely want to know something specific, not the entire story, as parents are afraid they might. With questions of sex as well as of adoption, parents are well advised in trying to answer freely and openly as much as the child wants to know. If the child asks a further question a minute or a year later, he will get further answers.

During puberty and adolescence young people may be engaged in mental identity experiments. What if father or mother or both were not my true parents, they may ask themselves. Perhaps I was adopted. Questions such as these mostly indicate that the young person has begun to think about his future life and his existence. He (or she) does not really question his family background.

Adopted children may raise the same questions. On the basis of their experience they have no more reason to doubt where they came from and where they belong than do children who grew up with their real parents. Of course, the "truth" is something different. The parents are not of the same stock. If the adopted child were to meet his real parents now, they would impress him as perfect strangers; there would be no reason to change allegiance to them.

During adolescence adopted children often express the wish to see their real parents "just once." The adopting parents can ordinarily grant that wish without qualms; they would not lose "their" child in the process. Part of today's conditions of adoption include that the (often unwed) mother of the child who has been put up for adoption renounce any claim to the child; she may not visit him or even know his new address. These rules, by which many adoption agencies abide, make it hard, if not impossible, for the adopted child to contact his real mother or father.

Parents who have children of their own, but who add an adopted child, do not act much differently. They have not suffered the shock of learning that they cannot have children of their own. Even parents who have adopted a child and then have children of their own—not too rare an event, incidentally—act in ways similar to adoptive parents with no children of their own. Like them, they too have thought for a while that they could not have children themselves. Contacts and experiences with the adopted child, however, may have removed inhibitions and unconscious fears, particularly those of having a child. Such parents tend to remain forever grateful to their adopted child. Only in cases where the adopted child turns out to be severely disturbed or retarded might those parents weaken in their gratitude, perhaps for the sake of their own children, and neglect the adopted one or put him into an institution.

Adoptions occurring after the child has turned six months of age create problems, and these increase the older the child becomes before he is adopted. Adopting parents or foster parents can hardly hope to take the parents' place for a child who has been in an orphans' home or an institution for the first two, three, or even six years of his life. It will take an enormous effort of upbringing and loving care to undo what the institution has unintentionally done to the child. Growing up in an institution means sharing the attending persons with fifteen or twenty other children and, among other things, having to accept shifts and staff turnovers.

Adopting parents have a chance of being accepted as parents by such a child (albeit as substitutes for his true psychological parents, who, in this case, are the foster parents), only if the child has lived his first two, three, or six years of life with the same foster parents who were fond of him and who would not part with him if they did not have to. In the beginning, at least, adopting parents would be more successful in their efforts on behalf of the child the more they would resemble and act like the foster parents.

In many ways foster children are like adopted children. They may live with their foster parents, but they have not been legally adopted. If the reason for nonadoption is merely a technicality and not a special reluctance on the part of the foster parents to commit themselves, they may be no different than adoptive parents. Ordinarily, foster parenthood is of a somewhat more temporary nature. Their custody may be revoked by the authorities. Adoption, on the other hand is final. Legally, adopting parents are considered as the real parents.

4.   Other Influencing Factors

We have described special conditions that may determine the effects of losses of family members. Similar considerations are in order when describing the *presence* of a person or a family member. To say a person is present may mean he is around sometimes or often, at regular or at irregular intervals. He may spend his time predominantly with one member of the family, with some, or with all of them. The contacts themselves may vary in length. They may involve much talking, little talking, or no talking at all. The family members may work together, they may work for themselves while still in each other's presence, or they may live alone. Some family members may prefer to remain isolated from the rest even though living under the same roof with them.

Statistically speaking, so-called average conditions of the presence of persons predominate in many families. If we do not know the details, we assume that average conditions prevail, for in this way we can hope to be closer to the truth than we could with the assumption that special or extraordinary conditions prevail. In those cases where we have learned that special conditions do exist, we naturally have to consider them.

This holds true for the characteristics of family constellations, which we have already discussed: for age differences between siblings, between parents and children, and between the parents themselves; for permanent and temporary losses; and, as outlined above, for the various forms of a person's presence in a family.

This is also true for other aspects of family life. *Characteristics of residence,* particularly availability as well as the use of space in the home, clearly tend to affect family life. One may assume, however, that ordinarily a family can create or strive after the kind of living conditions that will afford the type of contact they wish with each other. *Changes of residence* must be mentioned here too. They are usually easier to find out about than the living conditions themselves, particularly since the latter are not only a matter of space and location, but also of what the family can do with them. Change of residence in any case means the loss of the previous residence, and sometimes also a change of school for the children, and a change of work or even of a profession for the parents.

Friends and acquaintances are a part of a family's life to a greater or lesser extent, depending upon the members of that family. Here, too, a family is not merely the recipient of what is available, but can choose and sometimes even shape their relationships with others to their own specifications. A change of residence may involve more or less of a change of one's friends and acquaintances. Sometimes such a change of friends is the very purpose of a change of residence.

School attendance and change of school is important for the children; *choice of a profession or a job* as well as a change in one's place of work are important for the adults, particularly for the breadwinner. A youth may have changed school once or never, or he may have changed school every year. Thus he has also changed his classmates and friends often, a few times, or never. Every such change may imply a loss of friends. The same applies for adults. Changes of school or of work are likely to affect family life.

Family members may fall ill or suffer accidents, and may be bed-ridden for a while, either at home or in a hospital. In addition to the physical effects of *illnesses and accidents,* the latter may also involve temporary or even permanent separation from the family. The victim could lose all contact with his family for a while, and the family would lose the victim. In other words, temporary and partial losses of family members may result. Depending on the duration of the illness or incapacity, a person and/or his family may be adversely affected.

Social class, ethnic origin, religious affiliation, and political predilection of the family or of the parents also play a role in the family's life. The mere belonging to certain groups, however, may often be less important than the relationship these groups have to the larger social environment. A family that is a member of a minority group in one or more respects might also develop internal psychological problems and different attitudes to the social environment of "the establishment" than would families belonging to other minority groups or to the majority. The point in time when a family moves into a community, as well as their familiarity with the language of a country or even of a particular district of the country may affect the family in ways that cannot be attributed to interactions of family members among themselves. The more democratic the family's new nation or community is and the more civilized its citizens are, the less likely it is that these kinds of troubles will exist for a family. Family life would then develop more freely than in a restrictive or hostile environment. Under such favorable macro-psychological conditions it is easier to study and compare family constellations and family relationships. Similar types of family constellations tend to produce more similar effects on the individual in this case than they do under less favorable macro-psychological conditions.

If all we know about a family constellation is the sexes and the age-ranks of the persons who constitute the family, either because we simply do not have the information and have not even seen the family ourselves, or because whatever detail we can collect from an interview with a particular member of the family may not be trustworthy—the person may suffer from misconceptions or be lying outright —then it is best to assume that average conditions prevail with regard to all aspects under consideration. We must assume that there are average age distances between the members of the family, average residential accomodations, and average numbers of changes of residence. We proceed from the assumption that there is nothing unusual in school or at work for any of the family members and that there have been no uncommon or severe illnesses. We do not assume that losses have been suffered if none are reported spontaneously, or that those reported have occurred under unusual circumstances. We also must take for granted that there are no extreme characteristics to be found with their friends and aquaintances and that even the family's ethnic, religious, political, or financial situation is not far from ordinary.

If we make the assumption that all variables are standard and average, we are less likely to err with our estimates about the family in question, about the relationship of its members with one another, and about the roles they customarily take within the family than we would be if we arbitrarily elected to postulate unusual or rare conditions. Average assumptions are even better than no assumptions at all or the refusal to give any estimates of a family about whom only certain objective data are known. If we do the latter, we may have no reasonable idea at all as to what to inquire about, whom we should try to ask first, or how pressing may be a crisis in the family that we so far only know from hearsay. Estimates on the basis of whatever data are available at a given point may be viewed as heuristic hypotheses about the life-situation and the family or a particular member of the family. Those hypotheses are tentative, and new evidence may very well make us discard them. Even then, however, having tried more than one version in our observing minds, we will have a better idea of how special circumstances in that family should be interpreted or how they fit into our theoretical reconstruction of the situation. Without tentative hypothetical reconstructions of what the family's objective situation is probably like, even hours of talking and a battery of psychological testing may not lead us very far. We might know all sorts of things about the person, but we would not know what the life-situation is to which he responds. We would not know what made him the person he appears to be.

In other words, we can either play stupid and stubborn and refuse to say something, or even to think about a person, if we cannot refer to standardized tests or rating scales, or we could think about a person while gathering information about him, we could think about his life- and family-situation, and confirm our views, if new information seems to require that. We can try to think *with* the person concerned as well as with those he is talking about. We can try to identify with them and continue questioning. If we are drawing our information from the persons themselves and not from written records, we will notice, as a ɪule, that those persons will appreciate our questions, our empathizing "theoretical reconstructions" of their life-situations, our attempts to understand and to clarify their story. Most people interviewed tend to interpret our curiosity as interest in them, something which it probably can and should be in any case.

There are still other influencing factors that ought not to be overlooked. A person's *physical constitution,* his *looks,* his *visual acuity,* his *memory,* his *intelligence,* his *temperament,* his *vitality,* his *frustration tolerance,* and other characteristics are partly hereditary. The genes rather than the environment or the family determine a good proportion of these characteristics, even if the environment may help to develop them.

Members of the same family tend to have similar levels of *intelligence*. There are medium correlations of about r = 0.5 (correlation coefficients vary between 0 and 1, whereby 0 means no relation at all and 1 a perfect relation between two characteristics). If children have not lived with their true parents, their intelligence and that of their parents are still correlated by about r = 0.40. Identical twins, on the other hand, show an r = 0.90 for their intelligence. Identical twins are supposed to have exactly the same genes. Their native intelligence ought to have a correlation of r = 1.00 (see also Skodak & Skeels 1949; Newman, Freeman, & Holzinger 1937; McNemar 1938).

At any rate, intelligent parents are likely to have intelligent children and unintelligent parents unintelligent children. In spite of that trend, however, there are variations of intelligence among the children of a given sibling configuration. Intelligent parents may have three children, one of whom may be extremely intelligent and the other two barely above average. Unintelligent parents may have three children, one of whom may be a little below average, the other well below, and the third an imbecile.

These variations, however, are independent of sibling positions. One cannot claim that the oldest or the youngest or a middle sibling or the boys or the girls in a sibling configuration are generally more intelligent or less intelligent than the rest. This is also true for all the other characteristics mentioned, that is, for visual acuity, memory, temperament, vitality, etc. These are not associated with particular sibling positions. Within the hereditary limits of a given family, the genetic portion of these characteristics varies by chance.

This does not preclude the fact that certain sibling positions appear to be favored in certain respects. For example, more oldest siblings and only children have been found to go to college than persons of other sibling positions. This is particularly true for males (Schachter 1963). We cannot conclude from this, however, that oldest siblings or only children are more intelligent. Oldest siblings and only children seem to earn better grades than middle and youngest siblings do. Tests of intelligence by special intelligence scales show that there are no typical differences between persons of different sibling positions. On the other hand, if we measure the intelligence of young people whose grade averages are the same, we obtain a contrary result: middle and youngest siblings suddenly appear more intelligent than oldest siblings and only children (see Toman 1973b).

Thus, we may say that there are no significant differences in intelligence between persons of different sibling positions, but there are preferences for different social behaviors. Oldest siblings and only children identify more strongly with their parents and teachers than do middle and youngest siblings. They do what their parents and teachers expect to a greater degree. Consequently, oldest siblings and only children may sometimes get better grades than their actual output deserves. Middle and youngest siblings care less about their parents' and their teachers' intentions, and might even openly oppose them. Thus they are likely to earn poorer grades than their ability would warrant.

This applies to all of the characteristics mentioned above. Their hereditary components vary independently of each other and of the person's sibling position, even when there seems to be some slight association due to differential motivations and expectations in the family, as well as in part to certain physiological differences.

The second and third child, for example, are often physically stronger, relatively speaking, than the first-born child. Even their birth weight is often greater. This probably has to do with the intrauterine physiological facilitations that occur during the second and all subsequent pregnancies as opposed to the first. The intrauterine road to life has been paved.

By *temperament*, younger siblings often appear more vivacious than older siblings. The former tend to be more impulsive and carefree, the latter likely to take charge and to be "afraid" of their parents and other adults. *Frustration tolerance*, too, seems to be more pronounced with older siblings than with younger ones. They have learned earlier in life to postpone pleasures or even to renounce them than the younger ones have. Often they had to do it for the benefit of the younger ones. The younger ones, on the other hand, are generally called upon to a lesser degree because of their age; they are excused and indulged, and often retain this attitude far into the time when they would be quite capable of standing a little hardship or making sacrifices.

Similar differences can also be observed between boys and girls in the family, often regardless of their age ranks. In some families girls are allowed or expected to be weaker, more friendly, more self-indulgent than boys. Girls may be pampered whereas boys must not be. They should be gentlemen and learn how to pamper girls. Boys may fight, girls may not.

These apparent differences, however, can usually be attributed to different positions and sibling roles within the family, at least to an extent. If one could place a fetus of the genetic stock of the first-born into the position of the second-born, and the fetus of the genetic stock of the second-born into the position of the first-born, the differences to be expected as far as physical constitution, temperament, or frustration tolerance are concerned would be more or less the same. Again the first-born might be somewhat weaker physically, be more subdued in his temperament and have a greater tolerance for frustration than the second-born.

This experiment cannot be performed in reality, of course. If nature or fate were to bring about such a situation, perhaps by taking the parents away through death and by dividing the children up among as many foster parents as there are children, so that a first-born may be the youngest in his foster family and the last-born the oldest in his, we would still see only part of the story. The children are likely to be much more severely affected by the loss of their parents and siblings than by their new sibling position in their foster families.

The morphology of the face and body, which is largely

determined by heredity, can create resemblances with certain family members rather than with others, say with the father, the mother, an uncle, or a grandparent. Certain forms of interaction- and/or identification relationships with family members may become more likely than others. A parent may see himself in the features of one of his children and may try to act the idol and example for this child rather than for the others. Or a parent may recognize one of his siblings or one of his own parents in his child's face, voice, or way of moving, and may behave toward him (or her) as he did toward his sibling or parent. Because of his physical likeness with a parent, the other children may grant more authority to one of their siblings than he would have merely by right of his sibling position.

All these hereditary characteristics might modify the role a person plays among his siblings and in the family. If an oldest sibling is mentally retarded, but his younger sister and his still younger brother happen to be very intelligent, one of the two, probably the sister, will take the lead and develop into an older sister of brothers. The mentally retarded brother will soon be treated like a youngest sibling. If a youngest brother is physically strong, whereas his two older brothers are small and slim, the younger one will soon become the strongest of them all and assume the role of leader or at least of protector of his brothers.

If we do not know what the hereditary and constitutional characteristics in a given family are, we would again fare best by assuming that average conditions prevail. These characteristics are for the most part uncorrelated with each other. Their interindividual variations occur by chance. We are thus less likely to make a mistake when appraising a family or the roles played by its members than we would be if we assumed unusual or extreme conditions to prevail. Here, too, we have to keep testing how our tentative assumptions about a person and his family stand up against further evidence and what changes in our views of the person and the family might be indicated.

Judging from my experience and that of my coworkers,

I can report that our appraisals of family constellations and sibling roles, made on the basis of no more than a knowledge of what persons constitute the family, what their age-ranks were, and what losses, if any, they had suffered, were correct, on the average, in four of five cases. Even the fifth case, however, could usually be explained satisfactorily when further details about the family constellation, changes of residence, school, or jobs, and about illnesses or unusual constitutional characteristics of family members were considered.

5. Animal Families and Special Forms of Human Families

Animal families are not formed the way human families are. Their young are generally born as triplets, quadruplets, or by the dozen, and the most intelligent and most fit among them are the ones that dominate the others. In the human family, the first-born is at first usually stronger and more intelligent than the ones born after him. This difference diminishes gradually with time and aging. Only a sickly or poorly endowed oldest child can lose his advantage over the healthy and well-endowed second-born while still in his early childhood. In that case the second one becomes the leader and the authority.

Even those animals—such as the elephants or the anthropoids—who bear only one young at a time and the next one only years later do not ordinarily form human-like families. Rarely does the older sibling play mother for the younger ones. The older one more frequently runs around in the pack with his peers. Usually their fathers cannot even be identified. Animals do not know that their actions while in heat have anything to do with the birth of their young. Only among certain animals, especially among some birds, is the father a party to the hatching and feeding of the young. Even here the young of a given litter eventually scatter. They join other young of their own age, and they do so long before the next litter is due.

Man, too, has not always adhered to monogamy. Parents have not always been occupied with nursing and educating their children up to adolescence. At various times in history children have been put into educational institutions, some earlier in their lives than others. Teachers were to make ladies and gentlemen out of these children, sometimes for the explicit purpose of returning them to their original families prepared to take over their parental estates.

Nevertheless, over the past several centuries the overwhelming majority of people in the civilized and industrial nations have grown up in individual families. Most modern religions have advocated the individual family with both father and mother living with their children up to and even through the latter's adolescence. The fact that there were occasional instances of polygamy, as among the Mohammedans or the Mormons, probably carried no more weight on the whole than the custom in Western Europe of high-ranking gentlemen who would bestow on young girls from the poorer classes "divine" or, more bluntly, illegitimate children. Not all Mohammedans had many wives, and the Mormons are said to have taken additional wives into their families not so much in order to multiply their sexual pleasures as to provide for the unmarried women in the community. Even in the Middle Ages more than a few Mohammedans, especially the poor, had only one wife or none at all. Yet where there was polygamy, the children still had some sort of family life. The children born to a Mohammedan sheik or prince and his favorite wife formed the core family, and the children born to his other wives became something like the extended family. Such a father may have been physically less available for all his children (who, incidentally, were siblings and half-siblings to each other), but he was also more powerful than ordinary fathers. He could do more for his children, and his wishes and ideas were perhaps heeded more obediently and more promptly than those of fathers in monogamous families.

Special conditions, such as institutional day care for children of working parents, orphans' homes, or current experiments with communal family life may be viewed as the exception rather than the rule. In the early thirties Russia abandoned the idea of institutional care for all children from their earliest years on and returned them to their parents. In Israel, the kibbutzim do have something like day care nurseries for babies and small children; scientific observers, however, claim that this only represents an emergency solution. Even there, the children spend at least their evenings and nights with their parents.

Communal family life is still in the testing stage. So far, we can identify apparent complications: one stems from the fact that the parents who join other parents in such a commune are often financially unsuccessful and hence become bitter enemies of established society, the other that those parents have rarely solved their own practical and/or psychological problems to any great extent. Both conditions would have to have detrimental effects on their children, provided there is enough contact between them and their children in the first place. Often these children wander about insecurely and anxiously from one commune member to another looking for stability and warmth, for one or two persons who will consistently attend to them. It has been reported that the adults in such a commune, dedicated to their own "self-actualization," may not know an hour before their weekly kitchen-duty begins whether they will feel in the mood to do it. The children, however, want to know well in advance. They want to know who will feed them next. They want certainty. They want to know what to expect today, tomorrow, and even weeks hence.

Even incomplete families, that is, families with only one parent, usually the mother, are relatively infrequent. In certain places, however, they are being encouraged by peculiar reward systems. While children from such families are heading for a clearly lower-than-average quality of life and are much more likely to become delinquent and end up in jail than are children from intact families, the authorities in the large cities of industrial nations, particularly in the USA, have mysteriously moved to give an extra welfare bonus to the unwed mother for each additional child she bears out of wedlock. Often the children are not even the beneficiaries of that bonus. The careless mother may have to slip it into her ephemeral lover's pocket in order to get him to come again. The psychological situation of these children may fairly be described as grim.

If any conclusions can be drawn from the research on family life, including our research, it is the following: nothing is more important for the family, psychologically speaking, than that both parents by and large should have wanted and intended to have children. Even then it is a difficult and time-consuming chore for the parents to rear them. For the children, in turn, nothing is more important than to be reared by parents who care for them constantly.

This care can best be had from the child's true or natural parents. Usually they are emotionally and instinctively bound to their children by their love for one another, by the act of copulation and conception, by the period of pregnancy, the event of birth, and the nursing of the child during its first weeks and months of life. Even adoptive parents may form such ties (although these tend to be a bit weaker), if they get their children soon after their birth.

Children who were born as the accidental by-product of careless love relationships, or who may have been intended, but without any realistic thought of what would become of them—that is, children who were dropped from the mother's womb into the arms of the community— inherit a most severe psychological handicap in the process. The community does not really want these children. The authorities handling the matter have no emotional and instinctive interest in them. Whatever they do for those children cannot hide the fact that they are unwelcome to them, too. According to all practical experiences so far, the best service that the community can offer such a child is to urge the actual or natural parents to keep the child in their custody or to find adoptive parents or permanent foster parents who will take the child as soon as possible. This is the only way of securing a condition in which the child will feel welcome and loved. Without such a feeling, the child's social development is likely to flounder and eventually fail.

In the near future, perhaps in fifty or a hundred years, the most pressing task for all nations will be to control population growth. The limits of space and of terrestrial resources will force this task upon mankind. This means that governments may have to impose an average number of between two and three children per family. They will have to discourage, if need be by appropriate sanctions, particularly those individuals who have no realistic idea of what might and possibly can become of their children, who have neither the ability nor the means to provide for their children and to rear them themselves up to their adolescent years.

6.   Lovers and Spouses

We have already pointed out that animals and humans automatically tend to view new situations in the light of similar situations in the past. Men know that they do that from their everyday experience. In terms of learning theory, this is a process of generalization from past experience to present situations (see Hull 1943, also p. 4). In psychoanalytical terminology this is called transference (Freud 1916/17, also p. 4). Man transfers experiences and attitudes from the past to situations of the present — or at least he tries to.

Since family contexts are among an individual's oldest life contexts, since they are the most regularly effective, longest-lasting contexts stemming from the individual's earliest years, we may assume that generalizations and transferences from them to new social situations are likely to have occurred more often and may have influenced the perception and even the active shaping of contemporary life contexts more strongly than those life contexts that the individual has experienced only later in his life. Since the contexts experienced later were themselves influenced by contexts experienced earlier in life, the oldest life contexts are likely to affect contemporary contexts not only directly, but also indirectly via those older intermediary contexts from the past.

Naturally, these influences and effects are not inescapable. The expectations with which a person enters a new situation are continuously corrected—by the people who are parties to those situations, among others. Experiences with people in these new situations are added to the experiences a person brings with him, and both types together determine the expectations a person has when entering still other new situations. As a rule, only during psychotherapy is a person unable to collect new direct experiences about his counterpart, the psychotherapist. He can only learn more about himself and the persons interacting with him in everyday life, whether of the past or the present. The psychotherapist does not act like a person in everyday life. He merely comments and interprets the ideas, recollections, phantasies, affects, and motives of the patient.

Of course, even in everyday life situations it is true that a person in new social situations not only surprises others with his own expectations, which may or may not be appropriate, but the other persons have their expectations as well and tend, moreover, to judge the newcomer by what he does first. This may result in his rejection, without his even being given a chance to get to know the other people and to correct his expectations. On the other hand, he may also be accepted on the basis of his initial behavior and be consciously or unconsciously urged by the others to maintain that behavior in the future.

However, mutual modifications and corrections are more frequent. Everyone involved, the newcomer and the others whom he joins, have new experiences with each other. The members of a group tend to influence the newcomer more strongly and determine to a greater extent than he does just what his place should be in the group. This is even more true, the longer the group has been in existence and the more frequently and regularly the group members have met. It is most true of the family, where a newborn, of course, has no idea at first about what kind of continuing social context he has entered. The other family members have adjusted themselves to the newborn before he knows what it is all about. The positions and roles in any such groups, especially in the family, are not ordinarily chosen by the entering individual, but rather assigned to him (or her) by a "collusion" of the group. If the newcomer wants to change his role or position, he meets with resistance from the group. They may force him not to deviate from the direction of development they have chosen for him, whatever his own inclinations may be.

If ontogenetically older contexts do indeed affect more recent contexts, this should apply particularly to all situations in which long-term relationships to other people are being formed and developed. If a person enters a new partnership, friendship, or love relationship—potentially long-term relationships, in other words, for which he usually has several options and which he can shape himself—it is likely that enduring social contexts in his early life and in the life of his partner, friend, or lover will bear on the expectations and ideas about their relationship with each other. There can be other influences. What the partners have gathered from reading, from plays and movies, or from gossip in their neighborhoods, may also affect their relationship with each other. Yet, how one really carries on with such a relationship from hour to hour and day to day and how one shares the home, the dinner table, or the daily chores, can hardly be learned from books, plays, or mere gossip. It takes actual practice in living together the way one has usually done in one's original family. Family life is likely to provide the core of experiences for life with friends or spouses. Literature, the movie industry, television, or gossip can only add a few romantic twists here and there.

The clinician, whether psychologist, psychiatrist, social worker, or minister, tends to be surprised at first to learn how important actual experiences with similar situations are when it comes to choosing and shaping new situations. Even if a person thinks that he has built a unique relationship with another person or with several other persons for that matter, much of it is rather similar to other earlier relationships. Only a few aspects are different. A boy, for example, who has grown up as a spoiled only child and who wants to join a youth group with the firm intention of being altruistic, of helping others, and of taking no presents, may find himself altruistic in only one respect: he gives away the money that his parents dole out to him more generously than other parents do. For this he wishes to be loved and praised, to be listened to whenever he so wishes, to be preferred to others, to be made their leader, or at least their unanimous pet. He may, deliberately or not, incite antipathy against those who do not wish to play along in this. In other words, he still wants to be the favorite, the "only child," just as at home.

The Complementary Nature of Certain Sibling Roles

We can summarize what has been said as follows: other things being equal, new social relationships are more enduring and successful, the more they resemble the earlier and earliest (intrafamilial) social relationships of the persons involved.

This rule has been called the *duplication theorem* (Toman 1959b, c, d, 1962a, 1965a, 1971). Of course it is not very specific in this form. It may be easy to determine the duration of a relationship, but the success of a relationship is another matter. It is ambiguous unless defined as the voluntary continuation of the relationship on the part of the individuals involved. We might postulate, however, that the divorce or separation of a married couple, the lack of children of their own, or only a few children, as well as the children's problems with their social environment—either as neurotics or delinquents—all constitute failures of a sort, or at least a lack of success of the spouses' relationship with each other. Ultimately, the success of the spouses' children when married themselves would indicate success of the spouses' marriage. In other words: a permanent heterosexual relationship may be called successful if it is not separated, if it leads to having children of their own, and if these children in turn get married themselves and also have children. This is, unquestionably, a rather moderate, though objective criterion of success.

In order to appraise a contemporary love-and-marriage relationship, one cannot ordinarily wait this long. We could consider the spouses' relationship with each other as an indicator of their parents' successful or unsuccessful marriage only if the parents are undergoing psychological evaluation.

There are many other indicators, to be sure. We could interview the persons themselves, or their parents, or their children. We could have them report to us what the couple in question does, and how they have arranged their life together. We could explore their phantasies, their dreams, their letters, or their vacation plans. We could try to find out how much of their time is spent together, how many friends they have in common, what their friends are saying about them, etc. From this mosaic of data we could get an impression of the success of their relationship. As a rule, only time will tell whether their success can be compared with the success of other people's relationships with one another, whether the information is accurate and correct or only pretense or lie. That means, however, that it will be the duration of the relationship under investigation, the extent of their living together, and the happiness of their children that we will go by, and the happiness of their children will be ultimately proven only by the children's own successful marriages.

There is a third aspect in the duplication theorem that needs clarification: the resemblance or similarity of relationships. When is a relationship similar to another relationship? Here we are on safer grounds, particularly when comparing a contemporary relationship with relationships in the partners' original families. The characteristics of family relations and sibling configurations, which we have discussed at length, can help us here. The position that each partner in a love or marriage relationship had in his original family can be characterized, among other things, by his age rank among his siblings and by the sex distribution among them.

A husband, for example, might be the oldest brother of two sisters. This would imply that he has learned to lead girls, to feel responsible for them, to protect them, and to help them. Depending on his wife's sibling position, she may be able to accept her husband's role easily or only with difficulty. No troubles are likely if she is the younger sister of brothers. In that case she would have learned to let boys take responsibility, to submit to their leadership, as well as to be protected and spoiled. We could argue that these two partners complement each other by their age ranks. He is the oldest and she is the youngest. Moreover, both of them have been accustomed to life with a peer of the opposite sex in their original families. Their relationship with each other is *similar* to earlier relationships they have had.

By using the letters b for brother and s for sister, we can not only represent a person himself, but his siblings as well. The siblings, however, would be enclosed in parentheses. In this way, we can symbolize the older brother of a sister as b(s), the younger sister of a brother as (b)s, and the relationship between those two people as b(s)/(b)s. If the husband had two sisters, and the wife three brothers, their symbolic representation would be b(ss)/(bbb)s. In both instances we would call it a *complementary relationship.* By age rank and sex, their experiences in their original families complement each other.

There are other complementary relationships of sibling roles, namely the relationship between a younger brother of sisters and an older sister of brothers. One would expect that she provides the leadership and maternal care, whereas he relies on her, lets her nurse him, and acts as he pleases. Here, too, the age ranks supplement each other, she being an oldest and he a youngest sibling; and both of them have been used to life with a person of the opposite sex in their original families.

If both partners have only one sibling as indicated above, we would symbolize their situation in this way:

(s)b/s(b). If he had several older sisters, their relationship might read (sss)b/s(b). This is also a complementary relationship.

There are also *partially complementary relationships* of sibling roles. In their psychological significance these may be included under complementary relationships. A partially complementary relationship is one in which the lovers or spouses have had sibling relationships in their original families that are complementary to each other in addition to noncomplementary ones. When marrying, an oldest brother of a brother and a sister, for example, b(bs), brings with him experiences of living with both a younger brother and a younger sister. The experiences of living with his brother are obviously irrelevant for his love and marriage relationship. If he marries the middle sister of an older and a younger brother, (b)s(b), she could utilize both types of experiences in love and marriage: her relationship with her older brother and that with her younger brother. What "fits" her current relationship, however, is her sibling relationship with the older brother. She can utilize her experiences with him more easily and more usefully than she can her experiences with her younger brother. Probably her love- and/or marriage-partner will suppress her role of older sister of a brother (which she has also learned to take), and reinforce her in her role of younger sister of a brother.

Thus a partially complementary relationship is one in which one or both partners have had several sibling relationships in their original families, but among them both have had at least one sibling relationship that, by age-rank and sex of siblings, is identical with at least one of the sibling relationships of the other partner. In our example, the husband has, among others, a younger sister, and the wife, among others, an older brother. Written symbolically, their relationship is b(bs)/(b)s(b). The complementary sibling relationships are b(s)/(b)s( ).

We can assume that in a new situation, man is inclined to utilize the one past experience among several different types of past experiences that seems to fit best, that is, the one that stems from the relatively most similar situation in the past. If we assume this, then we may also treat complementary and partially complementary relationships alike. They belong under the same heading. We may presume that the prognosis for such a complementary or partially complementary love or marriage relationship is better than for other types of relationships. Other things being equal, complementary and partially complementary relationships ought to be more enduring and successful than any of the other types of relationships.

Noncomplementary Relationships

If each of two lovers or spouses came from families with only two children, each of them will have held one of four possible sibling positions in his original family (see p. 8). Since each of these four types can combine with any one of the four types of the other sex, there are 4×4 or 4^2 possible combinations of two partners. Two of these 16 types—complementary relationships—have already been discussed. The other extreme would be completely *noncomplementary relationships*. They also come in two versions.

If the oldest brother of a brother enters a relationship with an oldest sister of a sister, we are led to expect that both of them will vie for the position of leadership and of responsibility, and neither will want to subordinate himself or let himself be helped or supported. Since both of them have only had siblings of the same sex in their original families, neither is used to life with a peer of the opposite sex. They cannot quite figure their partner out. We may say that both of them have a *rank and sex conflict* with each other. It is a completely noncomplementary relationship. Written symbolically, examples would be b(b)/s(s) or b(bb)/s(ssss). In the second case, the oldest brother of two brothers is affiliated with the oldest sister of four younger sisters.

A somewhat similar condition prevails when a youngest brother of brothers marries the youngest sister of sisters. Both of them would like to be dependent and to find leadership and responsibility in the spouse. However, this they do not find. In their original families, moreover, both of them have been accustomed to life only with peers of the same sex. In the long run, they do not quite know what to do with each other as man and woman. They have a rank and sex conflict with each other. By sibling position, both of them are juniors. In many ways they get along better with a person of their own sex than with one of the opposite sex. If both of them have but one sibling, this would read (b)b/(s)s. The relationship (bbb)b/(ss)s (the younger brother of three older brothers and the younger sister of two older sisters) would also have a rank and sex conflict. It would be completely noncomplementary.

When we speak of *rank conflict,* the partners or spouses have had similar or identical age ranks in their respective original families. Neither of them is used to the age rank of the other. In their relationship they claim that age rank for themselves.

When we speak of a *sex conflict* among lovers and spouses, a partner has had no siblings of the opposite sex in his original family. In love and marriage that partner is expected to have trouble in his or her daily life trying to get used to the sex of his partner.

A rank conflict always involves both partners. A sex conflict, however, can involve one or both partners. Rank conflicts as well as sex conflicts are examples of noncomplementary relationships.

The extreme case, that is, a combined rank and sex conflict, has already been discussed.

There are *three more types of noncomplementary relationships* that occur between completely or partially complementary relationships on the one hand and those relationships in which both partners have a complete rank as well as sex conflict regarding their sibling roles.

The less extreme form of a sibling role conflict (after a

complete rank and sex conflict) is represented by those lovers or spouses of whom *both* have a *rank conflict*, but only *one* has a *sex conflict*. An example would be a match between an oldest brother of a sister with the oldest sister of a sister, that is, b(s)/s(s), or a match between a younger brother of a brother and the youngest sister of two brothers, that is, (b)b/(bb)s. In the first example, both partners are seniors by their sibling positions; in the second example both are juniors. In both cases, however, at least one of the partners has been accustomed to life with a peer of the opposite sex in his original family. By common sense as well as by the duplication theorem, we may anticipate that this is a little better for their life together than a situation in which both partners have identical age ranks and neither of them is used to life with a peer of the opposite sex.

A still milder form of sibling role conflict is represented by those couples where either both partners have a rank conflict but no sex conflict, or both of them have a sex conflict but no rank conflict. An example of a *rank conflict without a sex conflict* would be the older brother of a sister matched with the oldest sister of a brother, that is, b(s)/s(b). An example of a *sex conflict without a rank conflict* is a younger brother of a brother affiliated with an older sister of a sister: (b)b/s(s). We may infer in the first instance that both partners will claim the position of seniority for themselves and will not want to concede it to the other; in the second instance that the partners will have no authority conflict with each other, but will tend to treat each other like persons of their own respective sex. As far as the age rank and the sex of the partner goes, both couples have been familiar with only one of them in their original families.

One would also include in this type of sibling role conflict a couple that has a sex conflict and a partial rank conflict, for example, the younger brother of a brother and the middle sister of three sisters: (b)b/(s)s(s). As with partially complementary relationships, we may assume that in her current relationship the female partner feels called upon to act the older sister rather than the younger sister.

The mildest form of sibling role conflict would be partners who have *no rank conflict* with each other (or merely a partial one), and *only one* of whom *has a sex conflict*, as for example, the younger brother of a sister and the older sister of a sister: (s)b/s(s), or the older brother of a brother and the younger sister of a brother: b(b)/(b)s. In both examples the partners supplement each other in their age-rank experiences. One of them has been a senior among his siblings, the other a junior. Moreover, at least one of them has been prepared at home for life with a peer of the opposite sex. Only one of the partners comes unprepared in that respect. That partner, however, who brings the experience of living with a peer of the opposite sex into the current relationship, may be considered more likely to shape the heterosexual part of their current relationship than the other partner would be.

An example of love or marriage partners where one partner has a sex conflict as well as a partial rank conflict would be the oldest brother of a sister attached to the middle sister of three sisters, that is, b(s)/(s)s(s), or the oldest brother of a brother associated with a middle sister of two brothers: b(b)/(b)s(b). In the first example, the wife has a sex conflict, whereas the husband does not. Because she was not only the younger sister of a sister but also the older sister of a sister, she may have a little difficulty in accepting a junior role which her husband, the older brother of a sister, would probably like her to take. In the second example, the husband has a sex conflict, but the wife does not. In their relationship the wife is likely to utilize her experiences with her older brother rather than those with her younger brother, but the latter may sometimes interfere.

Only Children among the Partners

In all types of relationships discussed so far, both partners held identifiable sibling positions in their original families. There were no only children among them. Now we have to characterize those heterosexual relationships in which one or both partners are only children. We would expect that an only child is not ordinarily prepared for a peer relationship, whether of the opposite or of the same sex. In his home he could only collect experiences with his father and his mother. By common sense or by the duplication theorem it would seem likely that he would also unconsciously be looking for a father or a mother rather than a sibling-like person in love or in marriage. Nevertheless, since he will be searching for a partner of his own age-group, there are likely to be some difficulties in his love relationships and marriage, at least more than were to be expected between partners both of whom had siblings.

The relatively best prognosis could be given to a match between a single child and a person who has had a sibling of the opposite sex, for example, an only male child and the older sister of a brother: b/s(b); or the younger brother of a sister and an only female child: (s)b/s. The only child thus finds a partner who was able to collect life experiences with a peer of the opposite sex. A similar case could be made for a match between a single child and a person who, in his original family, has had siblings both of the same and of the opposite sex. Such a partner would probably bring his experiences with his opposite-sex sibling rather than those with his same-sex sibling into the new relationship.

A somewhat poorer prognosis is given to a match between an only child and a person who only had siblings of the same sex, such as an only child and the youngest sister of two older sisters: b/(ss)s, or an older brother of a brother and an only female child: b(b)/s. We may infer that the partners with siblings have become used to life with peers well enough in their original family, but not with peers of the opposite sex. Their contribution to their relation with an only child is based on less pertinent experience than it would be had they had siblings of the opposite sex.

The match between two only children would have the poorest prognosis, relatively speaking. Neither partner has had any life experience with a peer which he or she could draw upon in their relationship with each other. Both of them are likely to look for a parent figure in their spouse and unlikely to be able or willing to act that part for the other.

We have already pointed out (p. 28) that only children differ from other only children depending on the sibling position that their same-sex parent had held in his family. Vicarious experiences with the role of that parent may help the only child in his own relationships, particularly in marriage. If a male only child had a father who himself was an oldest brother, the only child will be more capable of taking the position of a senior with his own partner than he would be had his father been a youngest brother or an only child himself. Experiences of losses or of other hardships may, moreover, have compelled the only child to take some kind of a parental position, a role of responsibility and leadership, perhaps vis-à-vis his surviving parent or, at any rate, in the management of his own affairs. Where his now departed parent used to help and assist him, he now has to cope with matters all by himself. Such an only child may also be better prepared than other only children to act responsibly and helpfully toward his partner in love and marriage, even to make sacrifices for her (or him). Whether he really succeeds is these respects, however, depends, among other things, on the severity of the loss he had suffered. Grave losses, particularly those of a parent or of both parents in his early life, can make an only child, or anyone for that matter, so vulnerable that he himself will continue to need help far into his adult years rather than be able to give it.

The Complementary Versus the Noncomplementary Nature of Sibling Roles

Our diagnoses and prognoses of more favorable and less favorable love and marriage relationships imply, among other things, the longer or shorter duration of the relationship and the greater or the smaller number of children springing from it, and eventually even a higher or a

Table 1:   *Degrees of complementarity of sibling roles of spouses in various types of relationships*

(In all Tables b means brother, s means sister. A person's siblings are put in parentheses. The slash indicates association of marriage)

Degrees of complementarity 1 to 3	*Basic types*	*Other examples*
1a. Neither partner has a rank or sex conflict with the other	b(s)/(b)s (s)b/s(b)	b(ss)/(b)s (ss)b/s(bbb)
1b. Each partner has at least one sibling relationship that is neither in a rank nor in a sex conflict with at least one sibling relationship of the partner		b(sb)/(b)s (s)b(s)/s(bbs) (bs)b(s)/(b)s(bs)
2a. Neither partner has a rank conflict (or only a partial one) and only one of the partners has a sex conflict	b(s)/(s)s (s)b/s(s) b(b)/(b)s (b)b/s(b)	b(ss)/(s)s (b)b/s(bbb) b(s)/(s)s(s) b(b)/(b)s(b)
2b. Both partners have either a complete (or partial) rank conflict, but no sex conflict, or both have a sex conflict, but no rank conflict (or only a partial one)	b(s)/s(b) (s)b/(b)s b(b)/(s)s (b)b/s(b)	(ss)b/(bbb)s (b)b(s)/s(bb) (b)b(b)/s(ss) (b)b(b)/(s)s(ss)
2c. Both partners have a complete rank conflict and one of the partners also has a sex conflict	b(s)/s(s) (s)b/(s)s b(b)/s(b) (b)b/(b)s	(ss)b/(ss)s b(bb)/s(bbb)
2d. Both partners have a complete rank and sex conflict	b(b)/s(s) (b)b/(s)s	b(bb)/s(s) (bb)b/(sss)s

Table 1 (continued)

Degrees of complementarity 1 to 3	Basic types	Other examples
3a. One partner is an only child, the other has at least one sibling of the opposite sex	b(s)/s b/s(b) (s)b/s b/(b)s	(s)b(sb)/s b/s(bbb) (s)b(s)/s b/(b)s(s)
3b. One partner is an only child, the other has only (one or more) siblings of the same sex as himself	b(b)/s b/s(s) (b)b/s b/(s)s	b(bb)/s b/(s)s(s)
3c. Both partners are only children	b/s	

lower capability among these children to enter enduring and successful love and marriage relationships themselves in their later lives (see p. 80f). We suggested that the complementarity or partial complementarity of the partners' sibling roles boded well, whereas noncomplementary relationships, that is, relationships in which the partners' sibling roles imply age-rank conflicts and/or sex conflicts, have somewhat poorer chances. The chances of relationships between two partners, one or both of whom were only children, would have to be considered still less propitious. Table 1 summarizes these descriptions and distinctions.

One could argue that it is not the complementarity but rather the identity of sibling roles among lovers and spouses which leads to an enduring and successful relationship. A youngest brother of sisters and a youngest sister of brothers, for example, may understand each other well because both know how it feels to be the only one of one's sex and the youngest among peers. An oldest brother of brothers might get along well with an oldest sister of sisters because both of them have had similar problems with their siblings and have tended to solve them in a like manner. Both have had to provide leadership and responsibility to, and make sacrifices for, the younger ones, and neither has had much chance to practice contacts with peers of the other sex. A partner who might know more or all about the other sex may, because of his superiority, arouse their suspicion and discomfort. Even an only child may be able to empathize better with another only child than would a person with any other sibling position.

All that may be true. It is to be expected that persons with similar or identical role experiences can identify easily with one another. A relationship of *identification* with another person implies, however, that the partners can put themselves in each other's shoes and would thus feel and act like the other in that person's absence. A relationship of identification does not imply that the partners can get along well with each other, that they love to be with one another, or that they will cooperate and complement each other.

In contrast, an *interactive relationship* involves the fact that each partner wants to do things that the other does not want to do. The partners have partly different interests and preferences. One of them plans things, the other carries them out. One likes to go out to work, the other likes to stay at home. The latter may like to shape family life, whereas the former might prefer to follow in this respect. One likes heavy work, the other subtle work, one is a handyman around the house, the other loves to cook. One cares for the children at home, the other takes them on hikes and vacations. One prefers to help the children emotionally, the other intellectually and in school. One manages the family's financial problems, the other its social affairs.

We cannot claim *a priori* that one type of relationship is better than the other, that the similarity of partners or rather their dissimilarity and complementarity is more conducive to an enduring and successful relationship. Couples could conceivably be happy with each other whether they are of one type or of the other. Those couples, however, whose relationship with each other consists of one of identification rather than one of interaction are more likely, as a rule, to live side by side in relative independence from one another than are couples with whom interaction and the complementarity of roles are relatively more dominant. If spouses have chosen to pursue their separate careers and to move and work in different areas, if they grant each other a certain freedom for their private lives and a somewhat separate set of friends, at least in addition to their common friends, if they raise their children in a more parallel way, perhaps by assigning the sons to the husband and the daughters to the wife (which may entail a kind of separation of the sexes among their children), or if they put someone else in charge of their children, the husband and wife may well be like each other without creating trouble for themselves.

In such an identification relationship, one appreciates the partner because one can recognize oneself in him or her. On the other hand, in an interaction relationship, one appreciates the partner more, the less one can recognize of oneself in him or her or, in other words, the greater the difference is between them, relatively speaking. According to Freud (1916/17), a relationship of identification would sooner qualify as a narcissistic relationship, a relationship of interaction as an object relationship. The way Freud viewed it, an object relationship is a more mature relationship. It satisfies the partners more deeply and enduringly, as a rule, than does a narcissistic relationship. We should concede, though, that there is hardly an object relationship that is completely void of narcissistic or identification aspects, and there is hardly a pure and exclusively narcissistic relationship based entirely on identification with the partner.

In our times people continue to proclaim the equality of men not only before the law, where it has to be taken for granted, but also in their biological and psychological make-up. However fashionable this may sound today, it is probably an ideological exaggeration. Many differences between men are determined by nature and genetic constitution, others by social conditions, but even then they are not necessarily to the disadvantage of those involved. It is "natural" and even practical that the lawyer should help the plumber who has legal problems, and that a lawyer with plumbing problems should consult a plumber. It is "natural" that one teacher would rather teach small children and another teacher older children and young adults, or that one likes to work outdoors whereas another person loves to be in an office. To most observers in this world it seems natural that men do the heavier work, other things being equal, and women the more delicate work, that a man defends the family against outside attacks whereas a woman rather attends to the internal problems of the family. In the majority of cases, a husband is not only older than his wife (see p. 3), but also taller, physically stronger, more objective in his grasp of technical problems but more crude in his understanding of social matters; a wife is usually more graceful and beautiful, relatively speaking, she is more responsive to emotions and better in her psychological understanding of other people. A man tends to be the scientist or engineer, a woman the artist, a man the hunter, a woman the gardener, a man more patient with physical and technical problems, a woman with social, psychological, or medical problems, including her own.

There are, of course, other approaches. In some families the parents may change roles without harming the family life or their children. Difficulties may arise here, though, when it comes to appraisals by the neighbors, many of whom may find it somewhat difficult to accept such a reversal of roles. What should be noted, however, is the fact that even after such a reversal of roles has occurred the partners still supplement each other. They live and act in ways that are complementary to each other. In this instance it just so happens that the husband takes care of the house and the children, while the wife is the breadwinner and the family's outside advocate.

Some lovers and spouses want to be very much or completely like each other. Their ideal is, respectively, a feminine man or a masculine woman, or even a sexless individual whose anatomical sex difference is of secondary or absolutely no significance. Such couples are still more the exception than the rule. Each of them loves himself in the other person. Neither of them can tolerate it if the partner should deviate from his image of the partner. If the partner changes, they often separate, usually before they have had children of their own. It has been pointed out (p. 52) that in such a case their separation is of no great historical or sociological significance. Few people are likely to take them as an example, they do not campaign for their type of relationship, and, moreover, they have no children of their own whom they could really influence at an early age. If they do have children, these tend to grow increasingly unhappy because their parents cannot really accept them as persons in their own right with independent interests and wishes. Such parents feel that their children should follow after them, preferably all by themselves and without any educational efforts on the part of the parents. They should if possible be born already as adults.

Homosexual love relationships are often of this type. But even when one of the homosexual lovers tends to assume the role of the person of the other sex, the relationship does not seem to last. Where it does, it often becomes shallow and eccentric as the partners grow older. In any case, the relationship does not ordinarily produce one of the very important long-term and objective consequences of the majority of enduring heterosexual relationships: it does not produce children.

Statistical Tests of Complementarity of Sibling Roles

Although there are clinical-psychological and psychotherapeutic data that have confirmed the views expressed above on favorable and unfavorable love relationships and marriages, this casuistic and anecdotal evidence should be backed up by systematic and statistical tests of the thesis that noncomplementarity of sibling roles of partners does, on the average, reduce the duration and the success of a love relationship or marriage.

One of the negative criteria of the success of a marriage would be divorce. Obviously, in the judgment of one or both partners the marriage was so unsatisfactory that they decided to separate. If the complementarity or noncomplementarity of the partners' sibling roles does play a part in this, then there will be fewer cases of complementarity and more cases of noncomplementarity of sibling roles among the partners of divorced marriages than there are among a control group of intact marriages.

In order to test this, all divorced couples in a district of Boston who could be found, who were willing to cooperate, and among whom there were no only children were interviewed. The latter condition had to be met in order not to complicate comparisons with intact marriages. Only children, after all, have no sibling position.

Sixteen divorced couples were found. They were matched by 16 couples with intact marriages who were not significantly different from the divorced couples in age, in social origin, and in economic status. Intact marriages, moreover, had to have lasted at least ten years and have produced at least two children in order to qualify for our sample. Six of the divorced couples, however, were married less than ten years ago, and in seven cases the divorced couples had had no children. Table 2 shows the results.

We can see that 12 couples out of 16 intact marriages had complementary or partly complementary sibling roles, whereas only one couple did among the 16 divorced marriages. A chi-square test of the observed frequencies indicated that such a frequency distribution would occur by chance in less than 1 per mill of cases ($p < 0.001$). Therefore, the results of our test cannot be chance. Divorced spouses had significantly more rank and/or sex conflicts of sibling roles than did spouses who remained married.

In an experiment like this one, where a control group had to be matched with the experimental group (i.e., the

Table 2: Complementarity of sibling roles of spouses in relation to frequency of divorce

The sibling roles of spouses show	Number of	
	divorced marriages	intact marriages
complete or partial complementarity	1	12
rank and/or sex conflicts	15	4

$\chi^2 = 12.0$; $p < 0.001$

divorced couples), biases in favor of the theoretical expectations may have entered into the selection of subjects. The author is unaware of any such bias. Even so, a repeat experiment with a much larger group of subjects was indicated. By means of a questionnaire survey, 2300 junior-high-school students in Nürnberg and Zürich were asked about simple and objective characteristics of their family constellations, including losses of family members and a few questions about school, residence, and illnesses (see also p. 138ff). The latter included the sibling configurations of the students as well as those of their parents.

It turned out that we had 108 cases of divorced parents in the sample of 2300 families. Hence we could ascertain the frequency of different degrees of complementarity of sibling roles among the divorced parents as well as among the entire sample which could then be taken as representative for the families in the population as a whole. We again assumed that the incidences of complete or partial complementarity would be lower among divorced parents than it would be among the population of parents. Relationships with rank and/or sex conflicts of sibling roles or relationships with only children among the partners were expected to be more frequent among the divorced couples. Table 3 shows the results.

We again find that complementary and partially complementary sibling roles among divorced spouses are significantly less frequent than this would be expected by chance. Rank and sex conflicts as well as only children among the spouses were significantly more frequent than chance among divorced marriages. The frequency distribution reported would occur by chance with a probability of less than 1% (p < 0.01).

The differences are not quite as striking as they were in the first experiment (Table 2). One of the reasons may lie in the fact that in the second, or big, study, all of the 2300 families questioned had children. Access to these families was obtained via the schools. In the first, or small, study of 16 divorced and 16 married couples, seven of the divorced couples had no children. If the big study had also included

Table 3: Complementarity of sibling roles of spouses in relation to frequency of divorce

The sibling roles of spouses show	Number of divorced marriages	Relative frequency in the population
complete or partial complementarity	18	32
rank and/or sex conflicts	52	49
only children among the parents	38	27

$\chi^2 = 10.8$; $p < 0.01$

Table 4:   *Complementarity of sibling roles of divorced parents in relation to the duration of their marriage*

(Expected values are shown in parentheses)

The sibling roles of spouses show	Number of divorced couples who remained married	
	for less than 10 years	for 10 years or longer
complete or partial complementarity	2(7)	13(8)
rank and/or sex conflicts	22(20)	20(23)
only children among the parents	17(14)	14(16)

$\chi^2 = 8.2$; $p < 0.05$

couples who had no children of their own, the difference between the frequencies of complementary and partially complementary sibling roles among divorced spouses on the one hand and the spouses in the population in general on the other might have been larger.

By forming a group made up of divorced couples only, one could test whether those who remained married longer, say for ten years or more, show complementary or partially complementary sibling roles more frequently than do those divorced couples who had remained married for less than ten years. Table 4 shows the results. As can be seen, those divorced couples who remained married longer had complementary or partially complementary sibling roles significantly more frequently than those couples who separated sooner. Those couples whose divorce occurred relatively soon had significantly fewer complementary or partially complementary relationships with each other.

Relationships with rank and/or sex conflicts were more frequent among the couples who were divorced early. The frequency distribution in Table 4 could be expected to occur by chance only with a probability of less than 5% (p <0.05).

The sample of 2300 families also contained unmarried parents and parents who did not live together. It is probably fair to assume that this kind of relationship between parents who never married and never lived together represents another type of failure which is similar to the one represented by divorce. Again, we would suspect that those marriages that never came about would show fewer incidents of complementarity or partial complementarity of sibling roles of the partners than does the population of parents at large. Table 5 gives the results.

Here we notice that not only complementary and partially complementary relationships, but also those showing rank and/or sex conflicts were rarer among unmarried

Table 5: *Complementarity of sibling roles of unmarried parents of illegitimate children*

The sibling roles of unmarried parents show	Number of couples	Relative frequency in the population
complete or partial complementarity	5	9
rank and/or sex conflicts	6	13
only children among the parents	18	7

$\chi^2 = 22.9$; p < 0.001

parents than they were in the population at large. The fact that one or both of the unmarried parents were only children themselves, however, was particularly frequent among this group. The likelihood of this frequency distribution occurring by chance is less than 1 per mill (p <0.001).

Partial complementarity of sibling roles ought to be more frequent, the larger the number of siblings that each partner had had. This makes sense, since the probability of having siblings of both sexes increases with the number of siblings. For a person in a nondistal or middle position, the likelihood of having both older and younger siblings of both sexes also increases with the number of siblings. In any case, one of these different sibling relationships is likely to correspond to the configuration of any partner whom he (or she) might choose. Conversely, rank and/or sex conflicts between the partners' sibling positions are that much more likely, the smaller the sibling configurations from which they have come.

It could be that our tests of complementarity of sibling roles of spouses confirm our theoretical expectations of more enduring and successful relationships not so much because of the complementarity itself, but because of the number of siblings that the spouses had. Perhaps the partners get along well with each other because they grew up in large families, or conversely, perhaps they do not get along very well because they came from small families or are only children. Complementarity of sibling roles might only be a secondary consequence of the larger number of siblings, and this then might primarily determine how enduring and successful the relationship will be.

In order to test this possiblity, the number of siblings would have to be held constant. If the complementarity effect really is significant, spouses with equal numbers of siblings should have fewer complementary and partially complementary relationships of sibling position if they are divorced than if their marriages have remained intact. Those couples among the 108 divorced parents who had four or five siblings between the two of them (that is, one spouse had

Table 6:   *Complementarity of sibling roles when the number of*
the spouses' siblings is held constant

The sibling roles of the spouses show	*Number of divorced couples*	*Relative frequency in the population*
complete or partial complementarity	5	11
rank and/or sex conflicts	26	20

$\chi^2 = 5.1$; $p < 0.05$

two siblings, the other three, or one spouse one sibling, and the other three, or each spouse two siblings, etc.) were singled out from the rest. They amounted to 31 couples. The frequencies of complementary or noncomplementary sibling roles are shown in Table 6.

Again we can see that divorced couples have significantly fewer complementary and partially complementary sibling roles than the population of spouses at large. The frequency distribution shown above would come about by chance in less than 5% of all cases. While the number of siblings the partners have cannot be ruled out as a contributing factor to the duration and success of a marriage, we can be sure that the complementarity of the partners' sibling roles is also an influencing factor.

Comparison of the frequency of divorce among all those 2300 parents studied whose sibling roles were completely complementary, that is, where the spouses were either oldest brothers of sisters married to youngest sisters of brothers, or youngest brothers of sisters married to oldest sisters of brothers, proved particularly impressive. There was not a single divorce among them. Those parents, however, whose sibling positions showed both a complete rank and sex conflict had an empirical probability of divorce of 16%. These parents were either oldest brothers of brothers married to oldest sisters of sisters, or youngest brother of brothers married to youngest sisters of sisters.

Combining parents with completely complementary relationships and those with partially complementary relationships of sibling roles, we obtained an empirical probability of divorce of 3%. Hence, we might say that the probability of divorce among parents whose sibling roles show both a complete rank and sex conflict is five times as great as the probability of divorce for parents whose sibling roles are complementary or partially complementary. The frequency of divorce in the population at large was 5% for the generation of parents studied. Today's rate of divorce is obviously higher than that.

We also compared the duration of the marriage until the divorce occurred, and we found that parents with complementary or partially complementary sibling positions were married for an average of 16 years, whereas parents whose sibling positions had both a rank and a sex conflict were married for an average of nine years.

Let us now leave the failure criterion "divorce of spouses" and go on to test whether another criterion of success, children, shows differential effects depending on the complementarity or noncomplementarity of the parents' sibling positions. We would assume that parents with complementary or partially complementary relationships are relatively happier and more content with each other and would therefore (others things being equal) tend to have more children than would parents with rank and/or sex conflicts among their sibling roles, or parents one or both of whom were only children. Table 7 shows the results.

Obviously, the theoretical expectations were confirmed. On the average, parents have significantly more children than the population at large if their sibling roles are complementary or partially complementary. They have

Table 7:   *Complementarity of sibling roles of parents in relation
            to number of children*

(Expected values are shown in parentheses)

The sibling roles of parents show	Number of children		
	1	*2 to 4*	*5 and more*
complete or partial complementarity	110(146)	501(482)	71(53)
rank and/or sex conflicts	205(222)	749(732)	80(81)
only children among the parents	182(129)	388(424)	30(47)

$\chi^2 = 48.4$; $p < 0.001$

significantly fewer children than the average if one or both of
them were only children. The observed frequencies in Table
7 can be expected by chance only with a probability of less
than 1 per mill ($p < 0.001$). On the average, parents with
complementary or partially complementary sibling roles had
about half a child more than the average population; those
one or both of whom were only children had about half a
child less.

The question did arise as to whether the population in
general heeds the duplication theorem, even if unconsciously, and whether therefore more complementary
and partially complementary relationships are formed, on
the whole, than would be expected by chance. This could
not be confirmed for the total sample of 2300 families. What
could be shown, though, is that partners whose age at the
time of marriage was above the median age of marriage
(which was 27 years for the husband and 24 years for the

wife) had complementary and partially complementary sibling roles significantly more frequently than expected by chance. On the other hand, parents who had married earlier than the average had significantly lower frequencies of complementary or partially complementary sibling roles. The observed frequencies would occur by chance with a probability of less than 1 per mill ($p < 0.001$).

This means that, in a general way, the duplication theorem is being heeded and obeyed after all, at least to an extent. It is more likely to be heeded, the older the spouses are when they marry. Perhaps we can say that these couples have thought things over more carefully, that they have had more experiences on which to draw, and that they have come to know more people who may be eligible spouses, than would partners who marry early. More often than chance the former choose partners with sibling roles complementary or partially complementary to their own.

Of course, it cannot be concluded from our data that the duplication theorem by itself describes all or even major portions of married and family life as it actually occurs. The only thing we can be sure about is that it will have to be considered in family research. It is valid to an extent. Complementarity of sibling roles of lovers and spouses is one of the factors that seems to influence the duration and the success of a relationship.

Moreover, it was found that spouses with complementary sibling roles had their first child somewhat sooner after marriage than did those spouses with noncomplementary sibling roles. Losses of family members that spouses suffered in their original families tend to delay their date of marriage by one to three years, as well as to lead to a relatively poorer choice of partners. Complementarity or partial complementarity of sibling roles is somewhat rarer among them than in the population in general.

The parents of children and adolescents who consulted psychological counseling centers, as well as those of juvenile delinquents in reformatories and jails (as far as data on this were available), had not only suffered early losses of family members to a greater extent than the population in general, but also showed a greater-than-chance incidence of non-complementary sibling roles (Toman, Preiser, Gasch, & Plattig 1967). There were also more only children than expected by chance among the parents of neurotic children, that is, children who came to psychological counseling centers for help.

Other studies bearing on complementarity or noncomplementarity of the parents' sibling roles and its effects on behavior will be discussed in a separate chapter (p. 287ff). In summarizing what we have said so far, we may conclude that practically all tests of the duplication theorem turned out positive. Complementary sibling roles of lovers and spouses affect their relationship favorably, while noncomplementary sibling relationships, including those of only children, tend to have unfavorable effects. The field experiments we reported always dealt with hard, objective data that were quite unlikely to have been distorted by the subjects' self-evaluations or by the researchers' ratings.

Yet the reader should be reminded that noncomplementary relationships, including those that involve only children, need not fail automatically. Even in the group of spouses with the lowest degree of complementarity, that is, with complete rank and sex conflict of their sibling roles, only 16% were divorced, while 84% of them managed to get along with each other and stay together. Obviously all kinds of combinations of partners' sibling roles have a chance to last and succeed, although the probability of failure is clearly greater with some than it is with others. We can assume, however, that those couples who do not separate despite that greater probability—and this is the majority—shape their relationship with each other differently depending on their sibling positions and their degrees of complementarity. We will elaborate on this when we characterize in greater detail the various basic sibling positions and the various types of parent relationships.

7.   Friendships

Complementarity criteria for friendships among persons of the same sex are similar to those for heterosexual friendships. With the latter, as with love and marriage relationships, the existence of siblings of the opposite sex and of the same age rank that the partner has experienced among his own siblings tends to be relatively the best precondition for a successful and enduring relationship, other things being equal.

With friendships among persons of the same sex, the existence of a same-sex sibling of an identical or a similar age rank as the friend constitutes a favorable precondition for the friendship. An oldest brother of brothers, for example, would tend to get along better with a youngest brother of brothers, a youngest sister of sisters better with an older sister of sisters than with persons who hold other sibling positions. In both examples, the partners have neither an age-rank nor a sex conflict. One of them is a senior, the other a junior among their respective siblings, and both of them are used to life with a peer of the same sex at home.

Siblings of the opposite sex are less apt to prepare a

Table 8:   *Degree of complementarity of sibling roles among same-sex friends in various types of relationships*

(A slash indicates an association of two friends)

Degrees of complementarity 1 to 3	Friendships among men	Friendships among women
1a. Neither partner has a rank or sex conflict with the other	b(b)/(b)b	s(s)/(s)s
1b. Each partner has at least one sibling relationship that is neither in a rank nor in a sex conflict with at least one sibling relationship of the partner	b(bs)/(b)b(b)	(b)s(s)/(bss)s
2a. Neither partner has a rank conflict (or only a partial one) and only one of the partners has a sex conflict	b(b)/(s)b (b)b/b(s)	s(s)/(b)s (s)s/s(b)
2b. Both partners have either a complete (or partial) rank conflict, but no sex conflict, or both have a sex conflict, but no rank conflict (or merely a partial one)	b(b)/b(b) (b)b/(b)b b(s)/(s)b	s(s)/s(s) (s)s/(s)s s(b)/(b)s
2c. Both partners have a complete rank conflict and one of the partners has a sex conflict	b(b)/b(s) (b)b/(s)b	s(s)/s(b) (s)s/(b)s
2d. Both partners have a complete rank and sex conflict	b(s)/b(s) (s)b/(s)b	s(b)/s(b) (b)s/(b)s

Table 8 (continued)

Degrees of complementarity 1 to 3	Friendships among men	Friendships among women
3a. One partner is an only child, the other has at least one sibling of the same sex	b(b)/b (b)b/b	s(s)/s (s)s/s
3b. One partner is an only child, the other has only opposite-sex siblings	b(s)/b (s)b/b	s(b)/s (b)s/s
3c. Both partners are only children	b/b	s/s

person for same-sex friendships. Contacts with peers of the opposite sex would generally seem preferable to such persons. They would have a sex conflict with friends of the same sex. If a person has siblings of the same as well as of the other sex, he is likely to utilize his experience with his same-sex siblings in his contacts with acquaintances and friends of the same sex, and his experiences with opposite-sex siblings in his contacts with peers of the opposite sex. There would be a rank conflict but no sex conflict between two oldest sisters of sisters who become friends. There would be a rank and sex conflict between the oldest sister of brothers who befriends another oldest sister of brothers.

Here, too, we may order the various types of same-sex friendships according to the degrees of complementarity of the partners' sibling roles. If, for the time being, we only consider persons with one sibling, say the older brother of a brother, the younger brother of a brother, the older brother of a sister, or the younger brother of a sister, each can associate himself with a boy holding any of those four respective sibling positions. This makes 16 types of friendship partners, only ten of which differ from each other. The other six are only the symmetrical counterparts of relationships contained among the ten types. The relationship between an older brother of a brother and the younger brother of a brother, for example, is formally identical with the relationship between a younger brother of a brother and an older brother of a brother.

This reduced variety of types of relationships among same-sex friends may be one of the reasons for the greater value that is usually assigned to a friendship among persons of different sexes. Another reason is, of course, that friendships between persons of different sexes may lead to marriage and children and may thus contribute to maintaining the social system.

Friendships among girls and women are analogous to those among boys and men. The older or the younger sister of a brother or a sister may be friends with a girl of any of those four sibling positions. There are also ten different types of relationships here, if both friends came from two-child families and are characterized merely by their age ranks among their respective siblings and by the sexes of their siblings.

Following Table 1 (p. 90), Table 8 presents the basic types of friendships among men and those among women. Additional and more complicated examples of relationships would have to be presented in analogy to Table 1, but they have been omitted. The reader is reminded that friendships among partners having more than one sibling relationship of a given type (the oldest brother of several sisters, for example, who is the friend of the youngest brother of several brothers) are to be viewed in much the same way as those who have only one sibling (e.g., the older brother of a sister and the younger brother of brother). Likewise, the relationship b(bb)/(bbb)b would be considered as complementary as b(b)/(b)b. Moreover, the reader is reminded that partially complementary same-sex friendships require that among his sibling relationships a person has at least one that has neither a rank nor a sex conflict with at least one sibling relationship of the friend.

Table 8 has also been arranged according to the complementarity of sibling roles, whereby, in analogy to heterosexual friendships (Table 1), the similarity of a same-sex friend with a sibling of one's own family decreases by a growing number of aspects.

Friendships between two persons of the same sex were also shown to be subject to the duplication theorem, at least to an extent. If sibling roles are complementary, friendships tend to last longer and the friends tend to be more satisfied with each other. Friendships whose partners held similar or identical sibling positions in their original families tended to end sooner than those with complementary sibling roles (Kassel 1962, Schott 1966, Toman, Gasch, & Schmidt 1972).

The majority of marriage partners have been married only once. Love relationships may have been established with several persons, although usually not simultaneously but in succession. Friendships, on the other hand, may be maintained with several persons simultaneously, whether they involve persons of the same or of the opposite sex. Hence it is more difficult to compare one person's friendships with those of another. We do not know what set of friendships it belongs to and what its functions are in that set.

We therefore recommend that friendships be studied by inquiring about all the friends a person has and/or has had in his life. We found that, on the average, a person knows the sibling positions of 80% of his (or her) friends. He has also met a parent of 50% of his friends (more often the mother than the father), and with 50% of them he knows at least one of the friend's siblings. When questioned, a person will mention an average of 15 friends whom he had and/or has. Given the opportunity to talk about his friends in an unstructured or free psychological interview, a person will mention an average of five friends, three of whom tend to be of the same sex and two of the opposite sex.

Among friends mentioned or enumerated by males, the persons of complementary age ranks were somewhat more frequent than chance. Males who had sisters among their siblings mentioned relatively more female friends than did those males who had only brothers. Taken absolutely, however, all males (and females) tended to name more friends of the same sex than of the opposite sex. Both trends, that is, a preference for friends of complementary age rank and of the sex of one's sibling(s), were statistically significant (Toman 1972b, Toman, Gasch, & Schmidt 1972). The duplication theorem has therefore some validity with friendships too. Females of the sample studied, however, displayed no clear trend in their choices of friends.

The set or system of friends that a person has built for himself and maintained at a given time of his life is also an indicator of the preferences developed in his original family. If a person holds a middle sibling position, for example, (bs)b(sb), that is, if he is the middle brother of an older brother, an older sister, a younger sister, and a younger brother, the sibling positions of his friends tend to indicate which of his different relationships he may have preferred in his original family. If there are four oldest and one middle brother among his male friends, but not one youngest brother, we may interpret this to mean that he himself liked the role of youngest brother of brothers better than that of oldest brother of brothers. If, on the other hand, he tells us that his various girlfriends were an oldest, three middle and two youngest sisters as well as an only child, we may assume that vis-à-vis girls he likes being the leader and the person in charge about as much as he does being the person led, that is, being dependent and looked after. His relationship with his older sister could be just as good as his relationship with his younger sister. Judging by the numbers of friends, moreover, he seems to prefer relationships with girls to those with boys.

Likewise, the female friends of a female only child might be predominantly younger siblings. This would suggest that the person likes to assume the role of the oldest vis-à-vis peers of the same sex. The fact that her mother is the oldest sister of sisters would constitute a plausible reason for that. By way of identification, the person has partly adopted her mother's sibling role. If her mother were the younger sister of a sister instead, we would have to look for other explanations. Maybe the daughter, the only child, has been unconsciously urged by her mother to act the older sister for her. Mother may have made her a confidante and adviser with respect to her own emotional problems. The child would be hard put, of course, to try to accommodate her mother, but if the mother keeps at it and if mother's older sister is around the house a good deal, the daughter may have learned to play that role. We could also say the mother has unconsciously compelled her daughter to identify with her, the mother's sister, rather than with herself. Such a course of events is more likely, if the relationship between the father and mother was not very happy.

An oldest brother of a younger brother and a still younger sister might prefer oldest siblings among both his male and female friends. This would contradict our expectations. If we learn, however, that his mother as well as his father had been oldest siblings, both of them in monosexual sibling configurations (the father had only brothers, the mother only sisters), the behavior of the person in question may be more understandable. His father and mother may have found it difficult to get used to life with each other as man and woman. An attitude of war between the sexes may have prevailed in their relationship with each other. Because of their rank and sex conflict, the parents may have tended to pull the children of their own sexes to their sides to form a common front against the other sex in the family. If, moreover, their oldest son happened to be constitutionally weaker than his younger brother, or if the father, for reasons of his own, had a stronger than usual unconscious need to treat his first son like his own younger brother and to form an interactive relationship with him rather than one of identification, his oldest son may come to feel rather insecure in his seniority position vis-à-vis his siblings. He may feel he wants, or is wanted, to lean on his father rather than to assert himself, to identify with him and become a model for his siblings. Hence, perhaps, his preference for oldest siblings among his friends.

His mother, in turn, might have preferred her oldest

son, since he did not try to act authoritatively and as a leader. She claimed him for herself and left the second son to the father for identification with father or to assume a position of authority and seniority. If the oldest son sensed he could be sure of his mother's favor if he submitted to her and depended on her, we may have found the reason for his preference of oldest sisters among his girl friends.

Every person builds his individual friendship system as he (or she) grows up. This system of friends supplements his relationships with his original family. It grows in importance as he approaches the time when his own permanent love relationships and marriage are possible. Eventually it also supplements the family life he creates for himself. Some persons could not have or imagine family life except within the context and in interaction with a smaller or larger circle of friends, whereas others do not consider those extra-familial relationships and contacts very important.

Reasons for this can be found in the original family constellations of the spouses, as well as in the degree of the couple's compatibility with one another and with the child configuration they create for themselves. Parents with rank and sex conflicts of their sibling positions, for example, tend to remain more dependent on their circles of acquaintances and (same-sex) friends, some of whom they do not even want to share with the other parent. In contrast, couples whose sibling positions show complete or partial complementarity are likely to enjoy each other more and display no great need to pull many friends into their marriage. Parents who have come from large families themselves have a greater need than parents coming from a small family to perpetuate this style of their original family life by engaging in a more active social life. Last but not least, parents who have the type and kind of children that they had wanted, both consciously and unconsciously, are more inclined to stay home than are parents who have too few or too many children or whose children happened to have the "wrong" sex or to have come in the "wrong order."

Individual friendship systems, that is, the friends that a

person has had and/or still has, can be described by certain simple and objective characteristics. These include the number and duration of such friendships, the age and sex of the friends, the frequencies and durations of contacts with them, the familiarity of a person with his (her) friends' family situations, a person's ability to maintain friendships over varying geographic distances and separation spans, and the degree to which a person's friends either know each other or know about each other (see Toman 1968, Toman, Gasch, & Schmidt 1972, Toman 1973b).

On the whole, an individual friendship system may be presumed to be more mature and more gratifying and useful, the greater the number of friendships it comprises, as well as the more variegated the friends are by age (and sex), by duration of friendship, frequency of contacts and duration of each contact, by degree of familiarity with the friends' family members, and by the number of acquaintanceships or friendships prevailing among those friends. If a person retains no friends from his previous place of residence, if all his friends are of the same age and of only one sex, if he does not know a single one of his friends' family members, and if all of his friends also know each other or none of them knows any other, we are likely to be dealing with a more primitive or underdeveloped friendship system, perhaps with an unfortunate person who could do no better, someone who could not build a better individual friendship system for himself. If someone has many friends of both sexes who differ from each other by age, duration of friendship, frequency of contacts, familiarity with friends' family situations, if several groups among those friends also know each other; if the circles of friends that a person has overlap at least in part with those that his or her spouse had before marriage, if married couples had not only known each other's families but also each other's acquaintances and friends before they were married, and if they continue to maintain at least a part of those acquaintances and friendships, we are likely to be dealing with a highly developed individual friendship system.

Such individual friendship systems are partly dependent on social strata. In the upper and upper middle classes people know each other better and participate in each others' lives and fates in many more ways than do people in the lower classes. In a given social stratum, however, structural differences among these individual friendship systems usually indicate differences among respective persons, their family contexts, and their courses of life.

8. Parent-Child Relationships

We have already described the major types of relationships that siblings develop with each other (p. 9ff). There are $\binom{n}{2}$ dual relationships between the children of a sibling configuration. Each parent, moreover, develops his own specific relationship with each one of the children. This makes n relationships for each parent, or a total of 2n relationships. The number of relationships that exist between all of the family members is $\binom{n+2}{2}$. For example, a family with parents and three children gives us $\binom{5}{2}$, and that yields altogether 10 relationships. There are 2n relationships respectively between one parent and one child, 3 respectively between each of two of the three children, and 1 between the parents. If there are more children, say six, there are $\binom{6}{2}$ or 15 relationships between the children, 12 between parents and children and again 1 between the parents themselves. The total number of dual relationships should be $\binom{8}{2}$, which is 28. Computed the other way we get $15 + 12 + 1$, which is also 28.

What experiences do parents first draw upon and utilize when they have their own children? They might derive some of their knowledge and competence from the literature on education, which is not bad, but usually rather insufficient when applied in reality. More importantly, parents may draw on their own experiences when they were children themselves. Their own families taught them relatively most directly how to deal with children.

For one thing, there was their contact with their parents. They may remember how they themselves felt at the hands of their parents. They would also know, moreover, what went on in their parents' minds and what their parents wanted of them. An integral part of the process of education in the family is the understanding and adoption of the behavior and wishes of one's parents. This process is called *identification* with the parents, also introjection of the parents' wishes into oneself, or socialization. Identification, introjection, and acts of socialization also take place outside the family, but they start within the family (Freud 1916/17, Toman 1960c, 1968, Wurzbacher 1968).

Secondly, there was the contact with siblings. Depending on his own sibling position, a person has seen some of his younger siblings arrive after he did. Others had been around as long as he can remember. If all of a person's siblings had been around as far back as he can remember he is obviously likely to be a youngest sibling himself. His siblings may have been of the opposite sex, of the same sex, or of both sexes. A person's relationship to them may have been determined by the parents' wishes and behavior, while some of it has probably resulted from the direct experiences with his siblings.

In a certain sense, parents are less different from other parents than are sibling configurations from other sibling configurations. Parents are always of both sexes, which is not true of all sibling configurations. Most often the father works and provides a living for the family, whereas the mother takes care of the house and the children. On the average, the father is three years older than the mother, he is taller and physically stronger; the mother, in turn, is more graceful, prettier, more patient, etc.(see also p. 94). Even the children themselves differ more from their parents than they do from their siblings, not only by reason of age but also because of all those things that parents do alike for each of their children (such as feeding them, clothing them, putting them to bed, etc.).

Hence we may surmise that (former) children who have become parents themselves will tend, through identification with their own parents, to adopt similar characteristics and features vis-à-vis their children as do other parents toward *their* children. This is at least true for the direct interaction between parent and child. General differences between certain sets or types of parents, particularly those deriving from the compatibility or incompatibility of their sibling positions, will concern us later.

Experiences within one's own sibling configuration, however, not only tend to differ from the experiences of children in other families, but even from those of one's own siblings who hold different positions. It comes as no great surprise that most people experience their own position more immediately and emphatically than they do the positions of their siblings. They learn about the latter only by identification or occasionally imagining what is going on in the other person. If it is true that everybody knows himself better than anyone else, we might conclude from this that everybody knows his own sibling position better than other sibling positions.

All of this, incidentally, has nothing to do with how children should be treated as newborn babies. This aspect of child care is new for parents only with their first-born and is often not too difficult to learn. It is harder for them to accept the fact that from now on another person is here to stay, however small he or she may be at first, and that he will constantly call for the parents' attention and help. It is more difficult to realize that things do not merely repeat themselves with the arrival of the second child, but that the first child will react against the second, and eventually the second will react against the first, and the entire family situation changes. This continues with the third child, the fourth, etc.

The parents, too, have to develop a relationship with each of their children, as well as toward relationships that the children develop themselves. This is often felt to be even more true when a child configuration has become final, that is, when the parents have decided not to have any more children. After all, the children are growing up. Their relationships to each other and to their parents differentiate and become more stable. A given child increasingly accepts the role his parents and his siblings have assigned to him; they seem to be just as interested in his adhering to it as he may be himself. Even the parents still have a lot to learn, and it is here that their long-term experiences in their original families come in handy. Here they use what they think they have learned through identification with their parents as well as what they have experienced, suffered, and achieved in their contacts and interactions with their own siblings.

If a parent tries to understand how his child feels and to identify with the child's situation, psychologically as well as logically, he is more likely to have the greatest success with that one of his children who has the same position among his siblings that he had among his.

A father who was the oldest brother of brothers, for instance, can better identify with his oldest son than he can with his middle or his youngest son. If his oldest son is also his only son, his other children being daughters, the father may find it a bit harder to identify with him. He may have acted the leader and the model of his siblings, that is, his brothers, but his own son seems to be able to act the leader and protector of his sisters, but cannot very well be their model. He has to treat them like girls, kinder, more tolerantly, and more tactfully perhaps than his father treated his brothers, and that is where the father cannot quite follow him. If such a father (the oldest brother of brothers) happens to have only daughters, he may identify more readily with his oldest daughter than with the rest, but altogether less so than he would be able to with sons. The mother is more likely to become the daughters' model or idol, the father rather the friend and coveted partner whose favors must be fought for with one's siblings and, at best, shared with them.

The same would apply to a mother who is the youngest sister of brothers. She can identify most easily with her youngest daughter, particularly if the rest of her children are sons. If she has only daughters, she may have a little trouble understanding the behavior of her youngest daughter toward her older ones, particularly her knack for competition and opposition. If this mother has only sons, on the other hand, she will feel more familiar with the situation of the youngest than with that of the others, but she will, for the most part, interact rather than identify with any of her sons. In such an interaction relationship, for which all of her sons may be vying, the oldest son is likely to become her favorite.

As far as the *identification of a parent with his children* is concerned, we may thus postulate that he (or she) is likely to select that child first who is of his own sex and has a similar age rank as well as a similar sex role among his siblings to that of the parent among his own siblings. It is with that child that the parent can best identify, and the child in turn is likely to identify himself (or herself) better with that parent than would his siblings. Especially when it comes to handling his siblings, this child can learn more from his parent than his siblings can. The parent's conscious and unconscious lessons apply most directly to his own situation. After all, it is the situation which is relatively the most similar to the one in which he himself has grown up. If a parent treats any of his children preferentially at all, he is likely to intervene in favor of that child who has an identical or relatively most similar sibling position to his own.

Tables 9a and 9b show the various possibilities of identification and identification conflicts between a parent and his same-sex child. The greater the similarity of the sibling positions of father and son or of mother and daughter, respectively, the lesser the difficulties of identification with one another. In Table 9a and 9b, identification conflicts increase from top to bottom.

With respect to the interactions between parents and children, that is, asking for and giving help, cooperating and

*Table 9:   Possibilities of identification and identification conflicts
between parent and same-sex child regarding the basic
types of sibling positions*

a.

The son's sibling position	The father's sibling position is			
	b(b)	(b)b	b(s)	(s)b
is identical	b(b)	(b)b	b(s)	(s)b
shows a sex conflict	b(s)	(s)b	b(b)	(b)b
shows a rank conflict	(b)b	b(b)	(s)b	b(s)
shows a rank and sex conflict	(s)b	b(s)	(b)b	b(b)

b.

The daughter's sibling position	The mother's sibling position is			
	s(s)	(s)s	s(b)	(b)s
is identical	s(s)	(s)s	s(b)	(b)s
shows a sex conflict	s(b)	(b)s	s(s)	(s)s
shows a rank conflict	(s)s	s(s)	(b)s	s(b)
shows a rank and sex conflict	(b)s	s(b)	(s)s	s(s)

dividing the work, in other words doing things *with* the
other person rather than *like* the other person, a father who
was the oldest brother of sisters in his own family ought to
get along well with his youngest daughter among older sons.
If he only has daughters, he is likely to choose the youngest
or perhaps a middle daughter rather than the oldest for a
common enterprise in which he may need an assistant, a
helper, or a companion. If he only has sons, contacts with
them would be a little harder to maintain than with girls, but

the easiest for him to deal with and get along with would still be his youngest son, relatively speaking.

A mother who was the youngest sister of brothers in her original family usually finds her oldest son to be the most comfortable companion. This is especially true if the rest of her children are daughters. If she has sons only, she would still enjoy her oldest son's company best. If this mother only has daughters, she would find interacting with them relatively more difficult. As a rule the father may find it easier to interact with daughters even though they all strive for his attention and favors. One of them might get the lion's share or, if he intends an equal distribution, all of them may get rather little. If the mother develops any interaction relationship with any of her daughters, it would most likely be with her oldest daughter. In turn, the children thus chosen and favored by their parents find it easier than the other children to get along well with their parents.

In general we might say that *in his direct contacts and interactions, a parent prefers* that child who holds a position among his siblings that is similar or identical with the position of one of the parent's siblings. In other words, a parent can be with and cooperate best with that one of his children whose sibling position is relatively most complementary to his own. In the most favorable case that parent has neither a rank nor a sex conflict of sibling roles with that child.

Table 1 might be used to illustrate these relationships since it presents the different degrees of complementarity of sibling roles for the various types of love and marriage partners. All we would have to do is to substitute father/daughter or mother/son for husband/wife. In order to make sure, though, that there is no misunderstanding, different degrees of complementarity between parent and opposite-sex child are shown in Table 10a and 10b in a simplified form. Only the combinations of the basic types of sibling positions are presented. The reader is reminded that low complementarity involves similar or identical positions of partners and that an identification relationship between

Table 10: *Possibilities of interaction relationships and interaction conflicts between parent and opposite-sex child regarding the basic types of sibling position*

---

a.

	The father's sibling position is			
The daughter's sibling position	b(s)	(s)b	b(b)	(b)b
is complementary	(b)s	s(b)		
shows partial sex conflict	(s)s	s(s)	(b)s	s(b)
shows rank conflict without sex conflict, or sex conflict without rank conflict	s(b)	(b)s	(s)s	s(s)
shows rank conflict and partial sex conflict	s(s)	(s)s	s(b)	(b)s
shows complete rank and sex conflict			s(s)	(s)s

b.

	The mother's sibling position is			
The son's sibling position	s(b)	(b)s	s(s)	(s)s
is complementary	(s)b	b(s)		
shows partial sex conflict	(b)b	b(b)	(s)b	b(s)
shows rank conflict without sex conflict, or sex conflict without rank conflict	b(s)	(s)b	(b)b	b(b)
shows rank conflict and partial sex conflict	b(b)	(b)b	b(s)	(s)b
shows complete rank and sex conflict			b(b)	(b)b

two partners in general, and between a parent and an opposite-sex child in particular, is more likely, the lower the
complementarity of sibling roles. This implies that such partners understand each other and can substitute for one
another, but they do not supplement each other. Both of
them can do the same things equally well. They can take
turns or work in a parallel way, but they cannot easily be
with or work with each other.

Conversely, we can say of any identification relationship that increasing identification conflicts involve increasing complementarity of sibling roles of the partners in
question. As for the identification relationship between a
parent and his or her same-sex child (see Table 9), this implies
that such partners can sooner live with one another than
side-by-side or as each other's substitutes. They should be
the same, but instead they supplement each other. They are
not in each other's way, because one can do what the other
cannot do.

Naturally, the complementarity or noncomplementarity
of sibling roles of the parents themselves is not irrelevant to
their relationship with their children. If the parents have
complementary sibling roles and if among their children
there are some that have sibling positions complementary to
their own, the family constellation may be considered
especially favorable.

As an example, let us take a father who has been the
oldest brother of two sisters, a mother who has an older
brother, and a child configuration of boy/girl. Expressed
symbolically, it reads like this: b(ss)/bs/(b)s. In this expression the father is written on the left, the mother on the
right, and the children in the middle, between the two slashes.
This constellation is especially favorable because each parent
has exactly what he needed, both in terms of interaction as
well as of identification with his children. Parent and same-
sex child have identical sibling positions: the father can
readily identify with his son, the mother with her daughter.
Moreover the sibling roles of parent and opposite-sex child
are complementary. The father can interact comfortably

with his daughter, the mother with her son. The children themselves can develop their relationship with each other according to their experiences with one another and according to their vicarious experiences as observers of their parents and their relationship. Everything fits. Neither parent interferes with them. There is no inappropriate sibling role in the entire family.

The situation would be different if the same parents had a daughter first and son afterwards, that is, b(ss)/sb/(b)s. Father and son as well as mother and daughter have a certain amount of identification conflict with each other. Both parents as well as both children had and have a sibling of the opposite sex. The father, however, has been used to acting the senior for girls, whereas his son is taking the role of junior vis-à-vis his sister. He wants her to cater to him and care for him. He has been the younger one, also the little one, at least in the beginning. The father does not like his son's attitude toward girls, and the son does not understand what his father wants of him. The mother and daughter have a similar experience. The daughter tends to assume responsibility for her brother and to nurture him, but the mother does not quite see how her daughter dares to do that.

The interaction between father and daughter and between mother and son is also conflict-laden to an extent. The father does not like his daughter to take charge of men and to mother them. The daughter does not understand why her father does not want to be treated somewhat like her little brother. The mother wants to be approached kindly and politely and is surprised that her son, in spite of his father's good example, does not do so. The son, in turn, cannot see what she expects of him.

If the same set of parents had had three children, a son, a daughter, and a son, that is, b(ss)/bsb/(b)s, we are able to predict with some likelihood of accuracy which of the three children the parents are likely to consider the difficult one: the youngest son. Without him the parents and children would all live harmoniously with each other. All identification relationships and interaction relationships contain no conflict of sibling roles. The children's relationship among themselves duplicates that of their parents. The youngest son, however, has both an identification conflict with his father and an interaction conflict with his mother. In a sense we have already described his situation. He cannot be a senior of girls as his father and mother almost inevitably want him to be. He should take his older brother for an example. Moreover, he has little chance of breaking into the relationship that his brother and sister have built up with each other. What he has to offer, that is, dependence and a desire for her care, does little to wrest his sister from his brother. Things might change, incidentally, if they had a fourth child who happened to be a daughter. The younger brother and she would make another couple like the older brother and sister and like the parents.

If the same parents had had a daughter, a son, and then a daughter, that is, b(ss)/sbs/(b)s, the oldest daughter is likely to become the problem child. She would like to mother someone, but father does not enjoy being mothered and even encourages his son to reject her overtures. She would like to identify with her mother, but her mother acts quite differently toward boys and men. In contrast, the youngest daughter and the middle son, provided he concentrates on his relationship with his younger sister, have conflicts neither in their identifications with their same-sex parent nor in their interactions with the opposite-sex parent.

Parents who were only children themselves have more trouble than others in understanding the sibling situation of any of their children. Often they do not want any more than one child. Parents who have come from large sibling configurations and have only one child themselves find it equally difficult to identify with him or her. They do a bit better if they have been oldest siblings themselves. In that case and in order to understand their child, they can utilize the experiences they had before their siblings arrived, provided they were at least three or four years older than their next sibling. Otherwise even their experience as a temporary only child was usually too short and inarticulate to be of much use.

A parent who comes from a monosexual sibling configuration has more than average difficulties getting used to child configurations containing both sexes or just the opposite sex. Similar difficulties are encountered by a parent who comes from a bisexual sibling configuration, but who happens to have children of one sex only. If both parents were oldest siblings, they tend not to understand the younger as well as they do the older ones among their children, whereas parents who were both youngest siblings tend to puzzle their oldest children. Parents of this type are dependent and need to lean on some one. They tend to make their oldest child their adviser and confidant and do not notice that he needs a teacher or model which they themselves cannot provide. Sometimes an uncle or an aunt, that is, one of the parents' siblings, often the oldest, may become such a model for the child.

Each parent holds one of $n2^{n-1}$ possible sibling positions among his siblings, whereby n is the number of children in that sibling configuration. For both parents this number of possibilities must be multiplied. Since each of their children also has one of $n2^{n-1}$ possible sibling positions among his own siblings, a particular combination of the sibling roles of father, mother, and a given child is the product of all three sets of possibilities. If father, mother, and a given child all come from sibling configurations of three children, there would be $(3 \cdot 2^{3-1})(3 \cdot 2^{3-1})(3 \cdot 2^{3-1}) = (3 \cdot 2^{3-1})^3$, or 1728 different possible combinations of sibling roles of the parents and each of their children. If $n = 2$, again for both parents and for their own children, there are still 64 different possible combinations of sibling roles of parents and each of their children. If they come from sibling configurations of different sizes, n_1, n_2, and n_3 would have to be substituted for n.

These possible combinations would be too numerous and too confusing to elucidate, even if we used parents coming from two-child families only, who, in turn, have only two children themselves. Therefore, we shall proceed by describing the eight (if you like, 10) basic types of sibling positions in one of the coming chapters (Chapter 11) and the 16 (if you like, 19) basic types of parental couples and their effects on their children and the family as a whole in a separate chapter (12). Interactions with different types of child configurations can only be treated in a general way. In order to analyze and understand more complicated types of parental couples and their interactions with each other as well as with specific configurations of children, the reader would have to use the rules and principles described in this book and try to apply and combine them as best he can.

9.   Relatives

So far we have described families as if they existed without direct contact with their relatives. Only the indirect effects of the parents' brothers and sisters have been considered as far as they manifest themselves in the sibling roles of the parents, and the indirect effects of the grandparents, when they were lost during the parents' childhood or early adolescence, whether lost through death or permanent separation. In many families, however, the grandparents play an active part. They come to visit and participate in the family's life, at least sporadically. The same is true of uncles and aunts as well as of their children, if they have any. Unmarried uncles and aunts are the brothers and sisters of the parents, and of married uncles and aunts at least one of the marriage partners is at the same time a brother or a sister of one of the parents. Their children are cousins, that is, something similar to brothers and sisters. The difference is that cousins are much less frequently present in family life as are brothers and sisters. In most instances they do not live in the same house or apartment with them.

Under certain conditions or, more specifically, certain family constellations, such relatives—that is, grandparents, uncles and aunts, and cousins—are likely to be a more integral part of family life than under other conditions or family constellations. Only children or youngest siblings among parents tend to draw a grandparent into the house to a greater extent than do parents with other sibling positions. Often it is the grandmother who is thus drawn in. She is supposed to act as an additional parent not only for the children, but also for the parent himself (or herself).

Aunts and uncles are included in some family lives for similar reasons. If they are oldest brothers and sisters, they tend to assist their younger siblings-turned-parents. Some unmarried uncles, and even more unmarried aunts, may stay in the family for this very reason. They may forego marriage themselves because of the task they have taken upon themselves for their sibling. This is more likely to happen when both parents were youngest siblings. An oldest sibling of one of these parents may well be received in the family as the longed-for senior and advisor. Aunts and uncles who are youngest siblings themselves may also find a satisfactory place in the nuclear family. This is more than likely if both parents were oldest siblings and need a junior to alleviate their authority conflicts with one another. If the family of one of the parents had many siblings of only one sex, a father who had three sisters, for instance, or a mother who had four sisters or four brothers only, one of these siblings tends to stay in the newly founded family. In a psychological sense, such a course of events is not unnatural, even if rational arguments are sometimes raised against such solutions and if the solutions are expressly ruled out.

Parents who came from large sibling configurations may feel short-changed in ordinary monogamy. To them, marriage is something less than what they had at home. There are not enough people. This is not to say that polygamy and/or polyandry, that is, marriages with several wives or several husbands at once, should be admissible for those persons. However, there are no psychological objections to some form of participation on the part of a parent's sibling in his (or her) family life. Psychologically speaking, the children in such a family may have two fathers or two mothers, or both. If these parental figures act in unison with one another, if they supplement each other and if they do not disappear someday for good, there need be no adverse effects on the children. The inclusion of cousins in the family life can also result in good rather than harm. This is particularly true when one or both of the merging families have unbalanced child configurations, if one perhaps has only boys, the other only girls, or one family has two children with a large age difference and the other family has three children whose ages fit between them.

Aunts and uncles as well as their children are of interest in still another respect. They give an indication of the character and the atmosphere of the families from which the parents have come. If a parent of a two-child family has four siblings, three of whom are unmarried and the fourth married but without children, we may assume that special historical, geographic, or economic circumstances prevail that are counterconducive to having children, or that the atmosphere of the family in which that parent has grown up was not very good. Otherwise, why would three of the four siblings have avoided or never tried marriage and the fourth have shied away from having children of his (her) own (barring medical reasons)? Knowing no more about this parent's family and comparing him with the parent of another two-child family who has four siblings, all of whom have married and have had at least three children, one might surmise with some certainty that, historical, geographic, and economic circumstances being equal, the second parent has come from a more harmonious and favorable family situation than the first.

We have already pointed out that the success of a relationship between spouses manifests itself ultimately in the ability of their children to enter marriages themselves and to have children of their own (p. 80f, 91). In the present context, this means that the success of the grandparents' marriage is evidenced in the ability of the parents to conclude their own successful marriage and to have children. This is not to say that the grandparents' marriage is of prime interest. All we want to know is what the parents might have brought with them into their own marriage, and what kind of atmosphere they might be able to offer their children. A glance at the number of marriages and of children among the parents' siblings is rather revealing. We will learn from what population of marriages within the set of siblings the marriage of the parents in question is a sample.

We may presume, for example, that in the family first mentioned above, the parent in question is still better off than all his siblings. He has married and he has two children. As for the parent's original family as a whole, however, the atmosphere was probably on the unfavorable side. We do not know whether conflicts of sibling roles between the grand-parents or losses of family members or other hardships have played a part. It would be interesting to learn why this particular parent was able to found a family and why his siblings failed to do so or never even tried.

In the second family mentioned above, all of the siblings of the parent in question set up their own families. The parent in question has even one child less, apparently, than his siblings have. We were informed that he has only two, whereas his siblings each have at least three children. At any rate, the atmosphere of that parent's original family seems to have been more favorable than that of the parent mentioned first. If we wanted to interpret why the first parent outdid his siblings and the second parent stayed somewhat behind his siblings in number of children of his own, and, in addition, if we wanted to explain the supposedly less favorable family atmosphere of the first parent and the more favorable one of the second, we would have to ask a few more questions.

The marriage partner complicates things even more. As a rule, the spouse, too, has had siblings, and they too were either able or unable to establish their own families. In order to get useable estimates one could compute the number of children that all the siblings of both parents had, including the parents' themselves, and test whether the number of the parents' own children surpasses or remains below the average number of children of the parents' siblings. One could also make individual computations for each parent to find out the average number of children that the parents and their respective siblings had, and test which of the two parents may have been "more responsible" for the number of children they themselves had, the assumption being that it would be that parent whose sibling-generational average of number of children is most closely approximated by the number of children he and his spouse have had themselves. Finally, one could compare the number of children that the grandparents and their siblings had with the number of children that the parents and their siblings begot themselves and compute something like an increase or a decrease in the desire to have children from one generation to the next.

We can interpret these numbers of children only if they show large differences and deviations from the average or expected numbers. In practice, it may often suffice to check whether the parents' siblings had also married and whether they had any children at all, that is, at least one. In writing symbolic expressions for family constellations, we could indicate the marriage of a sibling by underlining the symbol of that sibling once. If that sibling also has one or more children, we can designate this by underlining the symbol for a second time. Thus b(s̲b)/sssb/(b̲)s(b̲s̲) would mean: the father (the expression to the left of the first slash) is the oldest brother of a sister and a brother. His sister is married but has no children. His brother is unmarried. The mother (the expression to the right of the second slash) has an older brother, a younger brother, and a still younger sister. All of the mother's siblings are married and have children (at least one). The father and mother in question have four children (the expression between the two slashes), three girls and a boy. The boy is the youngest child.

Provided comparable conditions have prevailed, we could conclude from this configuration that the mother came from a more procreative family than the father. The atmosphere of her original family was probably more favorable than that of the father's original family. If the father were considerably younger than the mother, one might say that his brother had not yet found the time to marry. On the average, however, he should be three years older than the mother. In lieu of more specific information we might assume that the age distances between the children are average too, which means about 3 to 4 years between successive children. The marriage must have lasted about 10 to 13 years by now (see p. 3f). The father may be 38 years old (average age of males at marriage plus duration of marriage), his sister perhaps 34, his brother 30. Even his younger brother may therefore be considered to be above average marrying age of males. Both of the father's siblings have probably had enough time by now to get married or to have children of their own. Having failed to do so justifies the assumption of a lower procreativity wish in the father's family.

Incidentally, all we need in order to confirm our assumption or to abandon it would be a few more data, perhaps just a single indication of the age of at least one of the family members. Even if we knew no more than that the two older daughters were married and that the second oldest had children of her own, the age picture for the entire family would change. The symbolic expression would now read like this: b(sb)/sssb/(b)s(bs). Assuming average conditions prevail, the second daughter ought to be at least 28 years old (the average marriage age of girls is 24, the average time elapsing until the first child is born is one to two years; since the report spoke of "children," we may figure at least two, and probably no twins; if the second child has just been born, the first one would be three or four years old under average conditions; this makes $24 + 1 + 3 = 28$). Assuming the oldest daughter is about three years older than the second oldest and her father to be another 28 or 29 years older than that (27 years being the average marriage age of men), the father may now be an estimated 59 or 60 years of age.

Persons asked about their family constellations can often tell us only little about their grandparents. Usually they know nothing about their sibling positions and nothing about their grandparents' parents. However, they do know the sibling positions of their parents as well as what became of the parents' siblings and can tell the questioner about it. They can also tell him, as a rule, whether their own grandparents are still alive or have died, and approximately when they died. These data are important since they allow inferences about the early or very early losses of family members, particularly of parents, which the parents of the person being interviewed might have suffered. If we merely want to distinguish very early losses of family members (occurring when the bereaved person was 6 years old or younger), early losses (occurring when the bereaved was between 7 and 14 years old) and other losses of family members (the bereaved was 15 years or older, and such a loss may be assumed to be no longer inevitably traumatic in its psychological consequences), we could do so in the following manner: we can put two dots above the symbol of the person who has been lost during the bereaved person's early childhood. We can put one dot above the symbol of the lost person if the loss occurred during the bereaved's early youth. Finally, we can put a cross above a person who has been lost later on in the bereaved's life (at or after his 15th year of age).

If the oldest brother of a sister and a brother lost his brother before he turned 6 years himself, we would symbolize it thusly: b(sb̈). Had he lost his brother only when he was 12 years old himself, this would read b(sḃ), and had he lost him still later, the expression would be: b(sb̸). As indicated above, the age limits do not refer to the age of the person lost, but to the age of the person who suffered the loss of another person. In the last example, the oldest brother of a sister and a brother was at least 15 years old when his younger brother died.

If we do not know the sibling positions of the grandparents, but want to present them symbolically anyway, we suggest using f for the grandfather and m for the grandmother. If we want to enter the grandparents in the example of the family constellation with four children given above, and if we have learned that the father lost his father in his early childhood, and the mother her father just a year ago, that is, quite recently, and that the father lost his brother in his early youth, the expression would look like this: f˙/m//b(sb̶)/sssb/(b)s(bs)//f⁺/m. Note that double slashes separate the grandparents from the nuclear family.

From this we can draw a few more conclusions. The recent loss of her father may have been painful for the mother, but it probably was not a traumatic experience. The father's loss of his father in his early childhood, however, must have been quite traumatic. Since the father also lost his younger brother in his early youth, we might assume that these traumatic conditions depressed the mood of the father's family and affected the family atmosphere. In addition to the financial difficulties that may have resulted for the family, there were probably psychological problems as well. The children grew up without a father. The youngest brother had barely been born when his father died. The mother had to be a father for her children, as well. She may have had to work and send the children to a day care center.

We have used this example to illustrate how family data can be handled, considered, and tentatively interpreted. These thoughts and interpretations must not be confused with reality. We do not yet know the reality. We hope to approach it as we continue to ask and to listen. In order to ask appropriate further questions and to listen properly, however, we will probably have to continuously separate the more likely interpretation possibilities from those that are less likely or outright wrong.

10.   The Data

What has been and will be reported is based on empirical data that have been secured by the author in various ways from various groups of people he studied. The first of these groups consisted of individuals undergoing psychotherapy during the years between 1951 and 1961 (51 cases) or those who had come for purposes of diagnostic evaluation (58 cases). Another group consisted of individuals selected in psychological guidance centers and psychiatric clinics (45 cases) as well as from among the author's circle of acquaintances, and all were selected according to systematic criteria (135 cases). Still another group consisted of the patients of counselors and psychotherapists whose work the author had to supervise (118 cases). This made a total of 407 cases.

In addition, the author had opportunities to learn about certain relevant aspects and characteristics of another approximately 1000 cases. These were those persons who played a direct or indirect part in the lives of the 407 individuals mentioned above. In some instances their unusual actions, their fates, their professions, and their relationships, or their comments made these additional people conspicuous.

These samples cannot be considered representative in a statistical sense, particularly since about one-fourth of the cases were Viennese and three-fourths came from the Boston area. However, since it was the correlations of relatively universal personality and behavior characteristics rather than the characteristics per se that mattered, the samples did not have to be representative, at least as long as the correlations observed were alike in all samples. This was true to a surprising degree.

Certain characteristics of a person's sibling position and his family constellation were significantly associated with certain forms of social behavior. Certain sibling positions seemed to correlate with certain personality characteristics, interests, and attitudes vis-à-vis a number of areas of reality. Certain sibling constellations of the parents correlated with characteristics of family atmosphere as well as with parental preferences for one of their children. Asked to describe their siblings, subjects furnished portraits that corresponded closely in terms of certain behavior and personality traits to those of other subjects according to the type of sibling position. The reversal of this procedure worked as well. If the subjects were given social behavior and personality characteristics arranged according to types of sibling position with the request to choose the behavior and character portraits that fit their own siblings most closely, they selected to a very significant degree the portraits of those sibling positions that coincided with their own siblings (see also Löhr 1966). In other words, they recognized their siblings from synthetic portraits of their siblings' positions. Numerous experimental studies on certain aspects of social behavior (achievement motivation, aspiration level, frustration tolerance, leadership roles taken among peers in childhood and youth, sensitivity to group pressure, aggression in phantasy and in reality, self-evaluation, evaluation of parents, siblings, superiors, colleagues, etc.) confirmed, on the whole, the behavior characteristics and personality trends found and described to be associated with different sibling positions. These and other studies have been reported on in another chapter (see p. 283ff, 293ff).

In order to learn more about the distribution of family constellation characteristics and to conduct critical field experiments (see p. 95ff), my coworkers and I explored large samples of the population, with the financial help of the Deutsche Forschungsgemeinschaft (or the German Research Association). We investigated 540 families in Zurich, 1530 families in Nuremberg, and 230 families in the area around Nuremberg; an additional sample of 620 grade-school students in Nuremberg, 180 children who had consulted psychological counseling centers, as well as 150 juvenile delinquents and prisoners and their families completed the study. A detailed report of that study has been submitted to the Deutsche Forschungsgemeinschaft (Toman, Preiser, Gasch, & Plattig 1967), and a compendium of its descriptive statistics has been published (Toman & Preiser 1973). The most relevant descriptive aspects of family constellations have been referred to repeatedly in this book. The field experiments conducted with the hard real data have been outlined in Chapter 6; these data concern the actual behavior of persons in their original families as well as in those they themselves founded. All the events studied had already taken place. The attitudes of the persons studied towards those events could no longer influence the events themselves. Even the investigators could not commit any errors of selection and interpretation worth mentioning, errors, that is, which may easily happen in psychological studies and which have indeed occasionally happened.

II.   Application and Practice

11. The Basic Types of Sibling Positions

In the coming chapters the basic types of sibling positions will be characterized according to their behavior, attitude, and interest preferences. The different types of parents will then be described in terms of their relationship with one another and with their children.

Sibling positions may be looked upon as roles that a person has learned to take in the family and tends to assume in situations outside the family, whether merely initially or more permanently. We have already pointed out earlier that these roles may be modified by regular and enduring social contacts outside the family and that both the roles learned in the original family as well as these subsequent modifications may be applied in new contacts (see p. 77f). The most elementary of a person's social behavior preferences, interests, and attitudes, however, are often retained. They may not appear on the surface, but if one looks out for the way in which a person actually arranges his life, what he does from day to day, how he shapes his relations with acquaintances and colleagues, with friends, lovers, and spouses, with parents and with his own children, what he does if given the choice, and under what conditions he feels relatively most comfortable and content, his original characteristics and social preferences can usually be clearly distinguished. Often the person himself does not know that he has those behavior characteristics and those preferences in his contacts with other people. Others do recognize them, however, and they respond to them instinctively and often unconsciously in their contacts and dealings with him. Hence, the reader should not necessarily expect to recognize himself in the portrait corresponding to his sibling position. Yet, if others tell him that the portrait does fit him, he should at least concede that they might be right and perhaps observe himself a little longer and more carefully. After all, the portraits describe what a person really does over and over again in his daily life and not what he thinks he does. They also do not describe what he might like to be.

More often the incumbents of particular sibling positions will recognize essential features of themselves in these portraits. However, dear reader, if both your self-evaluation and the evaluation your friends and acquaintances make about you seem to contradict a given portrait, particularly when you have neither a multiple distal nor a middle sibling position but rather a "pure" one, you would have to check a few things. The sibling position of one or both of your parents, unusually large or small age differences between you and your next older or next younger sibling, special circumstances such as changes of residence, separations from family, or losses of family members, all may have altered your family situation. If it is not yours, but an acquaintance's, a friend's, or a colleague's sibling position portrait that does not seem to fit, an informal inquiry into the sibling position of that person's parents or into special circumstances might be possible or even welcome. Other factors might be stronger than the composition of individuals making up a family and its effects upon the person in question. Living conditions, personal illnesses, special

physical likenesses to certain family members, even characteristics of the person's bodily constitution or special talents
may come into effect (see also p. 62ff).

It could also be that in an extrafamilial context, a particular person does not act his own sibling role but rather
that of one of his siblings. Since sibling roles are partly
forced upon a person by his parents and siblings, he may,
after a little scrutiny of the situation, resort to a role,
perhaps in school or among his friends, that someone other
than himself has played in his original family. The younger
brother of a brother may notice in a new group of people,
perhaps in kindergarten or in grade school, that he is better
liked if he behaves the way he saw his older brother act at
home. There is also another advantage to this. By identifying with his brother, he gains an edge of age over his
peers who are usually just as old as he is. Under ordinary circumstances, his older brother would be 3 to 4 years older
than he, he would know more and be able to do more than
the younger brother or his classmates can. There is also a
slight disadvantage in this. He is less able to convincingly
maintain a role adopted merely by vicarious experiences,
that is, by identification with someone else, than he can a
role that he has learned by his own direct experiences in his
family.

Another precondition might be a particularly favorable
milieu in the new group, possibly resulting from the fact that
there are no oldest siblings in the group. Moreover, in a new
social context such as kindergarten or school, there is the
possibility that a person will not only look for contacts with
children of the sex he has been used to through his siblings,
but also sometimes, or even predominantly, seek contacts
with children of a different sex. An oldest brother of
brothers, for example, may feel less enthusiastic about the
boys in his group than about one or several girls. Rather
than affiliating herself with boys, a younger sister of
brothers may join the girls. An only child who has not been
prepared at all for contacts with sibling-like peers might, af-

ter an initial shock over so many other children, turn out to be open-minded, eager for contacts with the other children, and popular.

Both the identification effect and the contact effect could be observed in a field study of nursery-school classes over a period of several months (Toman 1973b). Oldest siblings started out as leaders in the nursery school, but some of them were deposed after a few months or during the second year by youngest siblings. Children coming from monosexual sibling configurations sought contacts with children of the opposite sex after a while, and children who had siblings of the opposite sex only began to contact children of their own sex. However, both effects seemed to depend on the social atmosphere that the teachers and the school were able to create. They were demonstrable in a particularly tolerant atmosphere. On the other hand, in a more conventional school with stricter standards, the children tended to cling to those social preferences for which they had been prepared by their siblings in their original families (Sutton-Smith & Rosenberg 1970, Toman 1973b).

A person's relationship to his parents may also explain many deviations from the role in his long-term social behavior that would otherwise generally correspond to his sibling position. Persons with multiple and middle sibling positions always have more than one possibility when entering new social contexts. We have already suggested that we may actually be able to infer from the roles they take in new social contexts which one of two or more sibling relationships they prefer to practice and appear to value more highly (p. 112f). Moreover, we have also discussed how such preferences in new social contexts can be predicted from information about a persons sibling configuration (including age distances) and about the parents' sibling positions (p. 117ff). The reader would have to consider these possibilities if the portraits presented here do not seem to fit his family constellation.

The behavior and attitude portraits of the 8 (or 10) basic types of sibling position that will be presented in the following chapters have been drawn from routine psycho-diagnostic examinations and psychotherapeutic treatments. For each of the eight types, we needed a minimum of six cases, which moreover, had to meet the following criteria:

1. Their parents were to have had no incompatible sibling positions. Cases of complete rank and partial or full sex conflict were excluded. In accordance with Table 1 (p. 90f), the following degrees of complementarity were permitted: 1a, 1b, 2a, 2b, and, to an extent, 3a if a parent had been an only child but his same-sex parent's sibling position was compatible with the sibling position of the spouse or, if the spouse had been a single child instead, if the parent's sibling position was compatible with that of the spouse's same-sex parent.

2. Neither the person studied nor his (or her) parents could have suffered early losses of family members. Any person who had lost a parent before he himself turned 16 was excluded from the basic summaries of traits and features of social behavior and personality that constitute the portraits. The reactions of persons thus excluded to losses of family members and other persons, however, as well as their behavior toward parents, siblings, and friends were partly included in the portraits of basic sibling positions. Behavior patterns in psycho-therapy, whether as a patient or as a therapist, were taken from another group of individuals: namely, the author's professional colleagues, the apprentice psychologists and young physicians whose psycho-therapeutic work I had to supervise in the Boston area for over eight years, as well as the groups of their patients (see also p. 138ff).

The number of cases studied has increased considerably since the time these behavior and attitude portraits of the basic types of sibling positions were first worked out and presented (Toman 1960b, 1962). The minimum case number per type is now 20 persons, all of whom have met the two criteria mentioned above. Incomplete data are available for an average of 100 cases per type. Moreover, since 1960, many different aspects of the behavior and attitude portraits have been investigated and essentially confirmed in numerous experimental studies in the USA as well as in Germany, Austria, and Switzerland. The most important of these experimental studies will be discussed in a separate chapter (see p. 287ff).

The behavior and attitude portraits presented here are somewhat abridged and streamlined versions of the portraits given in earlier English and German editions of this book. They have also been the most popular portion of the book, as judged, among other things, by the number of journals, weeklies, magazines, and newspapers that reported about them. Other comprehensive publications on siblings and family relations have appeared which draw on my book to a greater or lesser extent; among them the works by Dechêne (1967), Forer (1969), Sutton-Smith and Rosenberg (1970), ought to be mentioned. Their contributions are discussed in chapter 15.

The descriptions of long-term social behavior and attitudes, interests, and social preferences that have been attempted in the portraits apply perhaps most directly to young adults. Of course, even young adults should not expect to find that all the characteristics of their sibling position fit equally well. The majority of characteristics, however, should be recognizable.

These portraits of basic types of sibling positions apply to children and adolescents too, although their life circumstances are likely to be somewhat different, and they also apply to older adults and to the aged. For mature adults who have found their desired profession and are satisfied with life, the portraits seem to fade. Such a person may impress others more by his position in society and by the tasks he is responsible for at work or at home than by his sibling position and his original relationship with his parents. However, he inadvertently expresses the fact that there is more to him than this impression would imply when he relaxes at home, when he chats and socializes at work, or when he speaks to friends and acquaintances about his child-hood and youth.

The old person tends to resume the sibling position of his childhood and youth. With relatives and friends he acts the way he was used to in the early years of his life, and he likes to be treated that way.

These portraits are, of course, not divorced from the social situation of our times. We cannot claim that these portraits have been valid at all times; the social structure implied in them is not the only one possible, nor are they immune to time. Our studies apply to industrial societies, to highly developed nations, and to urban rather than rural populations. Whether we are dealing with Western or Eastern styles of such highly developed and urbanized in-dustrial societies does not make very much difference for the role portraits of sibling positions, provided the family has remained a psychological, sociological, and economic unit that furnishes the early educational milieu for a child. One might anticipate, however, that even the less developed or predominantly agrarian nations will move toward in-dustrialization, and that, in turn, suggests that our role descriptions will become increasingly valid for them as well.

One of the implicit assumptions we make about the social structure in our portrait is the need to work. Adults have to produce goods in order to maintain themselves and their children and to survive, as well as to make life more pleasant, interesting, and worth living. This assumption is hard to refute in the temperate and cold zones of the earth, and probably even in any inhabited areas. Supposedly work-free paradisical enclaves that have occasionally been dis-covered in the tropics or subtropics have displayed on closer inspection that there, too, people work, fight, and cooperate, albeit in a more simple and relaxed way.

We also imply that, by current convention, and prob-ably also in the future, one parent will have to be the breadwinner in the family while the other takes care of the children as long as they are small. In the overwhelming majority of all families the father is likely to be the bread-winner and the mother the children's nurse. If the mother has a profession, she usually gives it up a few months before her first child is born and returns to it, or to one like it, at the earliest when her youngest child has started kindergarten or grade school. She frequently returns to work on a part-time basis at first. Some mothers take jobs only when their youngest child has turned 14 or 15, while still others never do.

Finally, the portraits do not rule out the fact that first-born children on the one hand and male children on the other are slightly privileged compared to those born later and to girls, respectively, be it as a result of economic, ethnic, religious, or legal customs. To state this is not to endorse it. I have attempted, however, to describe conditions as they appear to be and probably will continue to be in the near future. Moreover, I do not want to deny there may be objective reasons for some of the oldest child's apparent privileges. The oldest child has an edge over the second-born in experience and competence, he or she knows more than his or her siblings do at any given time in their childhood. Most often he also understands the parents' concern a bit better than his younger siblings do, and, in case of the loss of a parent, he makes a better substitute than his siblings could. This need not always be so, to be sure. The situation may not call for it. If the oldest child is incapable of taking over the parent's business, the custody of his siblings, or the royal throne, the second-oldest, or the child best suited, most qualified, and most interested, will generally assume the vacant position.

The professional handicaps that emerge for a woman who has taken care of the house and the children for a while and now wants to return to her job are hardly avoidable. If she has been serious about being a mother, she will not return to her former work for something like eight to fifteen years. After such a long time, however, she will have difficulty in catching up. In science or in the professions (medicine, economics, etc.), she will probably never make the connection again. She may have to resort to related professions that are easier — and less well paid — or take on easier tasks in her original profession.

The same would be true for a husband who cared for their children, while the wife earned the living. One might wonder whether a woman is not the more natural companion for small children than the man. It looks as if, perhaps because of the period of gestation and the time when she breast-feeds the child, a woman develops a more intimate, patient, and satisfying relationship toward her children than a man can. In order to really distribute evenly among men and women the burden of caring for the children and interrupting one's profession one would really have to persuade 50% of all husbands to become pregnant themselves, to breast-feed their children, and to stay with them at least for the first year of the child's life.

All levity aside, professional equality for the unmarried woman, the married woman without a desire for children of her own, and for the woman whose children have grown up, is a moral and social must, provided she has the right qualifications. Professional equality for the mother of small children, even if she has placed her children in the care of a hired nurse whom she merely supervises, is almost a contradiction in itself. The mother who stays with her children cannot fully devote herself to a job without some detriment either to her children or to the job. And the mother who delegates motherhood to a nurse makes that nurse the real and true psychological mother of her children. If she does not do this, if she tries to keep her relationship with her children, one of her duties will again be neglected: either her supervision of the nurse and children or her job.

The following portraits do not distinguish between a person who has several siblings of the same type and a person who has only one sibling of that type. This has also been expressed in the chapter headings. Nevertheless, we should mention that, for example, the oldest brother of a sister resembles the oldest brother of two sisters and often even the oldest brother of three sisters in his social behavior and attitudes to an extent that justifies combining all of them in a single portrait. If such an older brother, however, has four, five, or more younger sisters, the effects that this type of sibling position seems to exert may become distorted. He has too much of a kind. As a result, the sibling configuration may split into two subconfigurations, with perhaps a brother and two younger sisters forming one group and the remaining three sisters the second group. Another result may be that this oldest brother of sisters may try to get out of his family more determinedly than an oldest brothers of fewer sisters would, perhaps by marrying the first person who seriously crosses his path, or it may turn out that he can never break loose from his family.

When in the coming chapters we talk of an oldest brother of sisters, the youngest brother of brothers, the oldest sister of sisters, etc. the reader should think of one or two siblings, perhaps even of three siblings of the respective type, but of no more. If a person has siblings of only one type, but more than three of them, we recommend interviewing that person about his relationships with all of his siblings and about the relationships he thinks his siblings have among themselves.

Only children are being presented as a type of their own, although they do not really have a sibling position. Only by identification with the same-sex parent can they adopt that parent's sibling position in certain features of their behavior. There are also quasi-only children: those persons who do have siblings, but whose adjacent siblings are separated from them by six or more years. These persons not only bear the characteristics of their own sibling position, but also those of an only child. The latter characteristics are more dominant the greater that person's age distance is from the next older or the next younger sibling, or both of them, as the case may be. When encountering such a sibling position, it is advisable to look up not only the portrait of that position, but also that of the only child.

The Oldest Brother of Brothers: b(b..)

The oldest brother of brothers loves to lead and assume responsibility for other persons, particularly for men. He tries to take care of them and sometimes even to boss them around. He worries more about the future than others do. He may derive his claim for leadership from these worries. He would like to elevate his group to an elite position, and he works hard to do so. He requires the members of the group to offer their services and remain loyal to him in return, not to immediately want to know what they will gain from the situation, but to trust him. He thinks he knows what is good for them and for this reason he may send someone else to the forefront in critical or dangerous situations. As the leader, he believes he is harder to replace than the others. If needed, he will come to the rescue. If given a choice he would rather tangle only with opponents who are weaker than he is.

He identifies with persons in positions of authority and power more readily than others do. He can be content with conditions as they are, shows more understanding for them, and tends to become their advocate. His reputation is that of a man who can be relied upon, but he sometimes acts more popish than the pope. If a person in authority or power is not as strong as he pretends to be, the oldest brother of brothers is often the first one to notice this. Under given circumstances he can help to topple such a person better than others can. As the representative of a new order, however, he may overdo his care and concern. Supposedly in the interest of the others, he, rather than they, aspires for dictatorial powers. He is sure he knows better what is good for others, particularly for men and for his subordinates in power, than they do themselves. He can be tough, sometimes outright cruel. He likes to set a good example, he is self-critical, but he hates the criticism that others might express of him.

He is interested in property and possessions. He loves to create material as well as spiritual values. He cherishes order and regimentation, dislikes debts, and has realistic goals that can be reached by hard work and endurance. He does not rest on his past successes and even knows beforehand what should be done next. Often he foresees things better than others do. Failures do not discourage him, but they make him increase or change his efforts. He does not lose sight of the grand concept or master plan as easily as others do. In economics, science, art, and politics he appreciates the pragmatist, continuously inquires about the consequences and the relevance of a project, and can usually distinguish the expert from the charlatan more incisively than others.

With women he is sensitive and shy. He does not want to lose face. He has trouble admitting his interest in certain women. He loves it when a woman is more interested in him than he is in her. He likes to treat girls and women like boys, even wants them to look like boys, but unconsciously longs for that woman who defies her boyish looks and is willing to mother him inconspicuously and unreservedly. He may never forget an incidental hurt or insult from a woman.

His best partner would be the youngest sister of brothers. Other things being equal, however, she would fare better with an oldest brother of sisters than with him. A youngest sister of sisters can also entice him, but after a while he may tire of her. She presents too many puzzles and has no great skill in shaping their life together. He, incidentally, does not either.

An oldest sister of brothers could also please him. She tends to mother people, but he dislikes the fact that she does so too heavily. An oldest sister of sisters would be his toughest match. Both of them would tend to claim leadership for themselves, unless they have found a way instead of living parallel lives, pursuing their own careers, and recruiting the children of their own sex for themselves. He will take on the boys, she the girls. Even with an only child he would have trouble. Only if her mother had been a youngest sister herself, preferably of brothers, might things work out better. Among girls with multiple and middle sibling positions, the ones who most suit him are those who had at least one older brother among their siblings. He is also more likely than other men to choose women of the same sibling position as that of his mother. In all cases, it would be good for the marriage if he were permitted to maintain his contacts with his male friends.

As a father he is concerned and acts responsibly, but the family often regards him as too strict, too controlling, or not involved enough. He is known to be an efficiency fanatic, sometimes even a tyrant. He understands his oldest son best, and both of them can easily identify with the other. Of all the children, the oldest son thinks most like his father. He can also substitute for his father better than the others can. The father's best direct or interactive contact is likely to be with his youngest son, the second best with his youngest daughter. The latter, however, may create more problems for him than he cares to have. She finds herself under his jealous guard and does not like it very much.

Among friends, he is most at ease with youngest or middle brothers of brothers. He can identify well with other oldest brothers and with only children, but they do not get along well with him in their daily dealings. In groups of friends he can get along with all kinds of sibling positions and even likes variety as long as this does not include another oldest brother. If there is one, he can stand him only when he is absent; otherwise the two will have to divide the group, and the group members will have to decide to which of the two groups they want to belong.

The loss that would be most difficult for him to bear would be that of his mother or a motherly friend. His strongest guilt feelings would be associated with the death of a younger brother or of a good friend. The loss of any girl friend, under certain conditions even that of his wife, may leave him strangely unmoved, even if he does display all the customary signs of mourning.

Oldest brothers of brothers seem to flock to the following professions somewhat more frequently than by chance: economic leader, bank director, investor, naval officer or administrator, teacher, minister, social worker, judge, theoretical scientist, surgeon, (higher) government officer, contractor, construction engineer, trade union leader, head of an expeditionary force...

As a psychiatric patient, the oldest brother of brothers resents that there is an implicit dependence on another person. If there are no overwhelming personal or professional reasons for treatment, he would rather not even start it. As a psychotherapist he tends too much to try to settle his patients' affairs himself, to be over-solicitous, and to wish to help not only therapeutically but also by instruction or via his authority. He works better with men than with women and develops a therapeutic relationship more readily with younger siblings than with older siblings, but he can elaborate this relationship better and eventually terminate it more easily with oldest siblings than he can with youngest siblings.

Well-known oldest brothers of brothers are Lyndon B. Johnson, Henry Cabot Lodge, Harry Belafonte, Jonas Salk, Robert Oppenheimer, Sir Alec Home, and Hugh Hefner.

The Youngest Brother of Brothers: (b..)b

The youngest brother of brothers likes to lean on other people, particularly on men. He wants to have friends, to have men appreciate and respect him, and to be understood by them. In return, he is willing to accept responsibilities, but he does not want to be in top command. He does not mind being in a partly subordinate position, although it may not always seem so! He sometimes takes a long time to hear requests from those in his charge and he may oppose his superiors, at least on secondary matters. He usually does not oppose the master-plan itself that he has chosen to join.

Even so, he finds many things wrong with the world. He wants change. On closer inspection, it may turn out that it is not so much the change itself but the talk about the possibilities of change that he can engage in with others, especially with impressive men. What really needs changing will have to be decided by those men. If he can discuss things with them and even if his thoughts and objections are not necessarily followed but at least recognized and understood, he is happy and ready to apply himself, sometimes as a glowing and audacious disciple.

As a matter of fact, he can be daring, bold, and fresh. He likes to challenge opponents who are stronger than he is. He tends to wager higher bets than others. If need be, he will even risk his life. He can make sacrifices, and can work in tremendous spurts. However, he is also more easily discouraged and depressed by experiences of failure than others are. If successful, he is inclined to overestimate his powers and his chances. He sometimes appears volatile and impulsive, as well as ambitious and obstinate, regardless of what the situation may be. In this way, other men may occasionally determine his actions to a greater extent than he does himself.

Despite a certain obstinacy, despite the frictions he causes in some of his dealings with other men, despite the rough outer appearance he frequently assumes, and despite his considerable physical strength, he tends to be kind-hearted and soft. Even in the guise of an aggressor or a cynic, he shies away from the final consequences of aggression or sarcasm. He can forgive and forget.

His chief interest is the quality of life and the joys and sensations of the present, rather than the collection of goods and property. Material things do not matter as much to him as do moods and the meaning of his own existence. Hence he does not worry very much about where the money that he needs for his plans and his livelihood is to come from. He likes to live it up and to treat himself. Debts are not very important to him. He is also generous, although in an impulsive way. Too much order is harmful. More optimistic than others, he tends to live and plan beyond his means. Often a benefactor, a sponsor, or a lucky incident seem to come to his rescue when least expected. If they do not he may try to bluff or seek consolation with women or in night clubs. He pursues his scientific, technical, or artistic talents more avidly and with greater abandonment than other people. He is not concerned with the purpose or the context, however. He does not want to be tied to a particular content. If he is not engaged in forced or routine work he may accomplish great and unusual things.

He is relatively soft and yielding with women, even if he plays the part of a cynic or an erratic adventurer. He has a little trouble learning what women in general or his woman in particular really want, but if they cater to some of his desires, often relatively insignificant ones, he tends to be a faithful partner, sometimes to the point of servitude.

His best partner would be the oldest sister of brothers, although she would do better with a youngest brother of sisters rather than with him. An oldest sister of sisters would also provide the guidance and responsibility that he unconsciously seeks even though such a girl may impress him as being too strict or too spellbound by someone else's authority. The youngest sister of brothers would not be as mothering as he would like her to be, but at least she would know how to handle boys and men. Relatively the poorest match would be one with the youngest sister of sisters or with an only child, particularly if the latter's mother had been a youngest sister or a single child herself. In these cases both partners will look to the spouse for leadership, but they will not seem to get it. Among girls with multiple sibling positions or girls who are middle siblings, he would get along best with one who has had at least one younger brother among her siblings. At any rate, it would be important for him to be able to maintain some contacts with his male friends once he is married.

The youngest brother of brothers is not a conventional father. He does not like to be terribly involved with family matters. At first his children may even constitute a threat to his relationship with his wife. He wants her to take care of the children as well as of himself almost as another child and tends to compete with them for her affection. He may confide his thoughts and problems to his children prematurely. Sometimes it is clearly more important to him to be understood by his children than to understand them himself. He wants to be liked and admired. However, often he is also a good companion for his children, and as such he is probably at his best in his role as a father.

He gets along best with male friends who are the oldest brothers of brothers, or middle brothers who had youngest brothers among their siblings, or with single children whose fathers were oldest siblings themselves. Oldest brothers of sisters are not likely to be interested in him, whereas youngest brothers of sisters seem to get along with him rather well. Only other youngest brothers of brothers can offer him little of permanent value unless they act as co-followers in a group under someone else's leadership. In such a case, the two youngest brothers may jointly deplore their plight and comfort each other.

His gravest loss would be that of his mother or of a familiar motherly person. He would be relatively most confused over the loss of one of his older brothers or of a friend who had assumed that role with him. He would feel guilty over such a loss, think that he may have left the lost person in the lurch or hurt him emotionally, or he may feel that they had not talked things over enough. He would be less affected than it might appear at the loss of a girl friend who depended more on him than he did on her.

His preferred professions include announcer and entertainer, quizmaster, advertising agent or salesman, artist, writer, musician, actor, tutor, technical or scientific specialist, assistant or associate of leading men in business, politics, or science, a vote-rallying politician, opthalmologist, or anesthetist.

It frequently happens that the youngest brother of brothers seeks out something like psychotherapy, even if he cannot always optimally utilize the suggestions it offers. He is attracted by the fact that somebody is listening to him at last. He is startled when he learns that he eventually ought to be autonomous and independent. If he is a psychotherapist himself, he is inclined to be more carefree with a more laissez-faire attitude in his therapeutic work than other therapists are. He worries too little rather than too much about his patients. Even here, he is almost more concerned with the patient's understanding him than he is in understanding the patient or having the patient understand himself. He is more at ease with male than with female patients. Psychotherapy gets going a bit faster than usual when his patient is an oldest sibling. However, treatment can eventually be concluded more smoothly if the patient is a youngest sibling.

Well-known youngest brothers of brothers are Aldous Huxley, Gunter Sachs, Rudi Dutschke, Ingmar Bergman, Konrad Lorenz, Jacques-Yves Cousteau, and Vladimir Ilyich Lenin.

The Oldest Brother of Sisters:
b(s..)

The oldest brother of sisters is a ladies' man: he appreciates women, regardless of whether they are colleagues and fellow-workers, lovers, or spouses. There are no greater favors of fate, in his opinion, than the favors of (beautiful) women. He is a good worker, particularly when women participate or when he works on behalf of a woman. He does not refuse a leadership role when offered, but he will not seek it out. He likes to work, but work is almost never the main purpose of his life. Instead it is more a means to an end. He is in favor of "live and let live." He is willing to take risks and to fight for a good purpose, especially for a woman he has chosen. He would not do so, however, for a person claiming undue, or even due, authority.

He is not a man's man and thus not susceptible to the biases and prejudices of some male clans or clubs. If he joins such a club, or a crew, or a political group, he is likely to do so for the sake of a woman, his family, or his children rather than for the sake of an idea, of his compatriots, or for the glory of the fatherland. He is a realist.

He acknowledges professional authority without difficulty, but he bristles at an unfounded authoritarian demand. If women are his superiors at work, they should not try to rub it in, for this may turn him into their adversary. If he is in a leading position himself, he requires good work from his coworkers and subordinates, but he also likes them to have their fun. They need not make self-sacrifices at work. He is no tyrant, no dictator, no slave-driver, and he cannot stand any of these types of superiors himself. He will not accommodate them, yet he will not conspicuously oppose them either. He does not want to incite resistance. In such a case he will just change jobs, sometimes even his profession, more easily than would others, and even at the price of a lower income.

He preserves and takes care of property, a business, or an enterprise, but he does not become obsessed with it. He does not think that the goods of the world or his own goods have to be increased at all costs. He tends to be more cavalier than others if such possessions diminish instead of increase. For his beloved he would sacrifice more than others, economically or intellectually, but, thanks to his skill in matters of women and love, he is rarely put to the test. Even so, in his worldy pursuits and interests he is less likely than others to be affected by fashions, prestige, or by his colleagues and friends.

He knows how to handle women. He cares. He is attentive and understanding. He does not tire easily of dating. He is not ashamed of what he does on behalf of and "in the service" of a woman. He also tends to select, with greater certainty than other men, those women who will not reject him. If one of them should do so anyway, he can take it kindly and understandingly. He does not bear grudges. Disappointments in love do not shake him.

His best partner would be the youngest sister of brothers. He is better able than other men to show a younger sister of sisters how lovers or a husband and wife can arrange their lives with one another. An oldest sister of brothers is a bit too motherly for his taste, and he usually inadvertently avoids oldest sisters of sisters. He instinctively feels that they carry too much of the authority and strictness of their father with them. He could manage an only child better than other men could, particularly if her mother had been a youngest sister herself. He may take to girls of multiple and middle sibling positions, if they had oldest brothers among their siblings.

The oldest brother of sisters is a good father. He is concerned about the children and is willing to take family matters in his own hands, but he does not overdo his concern nor take his children overly seriously. To him, his wife is the most important person in the family. Her wish for children is usually more significant to him than his own wish for children. In contrast to other men, he can accept children in any temporal or sex order they may happen to come.

Male friends do not interest him very much. If he does not happen to be searching for a girl to love, he can entertain moderate friendships with men of almost any sibling position. Only with another oldest brother of sisters would he get along poorly, for by their nature each of them would rather have contacts with the other's sister. In groups of friends he tends to appear as the neutral and somewhat detached member, but if the need arises, if subgroups start fighting with each other, or if two or three members vie for the leadership of the entire group, he may step in as the mediator or may even become the leader himself. He is not eager, though, to maintain such a leadership position.

The loss of his mother would hurt him somewhat more than would the loss of his father, but the loss of a sister or of his beloved would also shake him temporarily. He feels a deep sense of loss, usually without ambivalence and guilt, and he can mourn quite efficiently. He overcomes losses faster than others, psychologically speaking, and can turn to substitutes or new persons sooner than other people can, but he does not forget or hide the fact of the loss in the process. The loss of a male friend tends to move him less.

Among the professions he chooses somewhat more frequently than chance are those of physician, pediatrician, gynecologist, scientist, linguist, movie or stage director, playwright (dramatist), architect, composer, personnel director, editor-in-chief, independent contractor, craftsman, dealer, or skilled worker.

He is an infrequent candidate for psychotherapy. Neither male nor female psychotherapists exert any great attractions for him. What they might offer, in his opinion, can be had better, more gracefully, kindly, and stimulatingly from real people in his everyday life, particularly from women. If he is a psychotherapist himself, he tends to get along better with female patients than with male ones, especially when they have brothers among their siblings. A female patient finds it harder, though, to break loose from him and the therapy when it ends; a male patient can do so more easily, and he can often benefit more through identification with his therapist than through identification with therapists holding other sibling positions.

Well-known oldest brothers of sisters are Robert McNamara, Leonard Bernstein, Albert Einstein, Shah Reza Pahlevi, and Mike Mansfield.

The Youngest Brother of Sisters:
(s..)b

The youngest brother of sisters is a great one with the ladies. They seem to love him and be anxious to care for him. They want to keep house for him, to handle his files or his suits, to cook for him, etc. This is the way it seems, and if those services happen not to be forthcoming, his sisters will have to step in. Being the first and only male among his siblings, he has usually been allowed to do or refuse to do more than others were. He has little competition. His sisters were expected to protect and serve him. He has been more important to his parents than were his sisters. Inadvertently and partly unconsciously he worked this situation to his advantage.

He is not likely to forego his privileges in life and at work, if he can help it. Here too, he wants to do or refuse to do whatever he likes; only his interests and talents should count. He does not like orders and leaves the details and trivialities to others, preferably to sympathetic women in his environment. He seems to be able to summon them almost by magic wherever he goes. They seem to want to help him, even if he offers them nothing very much or very concrete except ready compliments and occasional attention in return.

With this support he finds his own way of arranging his work and professional life. If the activities are to his liking, and if they capture his fancy, he may become a constructive and indispensable member of the team. If the main objective is to satisfy a superior or fulfil the team plans, not too much can be expected of him. His ambition is harder to arouse than is that of other men. He does not want to be pushed at work, he likes to set his own speed and deadlines. If he fails to meet them, so much the worse for his colleagues; he himself does not mind.

He can take charge of others and assume responsibilities of leadership. However, his colleagues, particularly the female ones, must help him. He attends to the grand design while his fellow women attend to the details and do the work. To him this is a matter of course, but he usually manages to keep the ladies happy with a little praise or a joke. Male colleagues, however, do not buy this. They are not satisfied that easily.

Property and wealth are no great concern of his, but he frequently finds a woman who is interested and willing to manage his affairs. He is not worried about where the money he needs for his enterprise or his own maintenance will come from. He is willing to decide how it should be used, however, and he does not waste it; but procuring it should be someone else's job.

He can be quite nice with the ladies, can flatter them and surprise them at times by his tact and care. However, he does not do so all the time. He does not really want to know what is dear or dearest to the ladies' hearts. They have him, and that in itself should suffice. Moreover, they are the ones who should know or try to guess what he likes and wants to do. He needs a kind, warm, and motherly person who is ready to overlook his flaws and keeps a skilful and supportive hand in his affairs. And she is not supposed to demand much recognition or credit for her share.

Accordingly, the best partner for life would be an oldest sister of brothers. An oldest sister of sisters would strike him as too self-righteous and strict, a youngest sister of brothers not motherly enough and too dependent, a youngest sister of sisters too impulsive and ambitious. He has no use for that. Girls who have held multiple or middle positions among their siblings would be compatible, provided they had younger brothers among their siblings. A single child is not much use to him unless her mother has been an oldest sister herself.

The youngest brother of sisters is in no hurry to become a father, but his wife usually cannot and does not want to spare him children of their own; she wants them. He often does not get involved himself, but leaves them, their care, and their education to his wife. He is not quite free of some jealousy of the children because of his wife's attention and care. To the children he acts as the companion and adviser, provided they do not consult him too often. If they do, he tends to evade them. He grants them more freedom and in-dependence than other fathers do, sometimes even more than the children can handle, and hopes that someday they will help him to realize his ideas and execute his plans as well as make themselves available to provide the comforts and do the chores at home.

He is less interested in male friends than other men are. He could accept an oldest brother of brothers, but the latter would become easily annoyed with him for his tendency of not committing himself to a common objective, of avoiding unpleasant tasks, and of enlisting women's help as a matter of course. The youngest brother of sisters, therefore, actually prefers a younger brother of brothers. This friend would not give him orders. On the contrary, he himself, the youngest brother of sisters, can suggest a thing or two to him without appearing as domineering as the youngest brother of brothers has learned to expect from his own and other oldest brothers. It may happen, however, that the youngest brother of sisters, being the first and only male among his siblings and untrained in the guidance of and care for men, will behave crudely and clumsily toward his friends. Since the youngest brother of brothers is more in need of guidance than he will admit to himself, he will not object. The youngest brother of sisters can do little with another youngest brother of sisters as a friend. That friend's sister tends to arouse more of his interest.

His most severe loss would be that of his mother or of his favorite sister, although the other family members will almost inevitably try to palliate the effects of the loss for him and to substitute themselves for the lost person. In this way he is usually spared the graver consequences of the loss and often appears a bit unmoved. If no one comes to his rescue and comfort, though, he might become agitated and depressed. He thus elicits the help of others after all. This also holds true for the loss of a motherly friend or of his own wife.

Among the professions for which he shows a certain preference are those of specialized scientist, technician, translator, editor, marketing expert, skilled mechanic, actor, artist, prosewriter, dancer, musician, journalist, reporter, or medical specialist such as dentist, internist, etc.

Under certain conditions he may like to undergo psychotherapy, provided the therapist is a motherly woman. In that case, treatment seems to be relatively most effective with him. He rarely becomes a psychotherapist himself; he finds the work psychologically too complicated. He is not too anxious to concern himself with other people's states of mind. If he has entered the profession, he would rather work with female than with male patients, and in particular with oldest sisters. He can complete and terminate psycho-therapies with males better and more promptly than with females, especially when the patients are younger brothers.

Well-known youngest brothers of sisters are Prince Philip, Curt Jürgens, Marlon Brando, Franz-Josef Strauß, Rudolf Nureyev, Warren Beatty, and Fred Astaire.

The Male Only Child:
b

The male only child is more used to dealing with considerably older people than are persons of other sibling positions. Even as an adult, he wants to live under the view of older people, including persons in authority and power. He wants to be their pride and joy, and he wants to be loved, supported, and helped more than others. What he does him-self often strikes him as more important than what anybody else is doing around him. Secretly he cannot quite rid himself of the thought that his job or his life situation has been con-ducted for the sole purpose of actualizing his needs and talents.

Since he received more attention and stimulation from his parents, as a rule, than an individual child who has had siblings, the only child is likely to display an edge over other children in intellectual maturity and expressed talent. If he enjoys the interest of his parents, guardians, and teachers, and if he discovers that he has the necessary skills, he may rise to great heights in that field of interest or work. He may also assume leadership positions, although he is not exactly made for them. His classmates and colleagues value his inner stability, the objective and detached way in which he pursues his, or even the common, interest, and the way he seems to be above the internal rivalries of the group.

Material wealth does not mean much to him. His greatest treasure, beyond himself, are his parents or those who substitute for them. He takes everything these persons bestow on him for granted. Although he says "thank you," to be sure, there is no real feeling of gratitude. It is also these older persons rather than he himself who should look after his material possessions and try to increase them. Only if property and wealth happen to be in his line of interest and talent, and if he notices that this may make him even more of a focus of attention in his environment, then material goods may strike his fancy after all, and he may be quite successful. Even then he does it ultimately for the enjoyment of life, for the sake of collecting art or participating in intellectual or cultural exchanges.

Among women he by far prefers the motherly person who admires him and is willing to subordinate her life and her interests to his career. If that woman is beautiful besides, all the better. He can be polite and considerate, but he uses these abilities at his own discretion rather than according to the woman's needs. More than males with siblings, he remains his own best friend.

He takes to oldest sisters of brothers and, if need be, also to oldest sisters of sisters. Women who are a few years older than he, or persons who had a similar or identical sibling position as his mother had, would be acceptable matches too. He may also get along with a younger sister, particularly if she is considerably younger than he is. Middle siblings may be attracted to him by virtue of the fact that he has no siblings and that he seems more autonomous vis-à-vis his peers than are other boys or men. If he comes upon another only child, the two cannot live up to each other's unconscious expectations of care and attention. Not infrequently such a marriage leads to an only child or none.

He would renounce children of his own altogether more readily than other husbands would. If they were to have a child, he feels it should be a boy. After overcoming his initial feelings of jealousy of his child, he may begin to pamper his son, or his daughter, and overprotect him, or her. This will occur particularly when he discovers his own traits in his son or those of his mother in his daughter. Occasionally a male only child will insist on having several children. In order to get them, however, he needs a woman who wants the same thing and to whom caring for children and mothering them comes naturally, hopefully because of her experiences in her original family.

Male friends are less important to him than fatherly patrons. An only child can best identify with other only children, as well as with oldest brothers. More than persons with other sibling positions, however, he can also get along with and interact with a person from an identical sibling position. Oldest brothers tend to lose patience with him too soon. They find it hard to share tasks with him, and they feel that he does not get involved enough and develops no sense of duty. They are likely to complain that it is difficult to arouse his ambition if he is not interested to begin with. Even if the only child is called upon to lead and direct, he prefers to be the adviser of another person rather than the leader himself. He willingly concedes the actual execution of leadership and its details to someone else, to someone, that is, who is better used to dealing with peers of both sexes.

An only male child is affected by losses if the person concerned is a parent, a parent-like patron and sponsor, or a motherly friend. Even then it is not always the objective loss or sympathy with the lost person as much as it is the immediate and direct impact on him that is the focus of his mourning.

Male only children are somewhat more likely than other persons to be found in the following professions: scientist, systematic philosopher, mathematician, art historian, archeologist, scholar, abstract painter or sculptor, poet, book dealer, estate manager, jeweler, technician, or fashion designer.

He is interested in psychotherapy as a service offered by experienced, well-meaning older people, but he has more trouble than others accepting the fact that it does not come free. Do not older people owe him such services, he may secretly ask himself, and in lieu of a positive answer he may actually forego the idea after all. Should he become a psychotherapist himself, helping the patient will not be the highest of his (unconscious) priorities. He is more interested in research, wants to fathom the secrets of psychic life, and someday earn a crown of laurels for it. He gets along better with male than with female patients, particularly with males who were only children themselves or who held a sibling position similar to the one his own father held. In the treatment of females, the beginning is relatively smooth and easy, but working through and terminating is more difficult than with males. This is especially true for female only children or for women whose sibling position is similar to that of his mother.

Through identification with his same-sex parent any only child may also adopt behavior characteristics and attitudes commonly associated with that parent's sibling position. Hence the question of the father's sibling position is even more important with the male only child than with men of other sibling positions. If the father's sibling position is known, one may also consult the role portrait corresponding to that sibling position in order to more comprehensively and pertinently characterize the male only child in question.

Well-known male only children are Robert Menzies, Arnold Palmer, Charles M. Schultz, Bob Hope, John Updike, Tom Mboya, Douglas Dillon, and Rudi Gernreich.

The Oldest Sister of Sisters:
s(s..)

The oldest sister of sisters likes to take care of things and give orders. She wants to know what is going on around her. She wants people to report to her, to be up to date and in control. She derives her claim to authority and leadership from another person with authority, usually an older man, a man in a high position, or from a law-maker.

This frequently includes her own father. She accepts this person's wishes or will unquestioningly and will remain faithful to him for many years. Only if the overwhelming majority of the people around her feel there is something absolutely wrong with these wishes or this design will she look for another new older man or law-maker to whom she will then remain devoted for the rest of her life.

Material wealth and property as well as cultural and intellectual goods are less important to her than responsibility and power over those people who were entrusted to her. These would include her siblings or her children, as well as her female and male friends and colleagues, provided they accept her surveillance and her control. She can demand generous means or money, which she will then spend without hesitation on behalf of those entrusted to her, in particular on behalf of her own children. She does the same for others, too, but she does not want to have to scrimp for herself either. Where the money is to come from or how the authority figure of her choice, her boss or her husband, drums up the money, is their business, she feels; if they cannot properly provide for her and those entrusted to her, they had better quit.

She can work hard for a good cause and sometimes tends to over-exert herself. She is tough and enduring. She does not take it easy herself and expects others, especially her charges, to fulfill their assignments and accomplish things. Her subordinates and colleagues rather dread than love her, even though she is convinced that she means well, and she would not be able to understand how anybody could possibly be afraid of her.

Not infrequently she gives men the impression of being an unconquerable fortress. She appears efficient, strict, and straightforward, and thus discourages many men from flirting with her or courting her. She is often annoyed that the man who has aroused her interest seeks contact with her but does not declare his intentions. She may be the one who does the proposing, and her beau may be taken off balance; but he tends to accept. He thinks, however, that now things will change, she will become kinder, more open-hearted, and will learn to give in at times, but she does not change much. She also stays tied to her father more strongly than the other women her husband might have contemplated marrying.

Her most suitable partner would be the youngest brother of sisters, although he would be better off, on the whole, with an oldest sister of brothers. She herself, the oldest sister of sisters, is inclined to consider him too soft and sloppy. He needs more tolerance and forgiveness than she cares to give. A youngest brother of brothers would also do for her; he can be converted to her life style more easily than other men. An oldest brother of sisters, on the other hand, strikes her as too conceited because of his experience with other girls and women, and she may never feel emotionally intimate with an oldest brother of brothers. They would tend to live side-by-side rather than with each other. Each of them would prefer to work on a job of his own. Even at home they would have to divide up their chores in order to avoid the frictions of direct interaction. Interaction does not work. They do not supplement each other. She could handle an only child, if he could tolerate her treatment. The same would apply for a middle sibling. She, more than other women, is interested in men who hold the same sibling position her father held.

Children are more important to her than her husband is. Sometimes she seems to have wanted to use him merely to father her children. In any case, the arrival of children is likely to relieve tensions between the couple. Her need for authority and nurturing, which her husband found somewhat overbearing, is now directed toward her children. She tends, however, to overprotect them and to subdue their desires for independence. She loves their dependence on her and her advice. She suffers more than other mothers do when the children eventually leave home, and she tries, sometimes to her children's regret, to wield power and control even from a distance. She can also forego men and a family of her own more willingly than other women can.

Her girl friends are more important to her than are her boyfriends. Only the prestige associated with men and their friendships may temporarily overshadow her interest in girl friends. Even in marriage, and as the head of her family, she still needs her contacts with girl friends and women more than other mothers do. Her favorite friend is usually a younger sister of sisters. Not only do the two get along well with each other, but her friend is surrounded by more men than she is herself and can bring one or the other of them along into her own house. She is also on good terms with an only child, particularly when this friend is a few years younger than she is and/or is the daughter of a mother who was a youngest sister herself. She can identify with another oldest sister (of sisters), but does not become close friends with her. In a group of friends the two would be rivals.

Her gravest loss would be that of her father or her elected (male) authority figure according to whose guidelines she has tried to arrange her life. Only in her first few years of life would the loss of her mother hurt her more. In later years she can more easily overcome this loss, possibly by assuming mother's role in the family. She can also cope with the loss of a female or a male friend, and she can frequently be a model for the other bereaved persons. If, however, she suspects that she herself may be in the slightest responsible for the loss, something she might feel without objective reasons if she were to lose a sister or her own child, she may struggle for the rest of her life to overcome this loss.

Among her relatively preferred professions are those of teacher, principal, head nurse, missionary, sister superior of a convent, director of a children's home or of a kindergarten, chief physician, surgeon, neurologist, supervising secretary, editor(in-chief), manager of an employment or theatrical agency, movie star, or judge.

As a patient of psychotherapy, her irritation with men as well as her ready subordination to her father and certain father figures would generally constitute the core of her problem. It is not easy to help her with this. More so than with other women, her pride can be her undoing. If she is a psychotherapist herself, she tends to be impatient, over-protective and domineering with her patients, particularly with men. She works better with female than with male patients and best with other oldest sisters. Younger sisters and men can entangle her more easily than other psychotherapists in interpersonal relations extending beyond psychotherapy. She must at least be more aware than other psychotherapists of these entanglements.

Well-known oldest sisters of sisters are Queen Elizabeth, Brigitte Bardot, Marlene Dietrich, Sophia Loren, Joan Baez, and Jacqueline Kennedy.

The Youngest Sister of Sisters:
(s..)s

The youngest sister of sisters loves change and excitement. She is vivacious, impulsive, even erratic, and easy to challenge. She finds herself in competition with girls and women, and men too, more often than other girls do. She is attractive, but also moody and capricious. Her mind may be changed and her intentions diverted more easily than other people's can be, particularly if the maneuver to distract her is not too obvious. If she notices that someone may be trying to manipulate her, she can respond with great stubborness and sometimes stick to an idea or plan for the rest of her life, even if it is against her own practical interests.

At work she loves to excel. Recognition and praise are very important to her, and she may accomplish good and even great things depending upon the extent to which these needs are fulfilled. If the working atmosphere changes for the worse, her motivation may dwindle. In that case she will not care whether such a change was the result of a plan or of the ill will of one of her superiors, or whether in fact a general economic crisis has caused it. She judges by what she experiences and feels. The context in which something happens is of secondary or of no interest at all to her.

She seems to need guidance from a woman or a man, as long as it is not too obvious and as long as the leading person at least goes through the motions of securing her consent. The youngest sister of sisters wants to be able to feel that she is listened to and respected as a person. If she is approached the wrong way, she may resist adamantly and unobjectively. She can show opposition and may take great pains to prove to her superior that he was wrong. Success makes her more exuberant than others, but failure also discourages her more than it does others except when someone patiently consoles and comforts her. If a person believes that she is capable of doing certain things, she tends to work very hard until she has indeed accomplished them, but if someone thinks little of her abilities, she may not even start the task in question. She is more suggestible than many, even though she tries hard not to be influenced by others. She is also more courageous and willing to take greater risks than others, and she is even likely to risk her life, especially when it will earn her the appreciation of a person dear to her or when she will thereby be in the limelight.

Material goods may be important to her, but she is not very consistent in this respect. She can try to amass things. She can put away savings for a long time, but she can also be quite wasteful and entice others to provide or squander goods themselves. Recognition by others and her own prestige and honor mean a lot to her. Her ideas about honor and a good reputation, however, are not always of the conventional type.

With respect to men, she tends to be ambivalent. On the one hand, she wants to stand out through the influence and effect she can exert over men, and she often succeeds at this. She can attract men better than other girls can. She may even make men lose their minds in the process, or she may play them against each other. On the other hand, she is inclined to compete with a man, if he only remotely indicates that he wants to take charge. These two trends may be the reason why men get tired of her after a while. If she notices that she has overdone it with a particular man and if he seems to want to leave, she may sometimes abandon all other men and even stop competing with this particular one. Not infrequently she marries under such a pressure, even if she regrets it later on.

Her best partner would be an oldest brother of sisters, although he is the least likely to fall for her tricks. It is more likely that she will attract an oldest brother of brothers, but the two would not find it very easy to live together as husband and wife. However, if they "conspire" to try a joint career or to cooperate in a special venture, they can get along with each other better. Youngest brothers offer her too little guidance, despite the fact that she acts as if she does not want any guidance at all. Middle siblings with younger sisters among their own siblings would also make feasible companions. An only child would be among the poorer matches, except if such a man is either considerably older than she or if his own father was himself an oldest brother.

The youngest sister of sisters finds it difficult to put up with children unless she has a governess, a maid, her own mother, or one of her sisters to assist her. If that is not possible, she needs her husband's support more than other wives do. He must be ready, explicitly or in the practice of every-day life, to assume responsibility for the children and to help her with them. If he does not like to do something, she does not like it either. If he is helpful, though, she is prepared to contribute her own share and take the burdens of motherhood upon herself. She feels, incidentally, that at least one of her children "must" be a boy.

Her best girl friend is often an oldest sister of sisters or a middle sister who had a younger sister herself. She expects this friend to provide her with understanding, opportunities to talk things over, and guidance. She is not indifferent to oldest and youngest sisters of brothers either, but men, often even the brothers of these girl friends, are an important link in her friendship, sometimes even a point of contention.

The loss she would find most difficult to bear would usually be that of her father. Ordinarily she has been "Daddy's girl." The loss of her mother would be softened by the presence and help of her older sisters. She tends to express her grief relatively most freely at the loss of a sister or a sisterly friend. She is troubled more than others are by vague guilt feelings. She feels she should have treated the lost person much better or should have talked to her more frequently and attentively than she did. She responds similarly to the loss of a boyfriend or of her husband. Nevertheless, she is able to accept other persons in lieu of the lost one relatively quickly.

She is more interested than other women in the following professions: secretary, singer, (comedy) actress, radio or television announcer, saleswoman, advertising agent, political speaker (also in women's liberation matters), interpreter, medical assistant, (employed) physician, dentist, artist, photographer, or fashion designer.

She loves psychotherapy. Treatment need never end as far as she is concerned, especially when her father, her husband, or a friend foots the bill. She feels that here, perhaps only here, she is really being understood. If she is a psychotherapist herself, she tends to be on the carefree side, convinced that things will work out for the patient all by themselves. She works better with women than with men, particularly when the women are youngest sisters. With oldest sisters as well as with men, she has trouble suppressing her own personal opinion and avoiding impulsive responses.

Well-known youngest sisters of sisters are Princess Margaret, Kim Novak, and Pat Suzuki.

The Oldest Sister of Brothers:
s(b..)

The oldest sister of brothers is independent and strong in an unobtrusive way. She loves to take care of men and does not insist on immediate or official recognition of the fact. She wants men to be satisfied with what they have to do. She gladly provides whatever she can contribute to make life and work more pleasant for them. If something big is at stake, she does not take it, nor the men involved in it, very seriously. She does, however, consider their subjective well-being and their belief in the project as being important. Some observers find her too condescending. The men in her charge are her main concern but she does treat them like little boys.

In her own work, she likes to appear superior, the person who stands above it all. She does not overexert herself, yet she does not avoid things either. She creates an atmosphere that her coworkers appreciate. Even her boss listens to her. She does not compete with men, but she rather acts as an umpire in their quarrels among themselves. Women, on the other hand, do not interest her much. In her opinion, they should help men or should help her help them. If they do not do that, they are not worth much.

Disappointments rarely discourage her. She is, or pretends to be, more optimistic than both men and women in her surroundings. What she cannot bear, however, is solitude. Being separated from men or rejected by a man whom she respects can hurt her deeply. She may not show it, but she will suffer from this sort of thing for a long time and may, under certain circumstances, turn into a man-hater. The first male, however, who is willing to listen to her and to trust her can change her mind.

Material possessions matter little to her compared with the "possession" of boys and men, but she may look after their properties and businesses. If she administers such properties, she does so more to please her friend or husband than to satisfy a basic need of her own. If she is well-to-do to begin with, she is more likely than other well-off women to choose her friends and her husband for other than material reasons. She may do so because of his talents and because his ideas and plans impress her. She is frequently the sponsor and benefactor of gifted men.

She does not fascinate men, but the man who wins her

can consider himself lucky. Since men feel quite comfortable in her company, they often take her for granted, and since she caters to their needs so attentively, they forget to inquire about her own needs. The man of her choice often requires a little encouragement to propose to her. She understands his simultaneous interest in other women a little better than her fellow-women do, but her tolerance is not unlimited. If she eventually pushes for a decision on his part, he is surprised to discover that he has unknowingly been giving her priority all along over the other women around him.

Her best partner would be the youngest brother of sisters. A youngest brother of brothers or a middle brother who has at least one older sister will also do. An only child would be acceptable too, at least if his own father was himself a youngest brother. An oldest brother of brothers would be relatively unfavorable, although he could still do worse. In their relationship a sense of fighting for leadership is likely to prevail, and neither of the two seems willing to budge.

She can handle children quite well: she loves them and takes care of them, even if her marriage is not particularly happy. She does favor the sons over the daughters, however, and urges the latter to concern themselves with the well-being of their brothers and boys in general, as she herself does. She expresses occasional irritation over the fact that her husband does not do enough in the family, avoids responsibility at home, or leaves too many decisions to her, but basically she is not nearly as disturbed by it as she seems. In any case, she values her own educational activities higher than she does her husband's or anybody else's, for that matter.

Girl friends are not important to her. The most likely friendship tends to be with a youngest sister of sisters. This girl can attract men, make them court her, and perhaps bring them along when the two girls get together. Some of these men may even want to recuperate with her, the oldest sister of brothers, from the tribulations that the youngest sister of sisters has put them through. A youngest sister of brothers is a somewhat less likely girl friend. She is too engrossed in her friendships with men and too dependent and yielding with them for the oldest sister of brothers to approve of or even tolerate.

In her early years of life the loss of her mother would be her gravest trauma. She needs her guidance and example to become the motherly friend of boys that her family needs, and which she wants to be. Somewhat later in life neither the loss of her father nor of her mother can really shake her up as long as her life's purpose is retained: to care for her brothers. Only the loss of a brother, or later on the loss of a good boyfriend or of her own son can give her emotional trouble. She fears she may have been negligent and at fault for the loss.

She elects the following professions more often than by chance: hotel director, inn-keeper, cook, head of personnel, union officer, social worker, actress, manager of artists or writers, nursery-school teacher, nurse, pediatrician, internist.

She neither wants psychotherapy nor does she ordinarily need it. She can help others and herself. Moreover, she realizes that there is no remedy in psychotherapy against the disappointments suffered at the hands of men. That, however, may be her only problem needing psychotherapy. If she becomes a psychotherapist herself, she can handle male patients better than females. Among men her preference is for those who have had older sisters. With other types of male patients, particularly with oldest brothers of brothers, she may develop more conflicts than is good for a psychotherapist. Female patients, on the other hand, tend to arouse too little of her interest, even though she can help a female patient better than she can a male one in eventually detaching himself from the psychotherapist toward the end of treatment. Even so, she is relaxed and friendly for the most part with both men and women. Her temperament tends to have psychotherapeutic effects all by itself.

Well-known oldest sisters of brothers are: Romy Schneider, Julie Andrews, Shirley McLaine, and Leontyne Price.

The Youngest Sister of Brothers:
(b..)s

The youngest sister of brothers attracts men more pervasively, as a rule, than other girls or women can. She does it quietly, though, or at least without much ado. Often she is all that a man would conventionally wish of a woman: she is feminine, friendly, warm, sympathetic, sensitive, and usually tactful. She can give in without being obsequious or servile. She is a good pal, willing to apply and devote herself if a person whom she loves requests it. She also gets what she wants from men. Sometimes she seems a bit spoiled or even extravagant.

Her enthusiasm for work and her professional motivation are for the most part average. If she has special talents, she may not necessarily develop them or use them in practice. She is not ambitious of her own accord, but may become so for the sake of an ambitious man. She is likely to adjust her life to the interests of one or several men. She often behaves as if there were no need for her to work, but she will do anything for a man she loves and has reason to love. Professional or other disappointments cannot discourage her.

Property and wealth mean little to her. However, she frequently happens to be better endowed than others. Her brothers usually take care that she suffer no dire need. She develops her cultural and intellectual interests in line with her brothers' interests or those of certain men rather than from her own initiative, but these brothers or men are willing to consider her their muse and devote their works to her. This may be why she can sacrifice all of her possessions more readily than other girls or women, if her lover, her husband, or circumstances require it. Her beloved man is her real wealth.

Men admire and love her. Wherever she goes, she finds suitors without trying and does not ordinarily abuse her good fortune. She is no femme fatale. She is nice and charming with almost all of them. Men adore her even when they know they will not be able to have her for a lover or a wife. Her first proposal from a man tends to come sooner than it does with other girls. On the average, she also marries a little earlier than others. If she happens to take her time, however, she is unlikely to lose her nerve as other girls might. She seems to realize that she can always fall back on her brothers. Even if she never marries, she has a boyfriend or a love relationship, perhaps one that may not be legalized because of certain conditions beyond her control.

Her best choice for marriage would ordinarily be an oldest brother of sisters, and of all types of girls she is relatively the most likely one to find the right partner for herself. She knows what she wants as a woman, but can adapt in all other matters. This is also what the oldest brother of brothers responds to. Unfortunately, she learns in the process that he cannot accept her for what she is; he may want to reeducate her. A middle brother would not be unfavorable either, as long as he had had a younger sister among his siblings. With a youngest brother of sisters she would miss the sense of leadership and responsibility she is used to with her brothers. A youngest brother of brothers or an only child would be among the least favorable matches, relatively speaking, and the latter would be particularly so if his father had been an only child or a youngest brother.

She loves her children, although she might impress them as being too dependent and "seductive." Even as a mother she is foremost a woman, and she loves her husband even more than her children. She thus inadvertently fosters a role of gentleman and protector in her sons. Her sons want to help their mother and do favors for her sooner than in other families. Daughters also learn, inadvertently as well, how one acts feminine, impresses men, subordinates oneself, and yet, or even because of it, how one manages to get what one wants.

Girl friends do not play a large role in her life. Before she realizes it, men come up and claim her for themselves. Her girl friends envy her good fortune with men. She attracts men not only fleetingly or for short periods of time (as the youngest sister of sisters succeeds in doing), but lastingly and for keeps. Still, there is no conniving in this, nor does she boast about it.

Losses can hurt her deeply. Among all the bereaved, she seems to be the worst affected. She suffers and mourns with great dedication, but by so doing, she also elicits sympathy and help. Unknowingly she even helps others bear and overcome their own grief. She is uninhibited in expressing what the others feel as well. Sometimes her grief over the loss of a family member, of a dear friend or of her husband, may exceed all manageable proportions, so that all the sympathy and comforting of others will not help. All she wants to do is to follow the lost person into the beyond. She would not commit suicide, but she may quietly refuse to go on living. It seems as if she just wants to wilt away from this world.

Professionally she shows fewer noticeable preferences than do girls of any other sibling position. She can turn to home-making and family life and give up her job more easily than others can. At work she is not bent on realizing her own high goals or her intrinsic potential. She wants to do what she enjoys doing or what her husband or other esteemed men want her to do. She likes to work in their company. Professions such as those of typist or secretary, medical assistant, nurse, laboratory assistant, scientific assistant, active participant in the family enterprise, admiring companion of another artist or explorer, as an actress the willing instrument of a stage director, these careers are somewhat more to her liking than they are for other girls.

She is no eager candidate for psychotherapy. This is partly connected with her successes with men. She hardly needs help in matters of love, provided she has not grown up under traumatic family conditions, but if she did have real troubles in love relationships, psychotherapy could not help her in any case. If she should become a psychotherapist herself, her great empathy could create more meta-psychotherapeutic conflicts for her than other psychotherapists would encounter, especially with male patients. This conflict will be there even if she does not give in to, but succeeds in defending herself against, her predicament. She instinctively understands men as a woman, but not necessarily as a psychotherapist.

Female patients with troubles in matters of love, on the other hand, would benefit from identifying with their therapist. If they could be like her in their attitudes and their behavior toward men, their troubles would soon diminish.

A well-known youngest sister of brothers is Elizabeth Taylor. Marilyn Monroe grew up partly as an orphan, partly as the youngest sister of foster brothers. Her life history is atypical because of rather traumatic circumstances, but her parts in movies are often reminiscent of the character of a youngest sister of brothers.

The Female Only Child:
s

More so than women with siblings, the female only child depends on the care and attention of relatively older persons. In school as well as at work and in her daily life, she wants her superiors, her colleagues, and her friends to be what her parents were for her. She leans on her superiors more than her colleagues do, tries to fulfill their wishes and plans, and wants to be their "dearest child," since she cannot very well be their only child. Thus she impresses others as a do-gooder with latent or manifest claims for preferential treatment. She can apply herself and get involved, but her fellow-workers, particularly the female ones, tend to find her egotistical. Sometimes she really is, and occasionally even her devotion to her superior is lacking.

Some female only children believe that their father or both parents owe them all the help or support that they can give, even after they have become adults and have entered a profession. She feels that her parents should pave her way;

they should continue to look after her and even protect her in her marriage. If she feels slighted or maltreated by her husband or his family, she is more apt than other wives to run back to her parents. The reason for such a proclivity may be traumatic conditions in her early family life, for example, conflicts between her parents or the early losses of family members that she or her parents have suffered.

Without her parents or paternal advisers, her career may falter. Even with sponsors, however, her chances for a very successful or independent career are slim. Here the fate of the female only child seems to be clearly different from that of her male counterpart. This may be connected with the fact that many professions are still dominated by men rather than by women, or with the fact that the female only child, when competing against other women or even against men, prefers to have a patron who will champion her cause. If he does not fight, she is prone to fail.

Material wealth is less important to her than an unswerving fatherly (or motherly) patron, but should this person be wealthy, look after his fortune on her behalf, and eventually give or leave it to her, she will certainly have no objections. In a situation such as this, however, she may easily misjudge the proportions and believe herself to be richer than she actually is or, in spite of a considerable fortune, she may feel poorer or more threatened by poverty than even the impecunious among her contemporaries. If she has gone through traumatic experiences in her early family life, however, she may have been shocked to her senses, may have abandoned her infantile and egocentric attitude, and may use cold intelligence in order to handle her own affairs. She treasures and enjoys her intellectual and cultural goods, provided she has no other worries.

She is hard put at first to hide her spoiled and egocentric personality in her contacts with men. She finds it harder than other girls to forego her needs in favor of a partner. She can be more heartless and extravagant than most girls and women, but may know better than others how to awaken and test fatherly traits in a suitor before she gets involved with him for good. Her mother assists her more than other mothers do their daughters and may even be the matchmaker. A man who takes an only child for his wife would be well advised to consider her mother (and her sibling position) carefully. Her mother often comes as a part of the package. This is not to say that the female only child cannot be a good wife, too. She may even be less inclined than other wives to become unfaithful. If she does leave her husband, she is more likely to go to her parents than into the arms of another lover.

Her best partner would be the oldest brother of sisters. An oldest brother of brothers may also provide the fatherly guidance, although not the doting affection, that she hopes for. A youngest or a middle brother of sisters would not offer her the leadership she needs, but may compensate for it by his implicit understanding of girls and their wishes as well as by his willingness to admire her. In such a case a greater than average age difference between the two would help, he being the older one. A youngest brother of brothers and a male only child would be relatively unfavorable partners unless special circumstances prevailed or the spouses accept that they would rather live side-by-side than in intimate interaction with one another. These special circumstances include a greater-than-average age distance between the two or early identifications on the part of the husband with a father who himself had been an oldest sibling.

A female only child cares less about children than other wives do except when her mother or a motherly person is willing to help and can be charged with taking care of the children. She would still rather be a child herself. If she is taking care of her own child, she wants to have the attention and the admiration of at least one older person. Her husband can help her too, mostly by praising her generosity and giving practical assistance. One child, preferably a girl, will often be enough for her. It becomes easier for her to care for a daughter and to suppress a certain jealousy of her parents' and her husband's attention for the child, if she can discover herself in her daughter. If she happens to have a boy, she prefers to discover and foster in him features of her own father rather than those of her husband. If she has several children, she expects her husband and his family to help and encourage her. Sometimes a conflict with her own parents or a wish to prove something to her parents may be the chief reason for a greater number of children. In that case, the prognosis for the children's development may not be very good.

She likes girl friends, if they are prepared to assume a motherly role toward her. They are either clearly older than she is, or they are oldest sisters of sisters or middle sisters who had other (younger) sisters among their siblings. Usually she loves individual contacts with her girl friends more than group contacts. She may become friends with the younger sister of sisters or of brothers, or even with another only child, only if she had had a hard time as a child and was forced to become self-supporting much sooner than other only children. In that case she might be able to offer the leadership, autonomy, and nurture that she longed for herself, but which she had to renounce earlier than other only children. She had to become her own motherly patron, one might say, and is even able to provide a little bit for someone else.

The loss she would find most hard to bear would be that of a parent or of a parent-like person to whom she had become attached. More than other women, however, she is occupied with herself rather than with other bereaved persons or with the lost person. "What is to become of me?" is her main concern. Losses of friends are less disturbing except when her paternal sponsor is also affected by the loss. In that case she must be careful to display her grief. Her tacit gain would be her sponsor turning to her even more than he used to before the loss occurred. To put it differently, she must be more careful than others not to show her feelings of rivalry toward the person who has been lost.

Female only children are more willing than other women to give up their jobs in order to marry, particularly if they are not expected to become mothers immediately. Among the professions they seem to prefer to an extent are: private secretary, secretary of a director, companion to elderly individuals, biographer, fashion designer, interior decorator, art historian, librarian, crafts woman, art restorer, or stage star.

The female only child has a weak spot for psychotherapy, but she is more likely than others to experience it as an end in itself. Here she finally meets the truly understanding and sympathetic person who will listen and respond to her. She finds it a bit difficult, though, to accept the fact that a psychotherapist does not do more for her, that he does not enter her everyday life as her permanent protector and helper, and that even the strictly psychotherapeutic relationship must end one day. If her development has been disturbed by early traumata, perhaps by conflicts between the parents or by the loss of a parent, and if she has eventually overcome these traumata, perhaps only with the help of psychotherapy, she may also become a psychotherapist herself. As such she will work better with female than with male patients, especially with women who were only children themselves or who suffered a similar fate in their family as she did. With male patients she remains somewhat insecure. She is more prone than other psychotherapists to be less than objective vis-à-vis her patients' problems. Her own problems, perhaps with her strong ties to her father or conflicts with him or with the losses of family members she may have suffered, may tinge her work.

Well-known female only children are Jeanne Moreau, Renata Tebaldi, Barbra Streisand, Lauren Bacall, Indira Gandhi, and Katherine Anne Porter.

Multiple and Middle Sibling Positions: Interpretation Guidelines

If the oldest brother has both a younger sister and a younger brother, we recommend consulting the role portrait of the oldest brother of sisters as well as that of the oldest brother of brothers in order to understand his behavior and attitudes. If a middle sister has an older and a younger brother, the portrait of the youngest sister of brothers as well as that of the oldest sister of brothers should be consulted. If she has a younger sister as well, the portrait of the oldest sister of sisters should be utilized in additic . . Of course, it is not an easy task for the observer to keep more than two portraits in his mind at once. If a person has a completely middle sibling position, that is, if he has an older and a younger sister as well as an older and a younger brother, the portraits of all four basic types of sibling positions would be pertinent. However, one could just as easily say that none of these four portraits applies. The synthesis or conceptual integration is not only difficult for the observer but also for the person concerned who, if he holds this kind of middle position, often cannot find his role in the family context. He is everything and, therefore, "nothing." Any of the four relationships he might develop with one of his siblings is already occupied by another one, who has usually solidified it with greater emphasis than he can. His oldest brother, for example, is a more convincing protector of his youngest sister, and his youngest brother is a more convincing follower of his oldest brother than he is himself. He is therefore frequently more impatient than his siblings to move out of the family (see also p. 18ff, particularly p. 21f).

If a person holds more than one role in his sibling configuration, these roles may not have been forced on him and he may not exercise them with equal intensity. As a rule, he will prefer one or two of his possible roles. In order to at least tentatively predict without additional information which of these several roles will be stronger than the rest, we can apply the following rules of sibling role strength or sibling role preference:

1.   Of several sibling roles that a person may hold in his sibling configuration, the one that will be stronger than the rest is the one he holds vis-à-vis the sibling closest in age to himself.

If a younger brother has a sister two years older and a

brother four years older than himself, his role of youngest brother of sisters should be stronger than that of youngest brother of brothers. If his sister is two years older and his brother is six years older than himself, the difference in strength of the two roles should be even greater. Here his role as youngest brother of brothers would be still weaker than in the first instance.

1a. Of several sibling roles that a person holds in his sibling configuration, the relatively stronger and more effective ones are those which he holds vis-à-vis immediately adjacent siblings.

If an oldest brother has a younger sister and a still younger brother, his role as an oldest brother of sisters should be more pronounced than that of an oldest brother of brothers. Similarly, if a middle sister has an older brother, a still older sister and a younger sister, the roles of oldest sister of sisters, and of youngest sister of brothers should ordinarily be more noticeable than that of youngest sister of sisters.

1b. The greater the number of siblings holding the same sibling role vis-à-vis the directly succeeding sibling, the greater the relative likelihood that another sibling other than the immediately preceding (or next-oldest) one may be the main representative of that sibling role for the succeeding sibling.

If three brothers, for example, have a little sister, the second-oldest or the oldest brother rather than the adjacent brother may become the person to whom the new sister mainly relates. Of two sisters, the oldest rather than the second-oldest may be the favorite older sister for a third girl born into the same family.

1c. The greater the number of siblings holding the same sibling role vis-à-vis the directly preceding sibling, the greater the relative likelihood that one other than the immediately succeeding (or next-youngest) sibling may be the main representative of that sibling role for the preceding sibling.

For example, if a girl has three younger brothers, the

middle of the two or the youngest one, rather than the oldest one, may be her favorite younger brother.

2.   Of the several sibling roles that a person may hold in his sibling configuration, the one that will be relatively more effective is the one he assumed earlier in his life and retained without interruption.

If an oldest brother has a sister three years younger than himself and a brother six years younger than himself, his role of oldest brother of sisters should be stronger than that of oldest brother of brothers. He had played the first role for three years before he began to play the second role as well. If a middle brother has a sister three years older and a brother three years younger than himself, his part as youngest brother of sisters would ordinarily be stronger than his part as oldest brother of brothers. He has played the first part since birth, the second part only since entering his fourth year of life.

This rule obviously implies that older siblings exert stronger influences upon younger siblings than vice versa. This should not surprise us. Each succeeding child is at first utterly oblivious of the situation into which he has been born, whereas the older siblings tend to realize very soon what the addition to their family implies. Moreover, with the arrival of the third child the oldest sibling repeats the experience of an addition to the family, while the second oldest does this for the first time. The psychological shock over a newcomer, however, can be more easily handled the more often one has lived through it. The milder the shock, in turn, the better the sibling concerned can exert his influences and shape the changed situation according to his own ideas.

The effects of rule 2 decrease in importance as the siblings grow older. This makes sense, considering the fact that a time difference of three years in the incumbency of different roles may be considerable with a 4-year-old and a 1-year-old child. It is three times the age of the younger child. With a 15-year-old and a 12-year-old, on the other hand, this difference has become relatively small, that is, one-fourth of the age of the younger child.

3.   The greater the number of sibling roles of the same type that a person holds in his sibling configuration, the stronger this role is likely to be compared with the other roles he holds.

If a youngest brother, for example, has an older sister and three older brothers, his role as youngest brother of brothers will ordinarily be stronger than his role as youngest brother of sisters. If a middle sister has two older brothers and one younger brother, her part as a youngest sister of brothers will probably be stronger than her part as an oldest sister of brothers.

4.   If the age difference between two successive siblings in a sibling configuration is considerably larger than all other age differences between successive siblings, two psychologically separate sibling groups may emerge. The younger of the two adjacent siblings, who are separated by the largest age difference, may assume the role of another oldest sibling.

Suppose five siblings show the following age distribution: a 19-year-old brother, a 17-year-old sister, a 10-year-old sister, a 7-year-old sister, and a 4-year-old brother. It is likely that the first two and the last three siblings will form subgroups or subconfigurations. The third child will presumably become, at least to some extent, an oldest sister of brothers and sisters, while the fourth child will become a middle sister of an older sister and a younger brother, and the boy a youngest brother of sisters.

5.   The greater the similarity between one of the several sibling roles a person holds and the sibling role his same-sex parent has held, the stronger will this particular role be compared with his other sibling roles.

If the youngest brother of an older sister and an older brother has a father who was himself the youngest brother of a sister, the son is likely to develop his role of youngest brother of sisters more strongly than his role of youngest brother of brothers.

6. The greater the similarity between one of the several sibling roles a person holds and the sibling role that a sibling of his opposite-sex parent held, the stronger this particular role will be compared with his other sibling roles.

If an oldest sister of a brother and a sister has a father who had an older sister himself, the daughter will usually become more of an oldest sister of brothers than an oldest sister of sisters. If a middle sister of two brothers has a father who had an older sister himself, the daughter's role as oldest sister of brothers will presumably be stronger than that of youngest sister of brothers.

These rules of sibling-role preferences can reinforce or counteract each other. According to rule 2, for example, a middle sibling of an older brother and a younger sister might prefer his role as a youngest brother of brothers. However, if his father is an oldest brother of sisters, the son may be reinforced in his role as an oldest brother of sisters. In any case, the two role preferences will counteract each other. If his father were the youngest brother of brothers instead, his role preference according to rule 2 would be reinforced by the same role preference according to rule 5. His role of youngest brother of brothers will outweigh the other role.

If it seems too complicated to bear in mind six rules of sibling-role preference in order to judge and evaluate multiple and middle sibling positions, one may restrict one's attention to the proximity rule (1a) and the identification rule (5). There are, of course, completely different ways of finding out about the person's preferred sibling role.

One might ask the person directly about his preferences for one or another of his siblings. Such a question is often answered ambiguously, to be sure, and sometimes also euphemistically or falsely.

One might ask the person about the sibling positions of

the friends he has had and has retained during the course of his life (see p. 112). The sibling position held most frequently by his friends is usually similar or identical with the one held by the person's favorite sibling or the one to whom he related most strongly. A middle brother of an older and a younger sister who has five oldest sisters, one middle sister, and one only child among his seven girlfriends thus indicates that he is looking for a relationship similar to the one he had with his older sister rather than the one he had with his younger sister. Other things being equal, we may in turn derive from this that he likes his role of youngest brother of sisters better than that of oldest brother of sisters. The former is stronger than the latter. There is an advantage in asking about the sibling positions of a person's friends: the question is more indirect and concerns the person's *actual behavior* in his choices of long-term friendships. The probability of ambiguous, euphemistic, or distorted answers is lessened.

Progressive industrialization and urbanization, as well as the need to control population growth, may have caused families to shrink in size. Two-child families are going to increase in number, whereas families with many children are becoming increasingly rare. This means that multiple and middle sibling positions will decline in frequency and significance. Even now the one-child, two-child, and three-child family together make up 80% of all the families studied in our sample of the population. About 20% are one-child families, 36% are two-child families, and 24% are three-child families. Persons coming from two-child families always have pure sibling positions, and exactly one-third of the persons coming from three-child families also have sibling positions that correspond to the basic types. A girl growing up in a three-child family, for example, can be the oldest of two brothers, or the oldest of two sisters, or the youngest of two brothers, or the youngest of two sisters. In another four configurations she would hold a middle position, in still another four a multiple distal position. In other words, even the difficulties of interpreting multiple and middle sibling positions might become rarer in the future.

Rearrangement of Sibling Positions

If a sibling disappears for good, the surviving siblings will have to rearrange their roles and relationships. If a youngest sibling has been lost, the second-youngest sibling or the next-youngest of the same sex is most likely to assume the position of the youngest, provided no additional children are born. If an oldest sister dies, the second oldest sister can take her place. It could be, though, that the brothers in the family will begin to focus on the middle or even on the youngest sister, abandoning their own roles of youngest brothers of sisters in favor of those of oldest brother of sisters. It could also be that they will urge the middle or youngest sister to take the role of oldest sister herself. If an oldest brother is lost, the second oldest may substitute for him and assume leadership and responsibility for the remaining siblings. If the sibling configuration consisted of two boys only, the younger one, after losing his older brother, can usually enter his brother's role to a certain extent by way of identification, even though he has no siblings left with whom to practice that role. Friends of such brothers, however, frequently report that this kind of transformation does indeed take place with the younger brother.

In cases where such changes of position occur after the loss of a sibling, one must assume that the original sibling position is likely to be preserved in varying degrees under the surface. The older a person is when he changes his sibling position, the less effective the new one will probably be. The person may satisfy the external requirements of his new part, or at least try to, but his attitudes and his social behavior may remain the same as before, especially when he feels he is not being watched or when he is trying to relax. One should relate the time during which a person has held a certain role among his siblings to the time during which he held another role. In a very simple model for evaluating the weight or the strength of those two roles, one would think that, other things being equal, the person would have to hold the new role for at least as long as he did the old one before the latter reaches the former in strength and behavioral effectiveness or before it can surpass it. However, as explained above (see p. 5f, p. 77f), earlier experiences should probably be given greater weight than later ones, perhaps in proportion of their time of effectiveness to the person's total lifetime or age. If someone has held a certain role from his fifth to his eighth year of life, but thereafter has had to assume a completely new role that he had never played before, we would conclude, other things being equal, that his new role would be as strong or stronger than the old one only if he has passed his 16th year of life. Only then will he have held his new role for half his lifetime, just as he had his earlier role at the time it stopped. If he occupies his second role while still holding his first one, or if his first role persists at least in part, the effects are more difficult to estimate. A middle brother of three boys who loses his oldest brother at the age of eight and takes his place vis-à-vis his youngest brother, had already partly been an oldest brother himself ever since his little brother was born. The effective time of a role, as expressed in relation to a person's lifetime or age, would also have to be weighed in relation to other roles that are effective at the same time (see Toman 1973a).

We can only deal with the general effects of such roles here. We are in a better position when observing family structures and sibling relationships even if we remember little more than that an earlier role is not erased by a new role but remains effective in some ways than we would be without such an assumption.

Prominent examples of persons who changed their sibling positions are John F. Kennedy and Richard Nixon. Both of them lost their oldest brothers, though at a time when they were already young adults themselves, and it is said of both of them that their style of leadership left something to be desired. Kennedy was a popular man, also with ladies, but he had very little success in the Senate and in the House of Representatives. Lyndon B. Johnson (an oldest brother of a brother) was able to get all of Kennedy's requests and his own through Congress with ease. Kennedy directed or tolerated the unsuccessful invasion of Cuban refugees in Cuba, could prevent the establishment of missile bases on Cuba only by a risky bluff, and had wanted to have a man on the moon before the Russians did.

Kennedy had brothers and sisters, whereas Nixon came from a family of five sons. He was the second oldest and is rumored to have been relatively unpopular with the ladies, although he spent a lot of time controlling his public image. He has been accused of wanting to have too much under his personal control, of being a manipulator and insincere. It looks as if he made pragmatic behavior and efficiency his uppermost guideline, but in a way so consciously and conspiciously as may be expected only of a person who tries to act the oldest brother of brothers by all and any means rather than by being the natural oldest brother of brothers.

Kennedy's oldest brother was an Air Force pilot killed in World War II. Nixon's older brother died of tuberculosis at the age of 23. Nixon, incidentally, lost his next younger brother in an accident when that brother was seven. This loss could also have contributed to the formation of his attitudes and social preferences.

Losses of siblings and rearrangements of sibling positions may also be caused by a sibling's illness, by chronic disability, or by physical or constitutional deficiencies. A sickly oldest sibling may bring about the fact that the second oldest assumes the position of the oldest even during childhood. A very gifted and ebullient youngest sibling may gradually climb to the top of the age-rank order among his siblings. Such developments are the exception rather than the rule, to be sure. Sibling losses as well as grave illnesses or inherited deficiencies of a sibling are relatively rare, too. If we have not been expressly informed about such special conditions, we would do best to assume that average conditions prevail (see p. 62f).

12.   Parents and Types of Parents

We have continuously stressed the significance of sibling positions. We have tried to show that the relationship between the parents is partly codetermined by their sibling positions in their original families. Their relationship may be happy or less than happy according to the compatibility of their sibling positions. We have even tried to explain the relationship between parents and their children as partly dependent upon the identity or complementarity of the sibling roles of the parent and the child.

All this should not obscure the fact that, as individuals, parents determine not only when they want to have children and how many they want to have; they also shape the lives of their children to a great degree. As was first pointed out by Freud (1900, 1916/17), and then by Jung (1912), Adler (1920), and Sullivan (1953), their influence can hardly be overestimated. The influence that their sibling roles and their compatibility with each other as well as with the configuration of their children exert on their family life and on their children's psychological and social development is only a portion of their total influence. Yet it can be more easily observed and objectively and systematically described than other influences emanating from the parents.

The following section should be understood in this light. My coworkers and I were and are not monomaniacs who know nothing more than sibling roles and combinations of sibling roles. I myself have seen many other things in my clinical and psychotherapeutic work as well as in my teaching and research that I would hate to have missed. Life is infinitely richer than I can depict it here. The principles of man's social development and his formation of groups are certainly much more complicated than anything I might be able to describe here. The model of social relationship development that I have presented is only a portion of the true model. Nevertheless, I would like to assure the reader that in my comprehensive experience and in my research efforts over many years, I have not come across any data sets that have appeared even remotely as objective and as easy to comprehend as are the data concerning family constellations. In order to screen and arrange an equivalent amount of data other than that concerning family constellations, I would have required much more time, and I could only have reported about it in a cumbersome and voluminous book. Even then, the information conveyed to the reader in relation to the time spent in reading would have been considerably less than it might be with the book presented here.

In this chapter, 16 types of parental couples where both parents had siblings and 3 types of parental couples where one or both parents were only children will be characterized according to the psychological and social atmosphere they are likely to want to create for their children. Different types of child configurations will also be discussed, in particular whether they consist of boys only, of girls only, and of both sexes. More cannot be done in this context; attempting to do more would probably make the principle more difficult to grasp and might put a strain on the reader. I hope, though, that, on the basis of what has been said and demonstrated so far and of the forthcoming descriptions of family constellations, the reader will be able to extract enough rules of procedure and enough intuitive understanding of the dynamics of family relationships to be able to decipher and analyze more complicated family situations by himself. More complicated family situations are, among others, those with parents and/or children having multiple or middle sibling positions as well as those afflicted by losses of family members.

The following descriptions have all been taken from the data already characterized (see p. 138ff, p. 147f). Like the descriptions of sibling positions, they may be considered valid provided average circumstances prevail, on the whole, or at least that no unusual circumstances are known (see p. 63). Parents have an average age distance between each other and between themselves and their children. No parent has been lost early in a child's life due to death or divorce. They are not constitutionally conspicuous, nor have they suffered from chronic illnesses. There is nothing unusual as far as their geographic, ethnic, economic, and political circumstances are concerned. In the case where one parent is considerably older than the other, unable to work, psychotic, or dead, where the family has changed residence several times and in radical fashions, where it belongs to an ethnic minority, has recently gone bankrupt, or is living in a country afflicted with a dictatorship or by war, some of the descriptions given may not apply in reality. Under ordinary circumstances, however, the reader may expect the descriptions to fit at least approximately in the majority of instances. Where they do not, we suggest the reader try to inquire further and to explore the possible reasons for this.

We assume that, with all types of parents and in all kinds of family environments, parents and children develop a relationship of identification and potential substitution on the one hand, and a relationship of direct interaction and supplementation on the other.

In an *identification* relationship, one person can take the other person's place. In a given context one person can replace the other. He (or she) can show the other person how to act. If they want to cooperate, they tend to get in each other's way. Often both of them want to do the same thing (see p. 92). In an identification relationship, moreover, one person can advise the other on the latter's relationship to a third person. The advising person has, or would have, a similar relationship to the third person as the advisee. If both of them were interested in the third person at the same time, they would become rivals. A mother may counsel her daughter, for example, in her relationship with her father or with a friend. She can empathize with her daughter.

In an *interaction* relationship, each of the two persons concerned works in a different way toward a common objective. One partner has different abilities than the other; one of them is different from the other. Each of them values the other exactly because he is not a duplicate of himself (see p. 92). In an interaction relationship, one of the two persons cannot easily advise the other on the latter's relationship to a third person. Each of the two individuals concerned has a different relationship to such a third person. The third person could or would become the rival of one of the two partners. A father would have a harder time, for example, counseling his daughter about her relationship with her mother or with a girl friend. He would have a man-woman relation with her mother or her girl friend, whereas the daughter would have a woman-woman relationship with them. The father cannot empathize with his daughter very well.

As a rule, a relationship of identification is formed between a parent and his same-sex child, and a relationship of interaction between a parent and his opposite-sex child. If there are only sons or only daughters, a parent and an opposite-sex child may also identify with one another, and a parent and his same-sex child may develop an interaction relationship. Such an inversion may even take place when there are children of both sexes, although it would be the exception rather than the rule.

In discussing each type of parental couple, we shall mention, among other things, which configuration of children would be most suitable for them. This will be done without much comment, whereas the less favorable configurations of children will apparently receive more attention. This can be justified in the following manner: the most suitable configurations of children are those in which the parents can readily identify with a child who holds a similar or identical sibling position as they themselves had and where they can interact conveniently with another child whose sibling position is complementary to their own. In other words, that child's sibling position would be identical in age rank and sex with the sibling position of (at least) one of the parent's siblings (see p.83).

For example: if the mother is the youngest sister of a brother and has an older son and a younger daughter, she can identify with her daughter and the daughter with her mother. The daughter, too, is the younger sister of a brother. Moreover, the mother has no trouble dealing with her son, for she had an older brother in her original family and her son, too, is an older brother of a sister. She can relate to her son as she did to her brother, and her son can treat her the way he treats his sister.

Parents more than anyone else tend to have the greatest impact on their children in the early years of their lives. Children are the products of their parents to a greater extent than they are of anybody else. Parents, however, are also influenced by their children. This influence starts with the arrival of the children and with the child configuration that the parents, with the help of fate, create for themselves. Starting at birth and depending on their sex and their age ranks, children can evoke new behavior from their parents or pressure them into resorting to roles different from their usual ones. These effects and responses are complicated and specific. Despite this fact, I will try to describe the general and crude influences and effects on the family members that emanate from particular types of parental couples and from particular child configurations. This will be done for reasons of economy and didactics. If we were to delve into the details of interactions between family members and of their relationships with each other, we would be lost before long. I do hope, however, that by studying the general descriptions the reader will gradually be enabled to evaluate family relationships as well as the play of effects between family members.

Parents without Rank and Sex Conflicts

Father the oldest brother of sisters /
Mother the youngest sister of brothers:
b(s..)/(b..)s

This is usually a good relationship. The father and mother understand each other, quarrel rarely, and supplement each other in their tasks as breadwinners, homemakers, and educators of their children. Both of them are usually attentive and thoughtful with their children. The father will ordinarily set the tone, but he is friendly and tolerant, while the mother is soft and submissive. Even so, she often gets what she wants. She is not afraid of showing their children her dependence upon her husband. Both parents try to instill a mutual understanding among the children. Parents of this type are significantly less likely to get a divorce than are average parents (0% versus 5%).

The best configuration of children would be one of a son first, then a daughter, or several sons and several daughters thereafter, or first a son followed by a daughter, another son, another daughter, and so on.

If their first-born is a daughter, followed by a son, there may be conflicts with their children. The son and father on the one hand, the daughter and mother on the other, cannot fully identify with one another because of the different age ranks of their sibling roles. In this case, the father and daughter easily tend to come into conflict with one another over leadership and authority, while the mother and son clash over who may depend on whom. The father does not want to be mothered and taken care of as insistently as his daughter wants to. The mother would prefer her son to be less dependent and lazy.

If they have only sons or only daughters, the

parents are still able to teach their children how a man and a woman may live together through their own example of a considerate and harmonious relationship. The oldest of the sons is usually identified with his father, one of the younger sons with his mother. Compared to other families who only have sons, the boys in this case are somewhat less competitive. If the parents have daughters only, the oldest is likely to identify with her father, the youngest with her mother. The oldest daughter, by virtue of her identification, tends to become less likeable to her father in interactive contacts than the youngest one does, even though he realizes that he can rely on his oldest daughter.

Father the youngest brother of sisters/
Mother the oldest sister of brothers:
(s..)b/s(b..)

Ordinarily, this is a good relationship. There is a great mutual understanding between the parents, but the mother is the person who sets the tone in the family. The father likes to submit to his wife's domestic regime. He even likes her advice in professional matters. He sometimes needs her encouragement. In essence, both of them agree on matters concerning the education of their children: she takes charge of them and decides what should be done. She keeps him informed, however, and he may have to examine an issue. He usually consents to what she suggests. Occasionally he may prefer not to be bothered. The mother tends to take care of the children and to be tolerant with them. Parents of this type are significantly less likely to be divorced than parents in the population at large (0% versus 5%).

The best configuration of children would be a daughter first, then a son, or daughters first succeeded by sons, or alternately a daughter, a son, a daughter, a son, etc.

If this couple happens to have a son first and a daughter second, difficulties may arise between the parents and their children. Being a younger brother himself, the father cannot identify very easily with his son, who is an older brother.

The mother, herself an older sister, finds it somewhat difficult to identify with her daughter, who is a younger sister. Moreover, the father and daughter encounter friction with each other. She strikes him as unmotherly and not reponsible enough. The mother and son, in turn, want submission from each other, and neither of them will submit.

If the parents have only sons or only daughters, the children can learn by vicarious participation in their parents' relationships with each other how peers of different sexes can live together. They will pick up an "inverse authority relationship" in the process, to be sure, a relationship in which the wife rather than the husband is the psychological leader. Among sons only, the oldest is likely to identify more with his mother, the youngest more with his father. The oldest son may be a little softer in character than other oldest brothers of brothers are, particularly since he notices in direct interactions with his mother that his younger brothers get along better with her than he does. If the parents have daughters only, the older one usually empathizes and identifies with her mother, the youngest one with her father. The father, in turn, responds more spontaneously and naturally to his oldest daughter than he does to the rest of them. He may admire the youngest, but tends to register with some regret that she will not do very much for someone else (namely himself).

Parents with a Partial Sex Conflict

Father the oldest brother of sisters /
Mother the youngest sister of sisters:
b(s..)/(s..)s

This relationship is a relatively good one. The parents understand each other, but the mother may have had some trouble at first getting used to living with a husband as wife, although usually he can teach her. She is inclined to oppose him on occasion and to compete with him, but these struggles do not last very long. He sets the tone in the family, but he must not do so in a conspicuous way or rub it in. She obeys him, as long as he does not question that she does so voluntarily. If there is a question in that respect, she may become stubborn and insist she is right. She also requires that he help her with the care and education of their children. He will even have to (publicly) attribute some of his professional success and recognition to her. Finally, it would be good for him to let her maintain contacts with her girl friends and sisters throughout their marriage and parenthood.

The best configuration of children would be a son first, then a daughter, or sons first followed by daughters, or a succession of son-daughter pairs.

If they have a daughter first and a son thereafter, they may encounter some difficulties. The father and son will have different opinions about the way girls should be treated. The father thinks that girls want to be guided and protected, whereas the son believes that girls should direct and mother boys. The father feels the daughter should submit and subordinate herself and should not try to control her brother. On the other hand, the mother would tend to reinforce her daughter's independence and to transform her into her confidante and big sister. She might hope that, between the two of them, they would become their men's masters.

The mother would be happier if all their children were sons rather than if they were all daughters. Her ambition vis-à-vis her own family as well as vis-à-vis other women and other families seems to require sons. Being the only woman in her family, she can dispense and shift her favors as she pleases or as she deems appropriate. In the company of her girl friends she loves to brag about her sons. This is so even though, by their experience in their original families, both parents could accept daughters only better than they could sons only. If all their children were daughters, the father tends to select the oldest as his own substitute. The mother also discovers that her oldest daughter can be her confidante and big sister and may even try to alienate her from her father. The youngest daughter can easily identify with her mother. She ought to get what she, the mother, could not get in life, the mother feels. The father, as well, is likely to pamper his youngest daughter more than the rest or at least more than his oldest daughter. Conflicts may result from this between the parents and their oldest daughter.

Father the youngest brother of sisters/
Mother the oldest sister of sisters:
(s..)b/s(s..)

This relationship may be considered relatively good. He and she are prone to get along with each other, although the steady company of a male peer is not easy for her at first. She is a bit tougher and more identified with authority than he likes, but by not contesting her claim to leadership or responsibility he can humor her and gradually make their relationship with each other a bit more relaxed. She sets the tone in the family, but does so much too seriously, he feels, and without winning the undivided sympathy of their children. The latter often get along better with their father, and although he does not have very much time for them and pursues his own interests, they still feel he is one of them. He sometimes defends them against their mother's claims for achievement and obedience. For the mother, justice and order in the family are important, and so is the opportunity to keep up her contacts with her girl friends or stay busy with some responsibilities outside the family throughout her married life.

The best configuration of children would be a daughter first, then a son, or daughters first, then sons, or a daughter and a son in two or more successions.

If they have a son first, followed by a daughter, the son would be handicapped in two ways when trying to develop his sibling role. As an older brother of a sister he cannot identify with his father very well. Moreover, his mother would tend to contest his interest in leading and caring for his sister. The mother would be inclined, instead, to transform her daughter into her own youngest sister and to band together with her against men in general and, at any rate, against the son she considers arrogant.

If they only have sons, the oldest is likely to suffer a similar fate. He cannot learn from his father how to treat boys, and his mother hampers him when he tries to collect his own experiences with his younger brothers. The mother often prefers the youngest or one of the younger brothers, the one who accepts her authority and leadership most willingly. This son can usually identify adequately with his father and thereby learns vicariously how to treat a female peer. Nevertheless, on the whole, the sons have the impression that life among spouses is not exactly easy. With some good will, however, it can be arranged.

If the parents only have daughters, the oldest will ordinarily identify with her mother and tend to please her father, whereas the younger daughters, or at least the youngest, are claimed by the mother. She may become mother's little sister. Some of the things that the mother did not grant to her own younger sister she can now grant her youngest daughter without inner conflict. The youngest daughter may thus become more dependent and less self-assured than other younger sisters of sisters would, particularly since her relationship with her father is not very close. Her father cannot make out his youngest daughter except perhaps when he recognizes himself in her. Incidentally, these parents can handle a configuration of children consisting of only daughters a little better than they can that of sons only.

Father the oldest brother of brothers/ Mother the youngest sister of brothers: b(b..)/(b..)s

This relationship is relatively favorable. He may be tough and self-righteous in his dealings with her and may inadvertently, even unconsciously, treat her like a younger brother at first. She, however, is so used to handling men, thanks to her older brothers, that she can usually tone him down and make him softer. Under her influence he seems to become more tolerant and more open to her wishes and concerns than are other oldest brothers of brothers to those of their wives. This is helped along, of course, by the competition he gets from her brothers. As a rule, they continue to care for their sister, she continues to love them, and he, the oldest brother of brothers, will have to try to adopt some of her brothers' ways of conduct, whether he likes it or not, if he really wants to please his wife. After all, if he has to satisfy his needs to lead and control, he can do it with his colleagues at work. She will also have no objections against his playing boss and provider with her children. It would be good for their family life if he could maintain his contacts with male friends on somewhat regular terms throughout his marriage and after their children have been born.

The best configuration of children would be a son first, a daughter second, or sons first, daughters thereafter, or a sequence of son, daughter, son, daughter.

If their son is born after their daughter, the father and the mother are both prone to find identification with their same-sex children troublesome. The father feels his son is too soft, playful, and dependent. The mother considers her daughter domineering. The father may try to transform his son into someone like his own little brother, but in this case he may increase his son's dependence and lack of autonomy. On the other hand, the father may recognize himself in some of his daughter's traits. If he and she want to do something together, however, they cause friction. The mother, for her part, misses a wish in her son to do something for a woman and to heed her needs.

If they only have sons, things would be a bit better than if they were to have daughters only. In the first instance, the father usually identifies with his oldest son and relates to the rest of the sons as an older brother. The mother feels somewhat excluded from this union of men, but this may teach the sons something about the needs and wishes of a woman. Their image of a woman may grow a little romantic and unrealistic in the process. The mother herself is likely to identify with her youngest son, but would also like to change him somewhat into a girl in her own imagination. If they only have daughters, the latter find fault with the unavailability of their father. If he does spend more time with his daughters, it may be with the unconscious intention of remaking at least one of them, and possibly several or all of them, into boys. He is identified to an extent with his oldest daughter, but does not appreciate the fact that she herself wants to be like him. If the parents' marriage is happy, the daughters will learn how one deals with men by watching their mother and by identifying with her. They may do so, though, in a somewhat romantic vein.

Father the youngest brother of brothers/ Mother the oldest sister of brothers: (b..)b/s(b..)

This relationship is a relatively good one. The father tends to be dependent on the leadership of others and opposes any attempt by others to patronize him, provided he recognizes that this is what they are doing. Yet he can take a woman's leadership and guardianship somewhat more willingly than a man's especially when the woman has learned to deal with younger brothers in her own family. She gradually gets him used to their life together as a man and a woman, but she retains a motherly position toward him. He wants perhaps nothing so much as to be understood, and he feels, incidentally, that she understands him. She treats him like one of her own children to a certain extent. Since her nurturing is usually tolerant and friendly rather than possessive, her children as well as her husband fare rather well. If he sometimes acts like a clown, they love it and laugh about it. If she concedes to him a certain amount of contact with men and male friends throughout their marriage, everybody could well be satisfied.

The best configuration of children would be a daughter followed by a son, or several daughters succeeded by several sons, or a daughter and a son in two or more successions.

If they have an older son and a younger daughter instead, there may be difficulties. Neither the father and son nor the mother and daughter can easily identify with one another. The son is too dependent and domineering for his father's taste, the daughter too dependent and obedient vis-à-vis her brother and men in general, as far as her mother is concerned. If the father learns to accept his son, though, if he treats him like his own little older brother, the two men may try to separate themselves from the girls in the family more than the girls may like. His daughter is somewhat less of a concern to the father than is his son. The mother, in turn, finds her son too autonomous and domineering. The two of them can't stand each other for too long at a time.

These parents would find it easier to accept sons only than daughters only. The father would identify with the youngest son and perhaps "appoint" his oldest son to be his leader and confidant. The mother would unconsciously urge her oldest son to identify with her, but would be prone to treat the rest of her sons the way she treated her own younger brothers. If the parents have only daughters, the oldest one would identify with the mother, and one of the younger ones would identify with her father. Neither parent, however, has become accustomed to dealing with girls and daughters. If the oldest daughter learns to mother and nurture her father and her younger siblings, and if at least one of the younger daughters changes into a "vivacious boy," the family may find a persistently tolerable way of life.

Parents with Rank or Sex Conflicts

Father the oldest brother of sisters/
Mother the oldest sister of brothers:
b(s..)/s(b..)

This relationship is only moderately favorable. In their original homes both partners have learned to live with peers of the opposite sex, but both of them are oldest siblings who tend to challenge the other's claim for leadership and responsibility. Each of them wants the other to give in, and both of them find it difficult to do just that. They do not fight a battle of the sexes, though, and that softens their conflicts. If they can divide up their tasks within their family life, their fight for dominance is further decreased. Both of them are prone, however, to recruit their children of the opposite sex for themselves, to keep them in a state of dependence a little too long, and to side with them against the other half of the family.

Any configuration of children containing both sexes is about equally acceptable to both parents. Twins might be even better, but they are too rare to count on.

If they have a son first and a daughter second, the father finds it easy to get along with the children, whereas the mother experiences difficulties in her identification as well as in her interactions with them. She considers her son too dominant, just as she does his father, and her daughter too submissive and passive. If they have a daughter first, followed by a son, the father is the one to have troubles. His daughter strikes him as overprotective, as acting too self-importantly, the son as undisciplined and spoiled. If the parents have a son, a daughter, another daughter, and another son, they could divide the two couples of children among themselves. The father would take to the two older children, the mother the two younger ones.

If all their children are sons, the oldest would tend to identify with his mother rather than with his father. The mother can show him how to handle younger brothers better than his father can. The father, on the other hand, would be inclined to treat at least one of his younger sons like a little sister and may in effect change him somewhat into a girl, psychologically speaking. Alternatively, if all their children were daughters, the oldest is more likely to identify with her father. He knows better than her mother does how one deals with little girls. The mother, in turn, would like to reshape one of her girls to be like a boy.

Father the youngest brother of sisters /
Mother the youngest sister of brothers:
(s..)b/(b..)s

This relationship is only moderately good. Both parents can get along with a peer of the opposite sex, but both of them also expect the partner to provide leadership and responsibility. Yet by character neither of them seems quite capable of it. In their original families they both became dependent on a person of the other sex. Each of the partners requires understanding, but feels insufficiently understood himself. Therefore, they are often less eager than other couples are to plan on children of their own. If they have them anyway, the parents tend to pressure the oldest child into the role of a confidant, an expert and an authority, earlier than he (or she) can take it. The child can usually oblige his parents only superficially in these respects. Intrinsically he (or she) remains insecure, since neither parent had been able to act as an adequate model for such a role.

Nevertheless, a configuration of children of both sexes would be a little better than a monosexual configuration.

If they have a son first and a daughter later, the mother can more easily identify with her daughter and come to terms with her son and cooperate with both of them than their father can. If they have a daughter first and then a son, the father is more at ease with the children than the mother is. The parent who finds his own sibling situation duplicated is likely to interact more intensively with their children and to push the other parent somewhat into the background. Such an isolation of one of the parents will also strain the parents' relationship with each other.

If they only have sons, it is the mother, and if they only have daughters, it is the father who finds it easier to get along with their children. Here, too, one of the parents may feel somewhat excluded from the family. In any event, however, the children are prone to lack and miss guidance by their parents. They cannot rely on the model provided by their parents when growing more independent themselves, for they offer no clear authorities. Hence the children's independence may impress an observer as one lacking in direction. These children may change their interests and goals more frequently than other children do. The parents even seem to encourage them in this.

Father the oldest brother of brothers/ Mother the youngest sister of sisters: b(b..)/(s..)s

This relationship can be appraised as only moderately favorable. Both parents supplement each other by the age rank of their sibling positions. The father is an oldest, the mother a youngest sibling. Yet neither of them had a sibling of the opposite sex. Neither has been accustomed to life with a peer of the opposite sex. They have no great troubles agreeing on professional matters or on housekeeping problems: he gives directions, and she acts impulsively or opposingly on occasion, but in fact she accepts his directions and the objective requirements of the situation. Their relationship as man and woman, however, is prone to remain tense for a longer time. There may be excitement in it at the beginning, but after a while it may also get tiresome. They can stick it out, on the whole, but neither their friends nor they themselves think of their relationship as being ideal. He is also the authority and the provider for the children, something that he may occasionally try to rub in. Still, she has to show him and the children at times that she too has something to say. Despite that, she needs his support and attention when caring for and guiding the children. She also gladly accepts her mother's or a sister's help. It is important for both parents to be allowed at least some contacts and get-togethers with their same-sex friends.

Their best configuration of children would be boys first, then girls, or a series such as boy-girl-boy-girl. If the father can curb his need to control and to lead, and if the mother can curb her inclination to intrude on impulse and to act out of ambition, the parents may be able to learn from their children, belatedly and in afterthoughts, how boys and girls as well as men and women can get along with each other and live as couples.

If they have a daughter first and a son second, the father tends to join forces with his son, and the mother with her daughter. However, identification between father and son and between mother and daughter is diminished. The daughter may identify with her father instead and adopt more masculine features than other oldest sisters of brothers would. The son could identify with his mother and as a result become softer and more capricious than other youngest brothers of sisters.

If all their children were sons, the family would fare a little better than if they were all daughters. The oldest son would identify with his father and one of the younger sons, or the youngest, with his mother. The father and the oldest son would offer guidance and support to the younger sons, whereas the mother may become somewhat excluded. She will bring herself to their attention, but the men in the family will not feel too comfortable about it. They learn to be prepared for surprises and occasional flare-ups and tend to grow more cautious with women in general than other men do. If the parents have only daughters, the oldest will, for the most part, assume the role of the older sister not only toward her sisters, but toward mother, too. One of the younger daughters, or the youngest, is usually identified with her mother. The father's relationship to her is often the most cordial, relatively speaking, whereas the oldest daughter, while following after her father and identifying with him, does not earn much warmth or gratitude from him. He takes her efforts for granted.

Father the youngest brother of brothers/
Mother the oldest sister of sisters:
(b..)b/s(s..)

This relationship is only moderately good. Neither he nor she have experienced life with a peer of the opposite sex in their original families. According to their age ranks among their siblings, however, they ought to be compatible. No one denies that she is the responsible leader in matters of family and housekeeping, not infrequently even of their professional life. He submits, for the most part, to her command which, incidentally, may be unnecessarily strict and brusque. He will only occasionally compete with her or oppose her, but once his reasons have been listened to and his feelings understood, he may quickly give in.

Their relationship as husband and wife, however, often leaves something to be desired. It rarely reaches the state of relaxation and contentment that they seem to see with other couples. She tells the children what to do; she advocates order and achievement at home, in school, and at work. The father is secretly against this, he sometimes encourages the children to oppose her, but when the children would need his support, he is often unavailable. For this reason, they eventually remain closer to their mother after all. Both partners would find it helpful if they could retain their contacts with same-sex friends and aquaintances. He needs his boys as she does her girls.

The best configuration of children would be a daughter first, a son next, or daughters first succeeded by sons, or an alternation of daughters and sons. If the mother can refrain from mingling in the relationships the children develop among themselves, they may learn to get along better with the other sex than their parents can show them.

If the oldest child is a son and the second-oldest a daughter, children and parents may have conflicts with each other. Neither the son and father nor the mother and daughter can easily identify with one another. The father considers his son as too independent, the son his father as inconsistent and irrational at times. The mother feels her daughter is not motherly and responsible enough, whereas the daughter occasionally complains about being over-taxed by her mother. Often, however, the mother is considerably more motherly and more tolerant toward her daughter than she is toward her husband and son. The father and the son can get along well with each other, if the father lets him be the leader or least if he does not intrude in his affairs. With his daughter, on the other hand, the father cannot seem to do very much. This configuration of children may bring about more of a confrontation of the sexes than one is likely to encounter in other families.

If all their children are sons, the oldest one usually identifies with his mother, one of the younger sons or the youngest with his father. The oldest may be prone to act the senior not only for his brothers, but also vis-à-vis his father. If that happens, the mother may feel left out and, in response, become even more adamant about duty, achievement, and the rights of women than other oldest sisters of sisters would. If all their children are daughters, the father may feel excluded from the family. The oldest daughter would tend to identify with her mother, to take care of and guard her sisters the way her mother does, but she lacks the experience (with brothers) to nurture and cater to her father. Moreover, the mother would not even let her. Father is hers, mother seems to imply.

Parents with Rank and Partial Sex Conflicts

**Father the oldest brother of sisters /
Mother the oldest sister of sisters:
b(s..)/s(s..)**

This relationship is more on the unfavorable side. Both partners were oldest siblings and are likely to be engaged in at least a latent fight for dominance in the family. Moreover, in her original family the mother has not been accustomed to life with a peer of the opposite sex. The father would be able to show her how men and women can arrange their life with each other, and he does and even succeeds at it to a certain extent, but her pride, her independence, and her obedience to her own father are also in the way. She feels that nobody can tell her anything except her father.

In the family he is the more sympathetic and tolerant authority, she the stricter and more rigid one. It would be good for her if she did not give up her job or her career altogether with her motherhood, but she should not be engaged in the same area or branch of work that her husband is. He might even be able to switch jobs more easily than she could. When they have children, she tends to bind the girls to herself and to enforce their opposition to men. She does not always succeed, though, and not always with all of her daughters, for their father knows how to get along with girls.

The most favorable configuration of children would be a son first, a daughter second, or sons followed by daughters, or first a son, then a daughter, a son, a daughter. The father would have no trouble identifying with his sons and getting along with his daughters, but the mother would not find it quite that easy. She would rather have children in the reverse order, one or several daughters first followed by sons. However, since she cannot show her daughters how they should deal with their younger brothers very well, and since the father would have difficulties of his own with such a reverse order of children, this latter configuration would be less favorable for the family as a whole.

The parents would do better with a configuration of daughters only than with sons only. The oldest daughter would try to identify with her mother and guide and guard her sisters in the way mother herself does. She notices, of course, that her father, too, is interested in her sisters and exerts no small attraction over them. Only she herself, the oldest daughter, feels somehow excluded from his interest. Therefore, she tries to identify with her father, but does not succeed very well. In this she and her mother might compete with the father over the affection of the younger daughters and might have to recognize that the younger daughters favor their father.

If the parents have only sons, the younger ones remain more exposed to the influence of their oldest sibling than would be true with daughters only. Neither the father nor the mother quite know what to do with their sons and are tempted to treat them a little like girls. The oldest son tries to learn partly from father, partly from mother, how he should handle his brothers, but he eventually has to resort to his own experiences with them.

Father the youngest brother of sisters/
Mother the youngest sister of sisters:
(s..)b/(s..)s

This relationship is rather unfavorable. Only the father has learned in his original family how to deal with a peer of the opposite sex. However, he does expect nurturance and care rather than opposition, leadership rather than competition. The mother, for her part, is not sure whether she should compete with men or submit to them. If she were to submit to a man, he ought to be able to guide her and to take family matters in his own hands, something that she notices her husband does not do. Thus, both of them long for a third person, he for someone who relieves him of the troubles of everyday life and lets him pursue his interests and talents, she for someone who allows her to be exciting, inspiring, even a little "wicked" at times. They would need a person to help them with their own children more than other couples would, perhaps her mother or sister, or else a brother-in-law or a male friend, who watches and admires her more attentively in her role as mother and who may be of more practical assistance than her husband is.

Relatively the best configuration of children would be a daughter, then a son, or daughters first, followed by sons, or an alternating series of daughters and sons. The father can readily identify with younger brothers of sisters, and he can get along well with older sisters of brothers. The mother, however, would prefer the reverse order of siblings among their children (older boys and younger girls). Only then could she identify relatively well with her daughters and accept her sons' independence, leadership, and "paternal" care.

In fact, she has less trouble accepting these traits from them than from men her own age. Even with her sons, though, she would not find it naturally easy to accept their attitudes. Since with this configuration of children, the father can neither identify very well with his sons nor get the secretly hoped-for mothering from his daughters, the sequences of boy-girl are somewhat less favorable, on the whole, than the sequences of girl-boy for this type of parents.

If they only have daughters, the parents will get along with their children a little better than if they only have sons. The oldest daughter will tend to become the leader and the person in charge vis-à-vis her sisters without being able to draw on her parents as a model to any great extent. She may learn to develop her role as a senior, however, from the way her father and mother want to be treated themselves, namely as juniors. The younger daughters would identify with their mother. This could lead to an increase of competition for attention, care, and guidance from the oldest daughter. Everybody in the family, father, and mother, and the other children, seems to want something from her. She may not be able to accommodate them; under the surface she could be more insecure than other oldest sisters of sisters.

If the parents have sons only, the burden of leadership is usually placed on the oldest son, again without proper apprenticeship and proper preparation from the hands of his parents. If he can indeed take on the assigned role, both parents are likely to have a fair-to-good relationship with him, even though their own younger children happen to be their rivals. They will also have certain difficulties identifying with their younger sons. The father had been treated with greater tolerance and more attention in his original family than his sons are being treated. More often than in other families the sons may leave the parents' home early, partly because of the leadership they lack and miss. They will look for authority figures outside the family.

Father the oldest brother of brothers/ Mother the oldest sister of brothers: b(b..)/s(b..)

This relationship is relatively unfavorable. Both parents are used to giving orders and bearing responsibility, the father usually in a more insistent fashion than the mother, but both of them find it difficult to admit that to their partner and to give in. Only the wife has been accustomed to life with peers of the opposite sex in her original family. She tries to show her husband how their life together might be shaped, but here, too, he is likely to resist her guidance. He may be annoyed by her condescendingly maternal air. Moreover, he feels she is too tolerant with the children. He requires achievement and obedience, whereas she seems to work for the realization of their children's wishes and interests, particularly for those of her sons. Despite these conflicts, however, the arrival of children is usually a perceptible relief for both parents. Both of them need juniors, younger brothers, dependents whom they can educate and for whom they can care. Both parents can also reduce their authority and leadership conflicts with each other by pursuing at least some of their interests separately. The wife finds it easier to give up her job or professional position in favor of her family and of home-making than oldest sisters of sisters would do, particularly if she has sons. Her husband should not interfere, though. He, however, tends to claim the sons for himself and to enlist them in his struggles against women. What irks him in the process is the fact that his wife exerts no negligible attraction on their sons and that all of them, except perhaps the oldest, find life with her more cozy than they do with him.

The best configuration of children, comparatively speaking, would be a daughter followed by a son, or daughters first, sons second, or a sequence of daughter-son-daughter-son. The mother can identify easily with her daughters and get along well with her sons. The father would have a harder time with them. He considers his sons as too dependent and passive, the daughters, at least the oldest of them, too bossy and protective. He would feel better with the reverse sex order among his children. For him, sons should be older and daughters younger. Since even then he cannot show his sons how to treat his daughters—he himself treats them like younger brothers—and since the mother would find it difficult to identify with younger sisters of brothers as well as to interact smoothly with her sons who are oldest brothers of sisters, the family as a whole would be better served by the first configuration of children.

If all their children were sons, family life would be a bit easier than if they were all daughters. The oldest son would have little trouble identifying with his father and relating to his brothers not only through his own trials and errors, but also through his father's example. He notices, however, that his mother exercises an even greater influence on his brothers than he or his father does. Only he himself seems to get the step-child treatment from her. Attempts to identify with her usually fail. He and his father may find themselves on one side of the family, with the mother and the younger sons on the other. In the contest for the favor and affection of the younger sons, the mother appears to win easily.

If the parents have only daughters, neither the father nor the mother can show their oldest daughter how to treat little sisters as girls. They themselves will tend to deal with them as if they were boys. The oldest daughter will have to learn how to care for and guide her sisters more or less on her own.

Father the youngest brother of brothers/
Mother the youngest sister of brothers:
(b..)b/(b..)s

This relationship is on the unfavorable side. Only the mother knows from her experiences at home how to handle a peer of the opposite sex. Both husband and wife, being youngest siblings, unconsciously search for someone who can offer them guidance and parental attention. Yet neither of them can give it to the other. The wife's experiences with her brothers are insufficient, for the most part, when she tries to win her husband over to her own idea of married life. He impresses her as erratic, competitive, and too dependent on other men. Not infrequently she herself, either as a person or for the sake of the family, develops an interest in one of the men whom her husband admires so much and tries to emulate. This man may be her husband's best friend, his oldest brother, or one of her own brothers. She would like such a person around for the children's sake, and, as it happens, the children often treasure such an uncle. Even the father himself may psychologically join the children vis-à-vis such a person and he may even compete with them for this person's attention and affection.

The best configuration of children, relatively speaking, would be a son first, followed by a daughter, or sons first, followed by daughters, or a son and daughter in alternation. The mother can identify with her daughters and handle her sons comfortably. The father, however, would feel uneasy in such a configuration. He would tend to recruit his oldest son for his own oldest brother rather than to identify with him. The son, however, will not play along in this. The daughters, on the other hand, are not motherly enough in his opinion. In fact, they impress him as being outright servile to their brothers. In any case, the father would prefer the reverse order, that is, daughters first, succeeded by sons. He can identify a little better with the youngest brother of sisters. His oldest daughter may provide him with more motherly care than his wife can, if he does not have a man whose guidance and direction he might prefer even more. The mother would have a more difficult time with such a sequence of children. She cannot identify very well with an oldest daughter, and her younger son will alienate her a little by his dependence and reluctance to commit himself.

If they have sons only, both the parents and the children tend to be better off with each other than if they have daughters only. The parents offer no example or model to their oldest son as to how he should handle his younger siblings, but he may inadvertently gather from their behavior what his parents want from him. He should not only be his brothers' guide, but he should even act as the parents' own counselor and adviser. This is what they unconsciously want, but it is usually too big a task for the son unless there is an authority figure outside his family, perhaps an uncle or a grandfather, who can help him with it.

If all their children were daughters, the parents would also tend unconsciously to assign a role of leadership prematurely to their oldest daughter. She should take that role not only vis-à-vis her sisters, but also vis-à-vis the parents themselves. The mother would have some difficulties when trying to identify with one of her younger daughters. She was treated for the most part more tenderly and attentively by her brothers than her younger daughters are treated by their older sisters. The father feels they do not understand him very well and exclude him anyway. These girls will try more than other daughters who had no brothers to get away from home and occasionally to run away, or move in with the first person who might offer them even a little bit of care and protection.

Parents with Rank and Sex Conflicts

Father the oldest brother of brothers /
Mother the oldest sister of sisters:
b(b..)/s(s..)

Ordinarily this is an unfavorable relationship. Their own sibling experiences have not prepared either partner for life with a peer of the opposite sex. Moreover, both of them have a rank conflict. They both claim leadership for themselves and expect their partner to submit, and neither of them can do this. Their relatively permanent conflict may sometimes be disguised as an ideological conflict of the sexes. They may attribute what they dislike in their partner to the partner's sex. If both of them have jobs or pursue separate careers, their conflict may be lessened. Both of them would be well advised to retain their same-sex friends throughout their marriage and parenthood, to take temporary leaves from each other, even to live in separate rooms, at least at times, and to seek each other's company whenever they wish to rather than from sheer habit or because of spatial proximity. Their situation may improve as soon as they have children, although both parents are prone to be too exacting and to overemphasize achievement and duty. Moreover, each of them will tend to recruit the children of his own sex and urge them to form a common front against the opposite sex. The father will teach his sons what is objectionable in women and how to beware of them, and the mother will do the same with her daughters. Parents of this type have a significantly greater chance of getting divorced than average parents (16% versus 5%).

In spite of the parents' difficulties with the opposite sex, a configuration of both boys and girls would still be better than a monosexual one. It would make little difference whether the parents have boys first followed by girls or vice versa. An oldest daughter would identify with her mother, an oldest son with his father. In both instances the oldest siblings would hardly learn from their parents how a boy and a girl can have a satisfying life together. They must learn it on their own while dealing with their siblings. The oldest siblings among the children tend to be more impressed and oppressed by the tense and belligerent relationship prevailing among the parents than the younger siblings are. The latter are buffered against such an influence stemming from their parents' relationship. They can avail themselves of their experiences with each other better than their oldest siblings can, and, later on, they can utilize these experiences outside the family as well.

If the parents have only sons, the father will find it easy to identify with his oldest son, to relate to his younger sons as he used to toward his own younger brothers and, in that respect, to set an example for his oldest son. The mother is rather excluded from this "men's club." As far as the father and some of the sons are concerned, the mother may cater to them and care for them, she should even consider it a privilege, but she should not have a voice in men's affairs. The mother does not exactly relish that, to be sure. She often tries to draw at least one of her sons to herself and perhaps to transform him into a girl, psychologically speaking.

If the parents have only daughters, it is the mother who can comfortably relate to the younger ones, identify with the oldest, let the oldest identify with her, and leave the father on the periphery of family life. He does not particularly like this condition, either. In both cases the children cannot learn very much from their parents that would make married life appear pleasant and enjoyable.

Father the youngest brother of brothers /
Mother the youngest sister of sisters:
(b..)b/(s..)s

This is an unfavorable relationship for the most part. On the basis of their sibling experiences, both partners have the same age rank. Both are juniors, accustomed to being taken care of and guided by their families. They feel someone else is responsible for them. Moreover, neither of them has experiences in living with a peer of the opposite sex; they are somewhat at a loss with each other. They can't seem to explain to themselves what is wrong with them; both of them are looking for someone who is willing to help them, who will guide them, listen to them, and understand them. Unfortunately, that person does not seem to be the spouse. A third person, perhaps his older brother or her older sister, a friend who was an oldest sibling himself, or one of the mothers- or fathers-in-law would qualify. Both partners should wisely try to strive for different professions and to pursue their interests and talents independently of each other. They should also try to retain their same-sex friends and see them more-or-less regularly.

Things do not seem to improve with the arrival of children. On the contrary, the parents even tend to let their children, or at least their oldest child, in on their own problems at an early age, and they try to turn their children into their own advisors. Needless to say, the children cannot ordinarily oblige them. They can only mimic their assigned role; they may impress observers as precocious and thoughtful, but underneath they are more insecure than other children. Often these parents have only one child. Parents of this type are significantly more likely to get a divorce than average parents (16% versus 5%).

A configuration of children of both sexes is usually more favorable than a monosexual configuration. Whether sons or daughters come first is more or less irrelevant. In both types of configurations the oldest siblings will have a hard time finding their place and role in the family. The parents offer them no examples for what they actually expect of their children. The parents can identify better with the younger children and vice versa.

If this couple only has sons, it is the father rather than the mother who will unconsciously convey to the oldest son how he should behave toward his siblings and toward his parents: he should lead and nurse them. The mother may feel slighted and not sufficiently a part of things. Her ambition vis-à-vis friends and aquaintances, however, tends to be better satisfied if all her children are sons rather than daughters. If all the children were daughters the mother could easily identify with the younger ones and make her oldest daughter her own "oldest sister." Yet in order to act the part of older sister, the oldest daughter can only resort to her experiences with her sisters. Her mother cannot provide an example except by interacting with her as a younger sister herself would. Here it is usually the father who feels, and often actually becomes, an outsider.

Whatever their configuration, the children do not learn very many positive things about how a man and a woman live together by observing their parents. As a consequence, they tend more than other children do to look for the longed-for authority figure or for a parental friend outside the family. Since they have been made to feel insecure at home, their attempts at contacts and ties outside the family are not always successful and happy.

Only Children as Spouses and Parents

If the spouse was not an only child himself (or herself), but had one of the four basic types of sibling positions instead, there are obviously four types of spouse relationships that the only child can enter. A male only child can have a wife who was an oldest sister of brothers, a youngest sisters of brothers, an oldest sister of sisters, or a youngest sister of sisters. A female only child can marry a man who was an oldest brother of sisters, a youngest brother of sisters, and oldest brother of brothers, or a youngest brother of brothers in his original family. We would assume that each of those types of marriages would look differently to the only child and impose on him (or her) a different role in marriage and parenthood.

However, the relationship of an only child with his spouse also depends, among other things, on the sibling position of the only child's same-sex parents (see p. 28, 170). Through identification with that parent, the only child adopts at least traces of the parent's sibling role. If his parent has one of the four basic types of sibling positions, the only child actually comes in four varieties, too.

Hence there would again be 16 different types of relationships between an only child and his spouse which would correspond to the ones we have described more elaborately in chapter 12. One could also draw upon these descriptions when dealing with a spouse or a parent who happens to have been an only child.

We may also assume, however, that only children differ more from children in all other sibling positions than they do from other only children. They would still resemble each other despite the different experiences they may have gathered by indentification with their same-sex parents. The actual experience of life without siblings seems to be stronger than the indirect vicarious experience of the parent's sibling role. In actuality they have *no* sibling position. For this reason it is probably worthwhile only in special cases to read up on the sibling role that the only child has possibly adopted through identification. This role may not tell us very much about his (or her) marriage; for this, the descriptions given below will generally suffice.

We will deal with the only child as a father, the only child as a mother, and parents who were both only children in their original families. The spouse's four basic types of sibling roles will be sketched for the only-child father and the only-child mother. As a rule, we might say that a person who had a sibling of the opposite sex himself and who marries a person who was an only child brings more experience of how a man and a woman live together into their marriage than does that person who only had siblings of the same sex. This latter person, in turn, brings more experience in living with a peer of one's own age into the marriage than does the person who happens to have been an only child.

Father an only child

This father more than others views himself as the focal point of the family. His wife would have to take the maternal role not only for their children, but for him as well. Often he does not want any children at all at first, and if they arrive, he finds it more difficult to subdue his jealousy of them than other fathers do. If his wife is an older sister, particularly of brothers, she is usually willing to take charge of her children as well as of her husband. If she is a younger sister, she expects more leadership and guidance from her husband than her husband is inclined to provide, at least in domestic and family matters. A larger-than-average age difference between the two may help. If his wife is considerably younger than he is, the husband may be prepared to assume the role of an oldest brother or even that of a father. In that case, it would help him to have had a father who had been an oldest brother himself, preferably of sisters.

Mother an only child

This person may be more inclined than others to remain a child herself even as a wife and mother. She wants to be pampered by her husband and watched and praised for all she does as a mother. In order to win her over to the idea of having a child of her own, her husband may have to persuade her or even beg her. She would like to consider it as a special favor to him.

If her husband is an oldest brother, particularly of sisters, he can usually give her what she wants. He recognizes more clearly than other men what he is letting himself in for and does not reproach her for any failings. A youngest brother, on the other hand, can hardly become the paternal friend and helper she is looking for. She sometimes has to play the paternal friend for him. If her mother was an oldest sister, preferably of brothers, she may even succeed. If she is considerably older than her husband, she will also be able to do it. If they have children, however, she usually manages to elicit not only recognition and admiration, but even her husband's practical help for her care and raising of the children, "using" him in the process, and directing his help.

Both parents are only children:
b/s

If both parents were only children, each of them will look for a parental friend in his spouse, but will hardly ever find it. However, they are at least able to identify with one another in this common plight and to understand their spouse's longings. As a result they may develop a tolerable way of life with each other after all. They tell each other what they want and cannot seem to get, they comfort and console each other, and they discover that each of them can offer at least something of interest to the other.

Even so, they do not necessarily want children. More often than other parents, they are content with an only child, upon whom each of them, especially the same-sex parent, projects his own ideas and partly unfulfilled wishes. The parents' hope is that these wishes will be realized and fulfilled for the child. While parents who were both youngest siblings themselves unconsciously tend to urge their child to become something like a big brother or a big sister for them, parents who were both only children tend to influence their child in one of two directions: The child will either remain a child even after he or she has grown up. He (or she) will learn less well than other children or even than other only children to really care for anyone but himself. Or the child will be psychologically transformed not only into a big brother or sister, but, according to the child's sex, into a father or mother. The child whose parents were both only children will be more gravely overtaxed by the task of becoming a "big brother or sister" than a child whose parents were both youngest siblings. This child seems precocious and sophisticated, but is actually very insecure underneath, awkward in matters of everyday life and occasionally even somewhat disoriented.

Incidentally, parents who were both only children show an increased likelihood of getting a divorce (9% versus 5% on the average).

It should be mentioned that the average divorce rate among parents is somewhat higher with today's generation of parents than with the parents we studied about ten years ago. The ratios of divorce rates, however, seem to have remained approximately the same.

Parents with Multiple and Middle Sibling Positions

If a parent was the oldest or the youngest among his siblings, but had both brothers and sisters (i.e., a multiple-distal sibling position), or if he was neither the oldest nor the youngest sibling, but had brothers and/or older sisters and/or younger brothers and/or younger sisters, it becomes considerably more complicated to determine the type of relationship under which he and his spouse may be categorized. If the other spouse also has a multiple or middle sibling position, things get still more complex. The observer may have to consult all the relevant types of parent relationships that we have outlined.

If a husband is the oldest brother of a brother and of a sister and his wife the middle sister of two brothers—i.e. b(bs)/(b)s(b)—the description of the following types of parental couples would have to be consulted: father the oldest brother of brothers/mother the youngest sister of brothers; father the oldest brother of brothers/mother the oldest sister of brothers; father the oldest brother of sisters/ mother the youngest sister of brothers; father the oldest brother of sisters/mother the oldest sister of brothers.

We have already stated that the synopsis of more than two sibling role portraits becomes unwieldy when dealing with a person holding multiple or middle sibling positions (see p. 188f). The same is true of parental couples. A synopsis of two types of parental couples may have to be made, but a larger number of types results in confusing their characteristics. Too many things are possible. The meanings of the portraits of different types of parents mingle and become redundant. Some of the many characteristics that are being combined are likely to be correct, but in a trivial way. Therefore, in studying parental couples whose partners have held multiple or middle sibling positions in their original families, we recommend that the observer determine for each spouse the dominant position among his (or her) sibling roles. This can be done with the help of the interpretation guidelines concerning the special characteristics or features of multiple or middle sibling positions outlined on p. 189ff, as well as by inspecting the person's friendship patterns. The sibling positions of those persons whom a spouse considers his friends can tell us which of his own sibling roles he may inadvertently prefer (see p. 112, 194).

If the father in the example given above happens to have

a brother two years his junior and a sister eight years his junior, we would expect that his role of oldest brother of brothers is stronger than that of oldest brother of sisters. If his wife's boyfriends before marriage were five oldest brothers (including her eventual spouse), one middle brother, and two youngest brothers, we may infer that she likes her role of youngest sister of brothers better than her role of oldest sister of brothers.

Even if we lack information about any special features of the spouses' multiple or middle sibling positions, and if we know nothing about their preferences in their friendships, we may assume that they would prefer that sibling role which is complementary to at least one of the other spouse's roles (we called this "partial complementarity of sibling roles": p. 83). We could view as dominant that sibling role of the spouse's several possible roles, which best corresponds to the other spouse and his sibling role, or at least one of several of them.

According to partial complementarity, in our example of b(bs)/(b)s(b), we would consider the husband's role of an oldest brother of sisters and the wife's role of youngest sister of brothers as the dominant ones. We would consult the portrait for father the oldest brother of sisters/mother the youngest sister of brothers. Because of the age distances from his siblings, however, the husband's role of oldest brother of brothers could also play a part. In order to be on the safe side, we should also consult the portrait corresponding to father the oldest brother of brothers/mother the youngest sister of brothers.

13.   Clinical Cases

In this chapter we shall discuss three examples of family constellations, and interpretations of their special features shall be given. In each case, these interpretations will be followed by clinical-psychological descriptions of the individuals in question, so that the reader may get an impression of how well the interpretations and predictions fit the facts. Before doing that, however, a few further details concerning the symbolic representation of family constellations should be discussed.

The Symbolic Representation of Family Constellations

We have already learned (p. 125) that a family in which the father had an older sister, a younger brother, and a still younger sister, and the mother had two younger sisters, may be symbolized this way:

$$(s)b(bs)/s(ss)$$

The slash means marriage and/or liaison. If we would also want to include the couple's children in the symbolic expression, say a son, a daughter two years younger, and another daughter seven more years younger, we would proceed this way:

$$(s)b(bs)/bss/s(ss)$$

The configuration of children is put between two slashes. The persons on either side are the parents.

If we know the age distances between family members, we could write them in index form:

$$(s)b(bs)/bs_2s_9/s(ss)$$

The age distances in a sibling configuration are given in years and in reference to one member of the sibling configuration. Our example shows it in reference to the son. The age distance between the youngest and the middle daughter is seven years, between the middle daughter and the oldest son two years. Hence, the age distance between the youngest daughter and the oldest son is nine years.

This expression is objectively equivalent to the expression:

$$(s)b(bs)/b_2ss_7/s(ss)$$

the difference being that now the middle sibling is the reference person. The person with whom we are dealing as a client and whose family constellation we are recording is not the oldest son, but the middle sister. If we do not know the ages and the age differences, or if we do not want to indicate them in the symbolic expression, we could use parentheses with the configuration of children, too, in order to designate which member of the family we have before us. If it is the boy, we could write:

$$(s)b(bs)/b(ss)/s(ss)$$

If it is the middle daughter we would write:

$$(s)b(bs)/(b)s(s)/s(ss)$$

Since the father is always written on the left and the mother on the right of the symbolic expression, confusion is unlikely.

If we do not want to designate the age distances in years but wish to record unusually large age differences between adjacent siblings instead (i.e. age distances of six or more years), we can indicate them by putting a semicolon between these two siblings:

$$(s)b(bs)/bs;s/s(ss)$$

It is possible, of course, to designate the actual age of family members insofar as we know it. If the son is 18 years old, the older of the two daughters 16 years and the younger daughter 9 years, and if we happen to know that the father is 46 years old, the mother 36, we could rewrite the expression this way:

$$(s)b_{46}(bs)/b_{18}s_{16}s_9/s_{36}(ss)$$

We advise against mixing indices of ages and those of age-distances in one-and-the-same symbolic expression, because it can result in confusion. If a person in a family constellation had died (which can be also be symbolized, as we shall see below), one should indicate that person's age as if he or she were still alive.

We have already learned how we can express the fact that a sibling in a family constellation is married (see p. 134): the symbol for that sibling should be underlined once: b̲ or s̲. If that sibling has also had at least one child, we underline the symbol of that sibling twice: b̲̲ or s̲̲. If a sibling should have children without being married we could omit the upper of the two underlines, but enter the lower one: b̲ or s̲. If that sibling is not married, but lives with a partner, we could replace the upper of the two underlines by a dot: ḃ or ṣ. If such a person has at least one child with his or her partner, we would symbolize this as follows: b̤ or ș.

Losses in early childhood (i.e. during the first six years of a person's life) are indicated by two dots placed above the symbol for the lost family member; for example, b̈ or s̈. If the loss occurred in a person's early youth (i.e. after the sixth and before the 15th year of life), we put just one dot above the symbol of the lost family member: ḃ or ṡ. If a family member has been lost later in a person's life we put a cross above the symbol of the family member: b̶ or s̶ (see p. 136).

If the sibling position of a parent is not known or is not needed, we can put f for father, m for mother. If a parent whose sibling position is not indicated has been lost, we can symbolize the loss in the following manner depending on the time of the loss: f̈ or ḟ or f⁺ and m̈ or ṁ or m̈.

If a sibling or a parent was lost before the person in question was ever born, we can indicate it by b̸, s̸, f̸ or m̸ respectively.

The family constellation of the example given above could have the following additional characteristics:

$$f/m//(\dot{s})b(b\underline{s})/\underline{b}ss/s(s\underline{s})//f⁺/\dot{m}$$

Note that the symbolic expression for the core family (i.e. the parents and children) is enclosed on each side by double slashes. These are only required when the grandparents are recorded as well. The symbols for the grandparents are put outside the double slashes, the paternal grandparents on the father's side, that is, on the left, and the maternal grandparents on the mother's side, that is, on the right. If the sibling positions of the grandparents should be known, their symbols rather than f and m could be filled in. If the grandparents are not included in the symbolic expression, we would assume that there is nothing unusual about them. No grandparent died or disappeared during the early childhood or youth of the respective parent. Hence, in the example given above, there was no need to record the father's parents at all in the symbolic expression.

The symbolic expression:

$$f/m//(\dot{s})b(b\underline{s})/\underline{b}ss/s(s\underline{s})//\overset{+}{f}/\dot{m}$$

means: The father's parents are still alive. His older sister died in his early youth, his younger brother is unmarried, and his youngest sister is married, but has no children. On the right side of the symbolic expression we see that the father of the mother is no longer living, but he died when the mother was already an adult. Her mother, however, died when she herself was a little child. The mother's middle sister is unmarried, her youngest sister is married and the mother of at least one child. Among their own children, only the son is married.

This same symbolic expression might also be written as follows:

$$//f/(\dot{s})b(b\underline{s})/m//\underline{b}ss//\overset{+}{f}/s(s\underline{s})/\dot{m}//$$

Here the double slashes are used in order to enclose the family constellations of each of the parents. The double slashes on the extreme left and right of the entire expression could also be omitted:

$$f/(\dot{s})b(b\underline{s})/m//\underline{b}ss//\overset{+}{f}/s(s\underline{s})/\dot{m}$$

In both instances f and m could also be replaced by the sibling position of the respective father or mother without rendering the expression ambiguous. The use of parentheses would also be permissible and meaningful:

$$[f/(\dot{s})b(b\underline{s})/m]/\underline{b}ss/[\overset{+}{f}/s(s\underline{s})/\dot{m}]$$

In some cases, we may have learned that someone had had older or younger sisters or older or younger brothers, but does not know their exact order. This may happen when collecting data with our short family questionnaire in which the numbers of older and younger brothers as well as of older and younger sisters should be indicated, but not their age order. To obtain the exact order in the questionnaire would require a more complicated procedure of questions as well as of answers. Not all subjects are willing or able to cope with the complication, even though they may have no trouble giving their sibling story in a verbal interview.

At any rate, if we do not know the exact age order of the siblings, we may use braces rather than slants when symbolizing family constellations. In algebra or set theory, the same braces would indicate a set. Using braces implies that the siblings assembled within them have not been ordered by age, but only listed by type.

If we received our information about the family constellation mentioned above merely with the short form of our questionnaire, the age order of some of the person's or his parents' siblings would be unknown. We may have to symbolize it this way:

$$f/m//(\dot{s})b \left\{ \begin{array}{c} b\underline{s} \end{array} \right\} /\underline{b}ss/s \left\{ \begin{array}{c} s\underline{\underline{s}} \end{array} \right\} //\overset{+}{f}/\dot{m}$$

From such a questionnaire it would be impossible to tell for sure which one of the mother's sisters is married and has children and which one is unmarried. Hence we need to write the braces, although both of the mother's siblings are of the same type: both are her younger sisters. Moreover, one cannot be certain from the questionnaire which of the father's two sisters died in his early youth and which one is married. Perhaps both characteristics concern the same person. However, this is not very likely. In order to indicate this uncertainty, we could use the "or" sign in logic: ∨ . We would have to write:

$$f/m//(\dot{s} \vee \underline{s})b \left\{ \begin{array}{c} b\dot{s} \vee \underline{s} \end{array} \right\} /\underline{b}ss/s \left\{ \begin{array}{c} s\underline{\underline{s}} \end{array} \right\} //\overset{+}{f}/\dot{m}$$

The "or" sign binds more closely than the simple juxtaposition of sibling symbols. It always means that the two signs adjacent to the "or" sign involve just one person. With regard to characteristics connected with the persons symbolized, one or the other or even both (or neither) may apply to the given person, and the other characteristic, or none, or both, may apply to the second person. Even if the uncertainty of information should be built into the instrument of investigation, in this case into the questionnaire which was used, the investigator should try to clarify the situation by additional inquiry.

If a person has half- or step siblings, this can also be expressed symbolically by indices; that is, by b_h or s_h or by b_s and s_s respectively. A stepfather whose sibling position is unknown or not recorded would be symbolized by f_s, a stepmother by m_s. If the stepfather's sibling position is known—perhaps he is an older brother of two sisters and a brother —we would write it this way: $b_s(ssb)$. This notation should be distinguished from the notation of the step siblings the father had. If the father had only step siblings of the same composition as above, this would be symbolised in the following manner: $b(s_s s_s b_s)$.

If a person had a stepmother and a stepfather, as well as fosterparents or adoptive parents, we recommend representing both the first and the second family constellation in which he had been a member. Let us take the mother of the family constellation used above repeatedly for purposes of demonstration. She is the oldest sister of two younger sisters. Suppose we have learned that she had a stepmother after the early death of her real mother, that her stepmother was an only child, that her real mother had been the oldest sister of a brother and a half-brother, and that her father was the youngest brother of a brother. We would symbolize this as:

$$(b)b/s(ss)/\dot{s}(bb_h) \rightarrow (b)b/s(ss)/s_s$$

Incidentally, from the sibling configuration of that mother's mother we can gather that she lost a parent herself, probably in her early youth. The existence of a half brother indicates that she had a stepparent and that her remaining parent had another child with that stepparent.

A Case of a Young Man Married at an Early Age

Emil K., an 18-year-old man, has consulted a psychological clinic. He filled in a family questionnaire and talked briefly to a social worker. The following data could be established:

Emil K. left high school at the age of 17, took a job as a salesman, left his parental home on his 18th birthday and, soon thereafter, married Bettina, an elementary-school teacher five years his senior. His reasons for consulting the psychological clinic were his uncertainty about what to do and his depressions. His wife had urged him to come and made his first appointment by telephone.

Emil has two sisters, one 2, the other 9 years younger than himself. Both of them still go to school.

Emil's father has a law degree and works for the government. The father has a younger unmarried brother and a still younger sister who is married but has no children. When questioned, Emil reported that his father also had a sister, who had died when his father was in grade school. This sister had been a few years older than the father. Emil's paternal grandparents come by for visits about once a month. At present, Emil himself has no contacts with his father's parents.

Emil's mother has two younger sisters; the older one is unmarried, and the younger one is married and has children. Emil's mother lost her own mother when she was still a child. She later had a stepmother who is still living, but there are no contacts with her now, as far as Emil can recall. The stepmother had no relatives, no children of her own, and no brothers and sisters. Emil's mother's father died eight years ago, but even while he was alive, contacts with him and his wife were few.

In symbolic notation the story reads like this:

$$f/m//(\dot{s})b(b\underline{s})/\underline{b}s_2s_9/s(s\underline{s})//\overset{+}{f}/\dot{m}$$

father   Emil   mother

Diagnostic evaluation of the family constellation data:

According to his sibling position, Emil ought to prefer girls and women who look up to him and who will let him be their leader. He does not seem to have married such a woman. He may have failed in school and taken a job that was probably below his father's expectations. His father had earned an academic graduate degree himself. Conflicts with his parents are also indicated in Emil's leaving the parental home and in his marriage, where, according to his phantasies, he may have been looking for motherly care and protection. This is suggested by the fact that his wife is older than he is and works in a position requiring an academic degree and regular contacts with children.

What might Emil's family have contributed to his failure at school and to his lack of training for a professional career as well as to his early marriage, where he may have sought refuge rather than fulfillment? And where do his feelings of helplessness and his depressions come from? An examination of the data will help answer these questions.

Emil's mother had lost her own mother early in life. Until her stepmother entered the family, Emil's mother may have had to act as mother for her two little sisters, to comfort them in the loss of their mother and perhaps to take over some of her mother's tasks even vis-à-vis her father. A while later, when her father married another woman, the three sisters might have had rather mixed feelings about their stepmother as is often the case in such a family situation. Emil's mother may have responded even more negatively since the stepmother, as an only child, may well have wanted to be the child of her husband herself, psychologically speaking, rather than the mother of his children. There may have been little mothering she could offer the children. Emil's mother could hardly learn how to be motherly and caring herself, either by identification with her stepmother or with her late mother, who had simply died too soon. We may gather from the fact that there is little contact between the mother's stepmother and Emil's family that the stepmother was not too successful in filling the mother's place.

One would expect that Emil's mother would find it difficult to live with a man and to take care of children, particularly boys, not only because there were no brothers in her original family, but also because of the early loss of her mother and the unsatisfactory substitute mother. Her unconscious accusation against her father that he betrayed his family through his remarriage and failed his children as a parent also may have had an effect on her relationship with her husband and even with her son.

Emil's father had lost his oldest sister. This loss was probably experienced as less severe by his father than the one Emil's mother experienced. His father's loss occurred a little later in life, and he did not lose his mother, but "just" his sister. The fact that the father and his siblings may have been traumatized more than would be expected, however, is indicated by the relatively low interest among his siblings to establish families of their own. Emil's father's brother remained unmarried, and his sister married, but had no children. Even the father himself suggests by his choice of an oldest sister of sisters that he was still looking for someone like his own older sister, and not for someone like his younger sister. Another mechanism may have been unconsciously at work in addition. He may not only have longed for an older and maternal sister, but also for a person with whom he could identify as a bereaved person, as a victim of a loss, someone, moreover, who would understand him and empathize with him.

The parents did not really get what they may have been looking for in their marriage. Emil's mother could not handle men very well and had trouble acting her mother-role. His father wanted a motherly and sympathetic woman, but got a sensitive, partly dominant and partly sadly reproachful woman. In order to reduce the conflict, he had to resort to his role of oldest brother of sisters, but he used it only reluctantly vis-à-vis his wife and only more willingly vis-à-vis his daughters, particularly his youngest. As an oldest sister, we would expect his wife to find it difficult to renounce the regime which she feels her father handed over to her and to submit to another man.

Emil was the first and most direct victim of this conflict between his parents. If he identified with his father's leadership role, his mother would not let him. His father, moreover, was an ambiguous model. If Emil identified with his father's dependency needs, his mother would not respond appropriately either. Where Emil could have excercised a role of responsibility and leadership, that is, with his younger sisters, his father may not have tolerated it. His father wanted to play that part for the little girls himself, particularly after the second daughter arrived, as it happens, seven years after the first one, which in itself could be an indication of trouble between the parents. Both parents had possibly expected to be comforted by Emil in their problems and sorrows, but he did not succeed in this.

These conflicts which probably bothered and burdened Emil, may also have affected his participation and interests in school. He noticed that he could not please his parents. If he failed them by his performance in school, too, things would at least be consistent and clear.

Even so, we can deduce from his sudden exit from school as well as from his parental home and from his early marriage that the situation may have become intolerable for Emil. He chose a type of person whom his father may have wanted, but did not get: a professional person, independent, and a little older so that mothering and care, perhaps even financial support, could be expected from her. Emil fled his family and fulfilled a wish that his father would have liked to fulfill for himself.

If these interpretations are correct, we would anticipate that Emil does not feel terribly comfortable in his new situation after all. According to his family experience, a girl younger than himself or, at any rate, a younger sister of brothers would have more to offer him than his wife does. Emil may realize that, while anxious to leave home, he nevertheless might like to accomplish things himself and even to take care of his girl, provided she lets him. If he could only overcome the difficulties that his parents had with each other, he might succeed. He would no longer have to try to fulfill their unconscious wishes, but could pursue his own wishes and interests. In that case he might even separate from his wife and look for another type of woman, unless his wife was a youngest sister, preferably of brothers.

Case history:

During his psychotherapy, which started about a month later and comprised 24 sessions, it turned out that Emil K. left home because he could no longer stand the tension and the smoldering conflict that existed between his parents. It was learned that his parents had drawn him into their quarrels and he did not know which side to take. If he supported one, he usually fell into disgrace not only with the other, but with both of them.

His mother, who was 36 years old, was always ready to scold men. She felt men abused women and pretended to be something better than women. She worried that her husband had a girl friend and might one day leave the family.

His father, who was 46, accused the mother in turn of being egocentric and rigid. She showed too little understanding of others, particularly of him and their children. To this day he continually praised his late sister as a model girl. Unfortunately, she had had to die at 13, whereas other girls much less worthy than she would live on to an old age, lead comfortable lives, and have children. According to Emil, his father also hinted at the troubles they had had in his original family. Things had not been easy there either. All of them, including his late sister, dreaded their father. Only after his oldest sister had died did the parents become a little more tolerant with their children. However, there has not been a really cordial relationship even up to today.

Emil's father also expressed his annoyance over Emil's poor work in school and accused him of not trying hard enough. The truth of the matter was that he had tried as hard as he could. He just was not good enough. The situation at home had always been more or less explosive. He felt sorry for his sisters, particularly for Elizabeth (the one nearest him in age). The youngest (Mila) was the parents' darling. She could do no wrong, and everybody tried to spare her any hardship. Even Emil himself had done this, but Elizabeth became the scapegoat in the process. Her father, mother, and even grandparents found fault with her. Only after he, Emil, left home, did things improve a little for Elizabeth. She also wanted to leave home, but reconsidered the matter.

Emil related that his wife Bettina was her parents' only child. Both parents had been teachers. Her father had had a younger brother, her mother two younger sisters. As a child, Bettina had often stayed with mother's middle sister. Bettina had a better relationship with this aunt than she had with her mother, although this aunt also had a daughter of her own.

Emil met his wife in the P. Club. He was totally drunk and she took him to her apartment. He had already left school by that time, had started working as a salesman and thus had fallen into considerable disgrace with his parents. His mother was shocked at first, but later she showed a trace of understanding. Neither parent came to his wedding. They did give their legal consent, however, his father with great annoyance and condescension.

Emil claimed that, looking at the matter frankly, he did not get along very well with his wife. What his father accuses his mother of being, egocentric and rigid, Emil himself could say of Bettina. He sometimes feels that she considers him her plaything. She does not take him seriously, but even so she watches over him jealously. He is not sure whether they should not separate. He is making a little more money now and needs no financial support from anyone. Maybe he would try to graduate from high school after all. If he succeeded, his father would also probably be appeased. He would not want to live in his parents' home again, though. He thinks he could do more for Elizabeth if he stayed away from his parents. If Elizabeth finishes school, she might want to leave home, too. If that happened, she could stay with them, with Bettina and him, provided, that is, they were still living together.

A Case of Parents in Family Therapy

Sylvia P. consults a psychological clinic because of her troublesome son who, she claims, is inconspicuous at school, but intolerable at home. He abuses and scolds his parents, refuses to heed their wishes or to do any chores around the house, teases his little sister, and maltreats the other family members' personal belongings. From a brief interview and a questionnaire that Sylvia P. filled out for herself and her husband, we learned the following:

Sylvia P., 38 years old, is married and the mother of two children, a ten-year-old boy, Jim, and a five-year-old girl named Chris. Her husband, Robert P., is 42 years old. He works as a chemist in a large corporation.

Mrs. P. had a brother two years younger than herself who had been conscripted for the Foreign Legion, probably by criminal deceit, and could not get a release in spite of every effort on the part of the family. He was killed at the age of 18 in a skirmish in Africa. Sylvia's father was the youngest of four children. He had an oldest brother and two older sisters. His oldest brother was an officer during World War I and was killed in the war. Both of his sisters are married and have children. He himself left the family in order to find better working conditions as a musician in another country, but died there when Mrs P. was six and her brother four years old.

Her father left some money that would maintain the family on a modest scale. Nevertheless, Sylvia's mother took a job as a language teacher after her husband's death and put both children into a boarding school. They lived there through all of their school years, but spent their vacations with their mother.

Sylvia's mother had an older sister and a still older brother. Both siblings are married. The sister has a child. For geographical reasons Sylvia's mother had no contacts with her siblings after her own marriage.

Of her husband, Sylvia reports that he was the younger of two boys. His older brother, three years his senior, is married and has children. His father is the older brother of a sister who is married, but has no children; his mother is the older sister of two brothers, the younger of whom died of tuberculosis at the age of 25. The other brother is married and has a son.

The symbolic expression of the family constellation reads like this:

$$b(\underline{s})/(\underline{b}_{45})b_{42}/s(\underline{bb})//b_{10}s_5//(\overset{+}{\underline{bss}})\overset{..}{b}/s_{38}(\overset{+}{b_{36}})/(\underline{bs})s$$

Robert   Jim   Chris   Sylvia

Diagnostic evaluation of the family constellation:

As an older sister, Sylvia P. would tend to assume a leading role and responsibility for others, particularly for boys and men. Her father would have responded well, had he not left and died so early. Her mother, too, wanted to be catered to and guided rather than lead and take charge of others herself. Sylvia's parents could not be of much help to each other. If each of them sought guidance and support in the spouse, they did not get it. If they looked to Sylvia for help and guidance, they were likely to overtax their daughter at first and to offer her no model themselves. Her mother's siblings could have acted as Sylvia's model, but there were no contacts with them.

Sylvia's brother and her father probably had no trouble identifying with each other while the father was around. However, that did not last very long. With her mother, on the other hand, Sylvia's brother would have experienced some difficulties. From his dealings with his sister he had learned that boys may and should let girls take care of them. His mother, however, appreciated those boys and men more who were able to offer direction and protection to a girl or a woman. By his less-than-average age distance from his sister, his relationship to her may have remained somewhat inarticulate and his dependence on her greater than it would be with other youngest brothers of sisters.

In short, Sylvia P. may have been called upon to act as an independent and responsible leader in her family sooner than she was able to meet these demands. She not only had to try to understand and support her brother, but her parents, too. She was witness to a less than happy marriage.

This was followed by the early loss of her father and the partial loss of her mother. Her father had probably been a focus of attention in his own family when his brother had died in the war. He may have been expected to take his oldest brother's place, to enter a military career or, in times of peace, to work for the government. He stuck with his musical interests, though, which seemed to lead nowhere financially. Because of these interests, he even left the family and eventually died in a foreign country.

Sylvia's father's family probably did not approve of her father's plans. This is suggested by Sylvia's brother's unfortunate decision to join the Foreign Legion. He may have tried unconsciously to satisfy his grandparents' wish which his father had ignored and to take up a military career as his late uncle, whom he had never known personally, had done.

Sylvia's mother, in turn, must have felt even less inclined to act motherly and supportively toward her children after she had lost her husband, since she sent them off to boarding schools.

Both losses must have been a grave shock for six-or seven-year-old Sylvia. After having come to know her parents as "weak personalities" she learned that they eventually disappeared altogether, that fathers cannot be trusted, and neither can mothers. If Sylvia managed to work her way through those traumatic experiences at all, she could be expected to become over-protective and motherly in an overbearing way. She fought for her family and forced her maternal care upon them. She probably required complete dependence and obedience from them, more than other older sisters of brothers would. Because of the lack of care in her early life, Sylvia may be prone to suffer from depressions and to turn to the panaceas of nibbling, eating, or alcohol, and she may possibly even erupt in diffuse aggressions. This tendency to become sad or irrationally angry at times may have been reinforced after the death of her brother.

As the younger brother of a brother, Sylvia's husband, Robert P., would be expected to prefer a spouse who would mother and understand him, especially with respect to the struggles and worries in his professional life and with other men. He himself had come from a family in which both parents were oldest siblings who had learned to accept each other as a man and wife, but who contested each other's wishes for dominance and control. Since he, as well as his older brother, only had the model of his parents but no experiences of their own to learn about life with peers of the other sex, a model that sisters would have provided, we suspect that Robert may have unconsciously recognized in his future wife her intensive need to take charge, to help and protect, but he was prepared to let her shape their relationship and their life together.

Robert's parents seem to have come from an ordinary background. His father's sister had no children of her own, but at least she did marry. His mother's next younger brother is married and has children. Her youngest brother died before he had reached the average age of marriage for men in general. Hence we cannot reasonably argue that he did not *dare* marry and found a family of his own. He was already dead before he could have done this.

Neither Robert's paternal nor his maternal grandparents seemed to have passed away early. We assume that both sets of grandparents were living during Robert's parents' childhood or youth. The same holds true for Sylvia's grandparents. None of them is known to have died early in her parent's lives.

Sylvia's and Robert's marriage probably suffers from Sylvia's need to dominate, control, and protect her children and husband, as well as from her erratic fits of anger and/or depression. A certain condescension not uncommon with oldest sisters of brothers in their dealings with, and care for, men might have been more striking due to Sylvia's difficult childhood and the less-than-average age difference between her and her younger brother. Robert might feel overwhelmed by the leadership and care she exercises even in matters she does not understand. He feels she does not approve of his contacts with other men enough unless these men are willing to display their reverence for her and court her favors and advice. She might unconsciously want to express through her behavior that she has enough to offer so that Robert should be as attached and admiring and exclusively devoted to her as her late brother used to be.

The children, Jim and Chris, have probably witnessed these tensions and conflicts between their parents, but they also arrived in the "wrong" birth order as far as the parents were concerned. Jim is the *older* brother and Chris the *younger* sister. While there was only Jim, Sylvia could treat him like her little brother. She may have done that to the point of making Robert jealous of their son. Moreover, having had too little motherly care and protection in her own childhood, Sylvia may have expected more help and assistance from Robert in her chores with the children than he was able or willing to provide.

When their second child arrived, which was somewhat later than the average distance for a second child, the parents' difficulties were increased rather than reduced. Their overprotected and overindulged son may have wanted to act as protector and guide for his little sister. Whether he was independent and patient enough to succeed may seem doubtful in view of the treatment he had been getting from his mother. Moreover, both parents unconsciously can not really accept this role for him. Sylvia would expect that her daughter would join her in caring for her son. She may even feel insulted by her son's attempts at independence from her, his mother. Robert, too, cannot empathize with Jim's possible leadership role vis-à-vis the daughter, and he might act toward Jim as if Jim were his own older brother. In his mind, Robert may make Jim the leader whose ideas and suggestions he needs and over whose favors he might even get into a scuffle with his daughter Chris.

From that we would conclude that Sylvia probably accuses her husband of being too soft and tolerant vis-à-vis his son and accuses her son of usurping a role to which he had no title. Robert, in turn, may reproach Sylvia for suppressing her son's autonomy wishes, for suffocating him with her motherly over-protection, and for acting like a master sergant at home.

Since Jim is said to have no problems in school and since the parents have no complaints about Chris anyway, it seems fair to assume that the psychological situation in the family is not hopelessly bad. Jim can be different, if he wants to be, and proves this in school. The parents, however, have conflicts with each other and with Jim. They exert an unconscious influence upon Jim that could hopefully be explored, better understood, and possibly changed through interviews with both parents. Although the son was the reason for Sylvia's consultation at the psychological clinic, she and their situation may be helped best, if the parents would talk over their relationship with each other and with their son. Anything else might change for the better by itself.

Case history

In the family therapy that Sylvia and Robert P. received from a male psychotherapist (who, incidentally, had been a middle brother of two sisters himself), both parents claimed that the other was doing something wrong in raising their children. Sylvia thought a boy should learn to obey, whereas Robert pleaded for free self-actualization. Jim should not be spoiled and pampered, which Sylvia seemed to do. It became apparent that Sylvia was very concerned that Jim should eat well and sufficiently. According to Sylvia, Jim had to have the very best and the first choice at the dinner table. It was also evident that Jim was a gaunt, but strong and sinewy boy. By nature eating did not really seem to matter to him. At least, this is how Robert saw it.

Sylvia also complained about Robert's unsteadiness and his inadequate concern about the family. She felt he worked too hard at his job. He took his profession and his colleagues too seriously, sacrificed too much of his private life in the process, and wanted to play the lord and master at home. She did not like forever cleaning up after him. Robert retorted that she was no good for anything else anyway and could not even do a good cleaning job. She should not talk about things she knew too little about. She had no talent, he assured the therapist. She had grown up like an orphan and she showed it. She kept bragging about her noble birth, he claimed, but her parents could not even provide her with a family life. Small wonder that she could not do it for her own children either.

During the course of the psychotherapy sessions, it turned out that Sylvia's father had been a dreamer, a soft and friendly man filled with unrealistic hopes for an artistic or musical career, while her mother, on the other hand, was a gaming, jealous, and ambitious woman, with little patience for the children.

Sylvia recounted that her brother had always been kind and attentive, and dearly loved his big sister. It had been a terrible misfortune that he had been lured into the Foreign Legion. She as well as her mother had tried to get his release via the French Embassy on the basis that he had been, after all, a minor when he had been conscripted, but their efforts were to no avail. While in boarding school, Sylvia and her brother had often tried to comfort each other, since the boarding school had been quite strict. They had also talked a great deal about their father. She suspected that he probably had girl friends, and had died from living it up at night in L. Eventually, he must also have run out of money.

Neither Sylvia nor her brother had ever got along very well with their mother. She had had interests other than and beyond her children. Sylvia professed that even today she preferred to have nothing to do with her mother. She had last been in touch with her four years ago. She also had no contacts with her relatives on either father's or on her mother's side of the family. This, however, was also due to geographical reasons.

Sylvia herself found it hard to start working at times. Once she had begun to work, however, she often had trouble stopping. If she felt depressed, she would eat a lot, but then she would suffer from how fat she was getting. Her marriage with Robert had been pleasant in the beginning. She had been overjoyed when their son was born and probably spoiled him. She may have neglected her husband, and other things too, at that time. That was when they had started quarreling. This was probably why it took them so long to have another child. Her son, incidentally, has been unruly and wild ever since he was born. He is a tough and strong boy, but sometimes filled with fury. Occasionally he is sad and whiney. They never have had any trouble whatsoever with their daughter, Chris. She is a charming and kind girl, has much more patience than Jim, and may even be more intelligent than he, but in any case she seems to be the wisest of them all.

Robert reported about the relationship his parents had had with each other. They were often cross with each other at first, but eventually their gripes subsided. His brother became a lawyer, is married, and has two children. On the whole he, Robert, and his brother had had a good relationship with each other. In the beginning he had had to take occasional beatings from him, but he eventually became his brother's match or even better. By that time, of course, they had stopped fighting. He, Robert, had always loved sports.

He needed vigorous physical exercise in order to counterbalance his meticulous work in the laboratory.

They were in touch with their relatives. His father's sister was married for the second time. She was a very feminine and attractive woman, and her first husband had died. They had no children. They probably did not want any. Robert's mother's brother had a son. There is a good relationship between that family and Robert's. The youngest brother of Robert's mother, who had suffered from tuberculosis and eventually died, had been engaged to someone before his death.

Sylvia, Robert, and the children enjoyed good contacts with Robert's parents. Sometimes the parents acted as go betweens when Sylvia and he had an argument. On occasion the children stayed with his parents. Unfortunately, they live 3000 miles away. Sylvia and his own mother are alike in many ways, Robert related, but when his parents were visiting them, or they their parents, the two women would have occasional controversies. They often had similar views and intentions, but even so seemed to be in each other's ways at times. Sylvia and Robert's brother got along well with each other, but they, too, would quarrel when they were in each other's company for long. Nevertheless, Sylvia admires Robert's brother and likes to hold up his image as a model for Robert. His brother's children and his own are not very close, but this may be due to their ages. His brother's children, a boy and a girl, are 16 and 13 years old, respectively.

During the therapeutic sessions Robert began to develop a little sympathy for Sylvia's sad childhood and youth. As a consequence, she mellowed in her attitude toward him and recognized that when she had been annoyed by him and started eating, she would also feed Jim and heap infantile favors on her son, apparently in an attempt to assure herself of his loyalty to her and of their alliance. She eventually thought, that the men in the family needed more of a life of their own and that perhaps she should "leave" Jim to her husband and concern herself more with Chris. When Robert began to noticeably appreciate Sylvia's accomplishment in her housework and with their children, she found it easier to do the work and even enjoyed it. Robert and Sylvia interacted with Jim in a more concerted way, and when Jim noticed the parents' common front, he became more reticent, at first rather grimly, but later on with an occasional smile. He grew closer to Chris who had never made a secret of how much she admired her brother. The parents agreed of their own accord to refrain from interfering with their children's contacts and dealings with each other. The children had to be left more to their own resources, Sylvia felt, and that was indeed what seemed to happen.

A Case of a Gang of Youths in Group Therapy

A group of nine youths aged 16 to 18, all of them high-school students, had been summoned by the Juvenile Court for breaking into the warehouse of a leather factory. Actually only one boy, Paul, had been caught by surprise by the night-guard and handed over to the police. It turned out that Paul, a girlish and soft-spoken boy and the only child of a high-school teacher of classical languages, did not really belong to the gang and had never been conspicuous in any way until this day. It became apparent that there was no intent of burglary; it was more of a prank played on Paul.

Two youngsters, Beppo and Fritz, led the quiet fan of their gang to believe, under the seal of strictest confidence, that they were diamond smugglers. They hoped to scare Paul off with this, because they did not like him. If he wanted to join them, he would have to pass a test. He was to keep the whole thing an absolute secret. If he squealed on them, his life might be in danger. Rather than being intimidated, Paul was enthusiastic and ready to do anything to pass the test. For their own fun, and perhaps also to frighten Paul after all, they took him by car to a secret meeting place, put a burlap bag over his head, and told him they were carrying him on their shoulders through the sewers of B. Actually they only "carried" him around the basement of an empty summerhouse that one of their parents rented. Merely pretending to walk, they put him down on the dirt floor a few times for a rest, twice in a puddle they had made themselves, and eventually took the hood off his head in the living-room of the "smuggler's house," lit by a petroleum lamp. They pretended to receive a coded telegraph call, pulled three air pistols when a noise outside seemed to worry them but put the guns away under their jackets when all remained quiet, and eventually they read the text of a telegraph message aloud: "Get shipment 138 from box labeled Madagascar, 3rd shelf on the left, warehouse, leather factory, Walnut Street 23. Simulate burglary."

In the subsequent discussion, the boys let it be known that this was an easy job that even a beginner could handle alone. Who wanted to do it? Paul volunteered immediately. Some of the boys expressed doubts that he could do it or that he could be trusted in the first place, but Paul insisted with sparkling eyes that he could. Four days later he did indeed break into the warehouse and, after having been caught, conscientiously refused to say anything about his mission. He claimed that he had wanted to steal a pair of soles for his shoes. However, there were contradictions in his story, which the police pointed out to him, and he eventually named the gang members. They all went before the court.

There the true story came out. Paul was found not guilty, the other boys were reprimanded, and they were ordered to attend a minimum of ten group therapy sessions with an experienced probation officer.

At this point, the group therapist wondered what, if anything, could be predicted on the basis of the boys' sibling positions about the structure of the group and about the presumable course of the discussions, which were to be conducted with a psychoanalytic orientation. The gang members were

Bavy ... younger brother of a half brother: $(b_h)b$
Beppo ... an only child: b
Ernest ... younger brother of a brother: (b)b
Fred ... younger brother of a brother: (b)b
Fritz ... older brother of a brother: b(b)
Guenter ... younger brother of a sister: (s)b
Kurt ... younger brother of a sister: (s)b
Ludwig ... older brother of a sister: b(s)

Paul, who was not a member of the gang and did not participate in the group therapy sessions, was an only child.

Diagnostic evaluation of the sibling roles and their interactions in the group:

There were probably two boys in the group who would claim leadership and contest each other for it: Fritz, the older brother of a brother, and Ludwig, the older brother of a sister. Less likely, but not out of the question, would be one of the younger brothers of sisters, and possibly also Beppo, the only child.

The two probable contenders for leadership, Fritz and Ludwig, had presumably different goals in mind. Fritz wanted a men's gang that would accomplish heroic feats. Ludwig would be less interested in heroism than in girls and would like to have his friends along when looking for a girl or recruiting girls for the group. Bavy, Ernest, and Fred were likely to flock to Fritz, whereas Guenter and Kurt would either vacillate or take to Ludwig. Beppo would claim only a secondary leadership role himself. He would prefer to be an initator and assistant to the primary leader of the group, but would expect in return to be recognized and given more attention than the others.

Beppo rather than Fritz may have conceived the idea of the prank. Paul was presumably viewed as an unlikeable boy, a do-gooder, and a sissy, and was therefore rejected by the group despite his admiration for them. It is possible, though, that Beppo would have wanted to get rid of this applicant for membership, even if he had been more attractive to the group. Beppo might have felt that Paul, another only child, could have put his privileged position in question. Beppo suspected Paul of striving for the position of "most important man" to the leader of the group and for those privileges from the group that he at present enjoyed himself.

The group would most probably try to ridicule the therapy sessions, but the group therapist would nevertheless initiate the group process. It might have been the judge's intention to make the youths aware of their brutality and recklessness when frivolously causing so much trouble for a naive and gullible fellow-student. The intention of the group therapist, however, would not be a lesson in morality or some reinforcement of the group's guilt feelings. If a sense of guilt was voiced, however, he would not change the subject, but rather give the group a chance to talk about it.

Despite all the fun they had had with their prank, it is likely that the group would eventually consider it a failure. If so, the contender for leadership who was more strongly identified with the prank and who may have organized it had probably fallen from the group's favor by now. A loss of prestige was the least he could expect from this. After all, they had been summoned to the court and penalized.

In the group sessions Fritz would either have to play it big once again and try to make a farce of the sessions, or he would have to stay in the background, watch what the therapist does with the group, and ultimately wrest the leadership from him again.

Ludwig, on the other hand, would be on top now. He would prefer to try to disrupt the group session in his own way, perhaps by bringing up girls, sex, and love in their discussions. Maybe he would form an alliance against Fritz with the group leader right from the start. He was less guilty than Fritz. He was never in favor of carrying a prank that far. Amorous adventures were more on his mind, and they would not land them in the court so easily.

It might also be that the younger brothers of brothers,

after turning away from their former leader, would prefer to align themselves with the younger brothers of sisters than turn to the oldest brother of a sister. They may sense instinctively that the oldest brother of sisters is actually more interested in girls than he is in the members of the group. The younger brothers of sisters, however, while also interested in girls, might nevertheless offer a sense of independence to the group without necessarily leading or dominating the others as obviously as oldest brothers of brothers tend to do. Moreover, they, that is, the youngest brothers of sisters, are prone to have less of an active interest in girls. The group might also split up in several such subgroups and perhaps fall apart. Beppo for his part could either stay with Fritz or go over to Ludwig.

Case history:

The question of guilt was the first to be raised in the group. Beppo had had the idea of the prank, and Fritz had been amused by it. Yet he had not exactly taken the initiative but played along with the others instead. Even so, the group considered Fritz responsible and guilty, Beppo innocent. Beppo had had lots of ideas before, but the perpetrators are responsible if these ideas are put in practice. As it happened, Fritz had suggested that they give Paul a warning after they had fooled him so successfully in the "smuggler's meeting." This had been rejected by the group, particularly by Ludwig. The argument was: if Paul was really that stupid he should pay for it. If he was not, he would not need a warning.

Beppo at first tried to disrupt the group sessions with jokes, and the group members played along. When they realized, however, that the group leader had no objections against jokes, they and even Beppo became more serious. Fritz seemed willing to take the blame for the whole affair on himself. Ludwig tried to divert the discussion to nightclubs and barmaids and to embarrass the group leader by direct and silly questions. He did not succeed.

The group members then discussed their experiences

with unlikeable people, pondered on what had made these people so unlikeable, compared Paul, as well as a few members of the group, with these people, and seemed to form two subgroups. One of them consisted of Bavy, Ernest, Fred, and Fritz, the other of Guenter, Kurt, and Ludwig. Beppo enjoyed the role of mediator for a while. Bavy, Ernest, and Fred explained their affiliation with Fritz as a wish not to let him down just because something had gone wrong. Guenter and Ludwig considered these expressions of loyalty too primitive for their taste. Kurt would not join the other two in their opinion, but when Fred, too, became unsure of his loyalty to Fritz, the two formed a subgroup of their own. Now Beppo tried to mediate between all three groups but eventually gave up.

Toward the end of the therapy they talked about the group leader and his experiences as a probation officer. He did not tell them anything concrete, but despite or possibly because of this the group members tried to guess what his work was like. From this they proceeded to discuss vocational prospects, and although one of them tried to ridicule the situation once again by saying he wanted to become a diamond smuggler, there were actually rather productive exchanges about various vocations and careers.

Treatment was terminated after 14 sessions, by mutual agreement. The members seemed to part in three subgroups: (a) Bavy, (Beppo), Ernest, and Fritz, (b) Fred and Kurt, (c) (Beppo), Guenter, and Ludwig.

14. Quantitative Aspects
of Family Constellations

In this chapter we will attempt to quantify and aggregate the degrees of conflict that may prevail between spouses and/or between parents and children, as well as those between friends of the same sex. Compound measures for all conflicts that can exist between spouses, parents, or friends were developed and tested empirically, although not always in a systematic fashion.

The severity of losses of family members that a person may have suffered was broken down into components, and an index aggregate was developed that could be tested more systematically than the conflict indices. It was proven valid.

The measures for the degrees of conflict and loss will be demonstrated and explained. The reader should not have any great difficulty in understanding these demonstrations and explanations. However, if he thinks he will, or if he wants to skip the whole chapter, this can be done without harm to his understanding of family constellations in general. The measures and indices merely articulate what the reader has learned by now from this book. In fact, they cover less than he already knows. The measures and indices may help, however, if a larger array of data about family constellations is to be absorbed and evaluated and their correlations tested. This is the reason for reporting them.

Measures of Conflict

It is possible to express the degrees of conflict between the sibling roles of friends or spouses more precisely than we have attempted to do in our complementarity and conflict tables (see p. 90, p. 108).

The degree of sex conflict prevailing in a marriage may be expressed by d_s for each of the two partners, where d_s is the coefficient of the sex distribution in the sibling configuration of the given partner. This coefficient d_s is a function of the number of same-sex siblings (n_s) in relation to the number of all siblings (formula 1):

$$d_s = \frac{n_s}{n-1} \tag{1}$$

In formula (1), n is the number of children constituting the sibling configuration of the given spouse. According to formula (1), a relationship such as b(sb)/(b)s would yield a sex conflict of 0.5 for the husband. If the relationship were b(bb)/(b)s instead, the husband's d_s would be maximal, that is, 1, whereas in b(ss)/(b)s it would be 0. In b(bbs)/(b)s his sex conflict would be 0.67, and in b(sbb)/(b)s it would be the same. The wife's sex conflict would be 0 in each of these examples. With only children, d_s would be indefinite (0 divided by 0), but we could meaningfully assume it to be $d_s = 1$.

The combined or total sex conflict (d_{s_m}) that exists between spouses according to their sibling roles is expressed by formula (2):

$$d_{s_m} = \frac{d_{s_b} + d_{s_s}}{2} \tag{2}$$

The sex distribution coefficient of the husband is d_{s_b}, that of the wife d_{s_s}. The maximal value of d_{s_m} is also 1.

Similar considerations apply to rank conflicts. The degree of rank conflict prevailing in a marriage is expressed by d_{r_m}, which, in turn, is the sum of d_{r_b} and d_{r_s}, the rank coefficients of the husband and the wife, respectively. The rank coefficient is a function of the difference between the number of younger siblings (n_{jun}) and the number of older siblings (n_{sen}) that a person has, devided by the total number of his siblings (formula 3):

$$d_r = \frac{n_{jun} - n_{sen}}{n-1} \tag{3}$$

A positive d_r indicates that we are dealing rather with a senior sibling, whereas a negative d_r indicates that we are dealing rather with a junior sibling. The absolute value of d_r reflects the degree of the spouse's seniority or juniority. A person like (b)b(sb) would have a $d_{r_b} = 0.33$, a person like (bs)s a $d_{r_s} = -1$. The husband would be somewhat of a senior, the wife a pure junior. With only children, the d_r is indefinite, but we could meaningfully assume it to be $d_r = 1$.

In analogy to formula (2), the combined or total rank conflict prevailing in a marriage can be expressed as d_{r_m} (formula 4):

$$d_{r_m} = \frac{d_{r_b} + d_{r_s}}{2} \tag{4}$$

Hence, (b)b(sb)/(bs)s would have a total rank conflict of $d_{r_m} = (0.33 - 1)/2 = -0.34$. The couple has a certain amount of rank conflict leaning toward the junior side. They are in a slight need of a senior. In the marriage b(sbs)/s(bs), there would be a rank conflict of 1, that is, a maximum of seniority conflict. Each of the two partners would be trying to change the other into a junior. The marriage (s)b/(b)s, on the other hand, would yield $d_{r_m} = -1$, which indicates a maximum of juniority conflicts. In contrast, relationships such as b(s)/(b)s or (bs)b(s)/(s)s(bb) would both have a total rank conflict of zero.

Formulas (3) and (4) could indeed be restricted to siblings of the opposite sex. A person's rank relationships with his opposite-sex siblings would obviously be more important to his marriage than his rank relationships with the siblings of his own sex. This is at least acceptable as long as d_s and d_{s_m} are being considered anyway. In that case the second version of d_r and d_{r_m} may even be preferable. The rank conflict of (b)b(sb)/(bs)s would thus be $d_{r_m} = (1 - 1)/2 = 0$. For (bs)b(s)/(s)s(bb), on the other hand, it would be $d_{s_m} = (0 + 1)/2 = 0.5$. As is to be expected, the two versions— considerations of all siblings or only of the opposite-sex siblings—may result in different values of the rank coefficients and of the total rank conflict.

Another type of conflict derives from the fact that marriage, at least in the civilized world, is a relationship between no more than two persons. Sibling configurations, however, may be composed of three, four, six, ten, and more persons. In many instances, therefore, a marriage will differ from sibling configurations in the number of possible person-to-person relationships. The discrepancy coefficient d_n expresses the degree of this type of conflict (formula 5), whereby n is the number of children constituting a spouse's sibling configuration.

$$d_n = \frac{n-2}{n} \tag{5}$$

In formula (5), the numerator should actually be $n - n_m$, where n_m is the number of persons that form a marriage. Where neither polygamy, polyandry, or group marriages are customary, formula (5) is sufficient. Only children would have negative values of d_n. They literally get more in marriage than they had at home in terms of peer relationships. Spouses who have only one sibling obtain d_n values of 0. The larger n is, the more d_n approaches 1.

For a given marriage, d_{n_m} indicates the degree of conflict resulting from the discrepancy between the number of spouses and the number of children in the spouses' original sibling configuration (formula 6):

$$d_{n_m} = \frac{|d_{n_b}| + |d_{n_s}|}{2} \tag{6}$$

The number-discrepancy coefficient of a married couple is half the sum of the absolute amounts of the number-discrepancy coefficients of the husband (d_{n_b}) and of the wife (d_{n_s}). Its maximum value, which can only be reached asymptotically, is 1. The marriage b(b)/(s)s represents a discrepancy of zero, b(ssss)/(b)s a discrepancy of 0.30, b(ss)/(bb)s a discrepancy of 0.34, and b(ssss)/(bbs)s a discrepancy of 0.55, whereas b/(bb)s yields a value of 0.67.

In analogy to formulas (3) and (4), formulas (5) and (6) could be restricted to a person's opposite-sex siblings. In this case, n would be the number of opposite-sex siblings plus 1. It should be mentioned that an only child and a spouse with siblings of his own sex only would have the same d_n value $(d_n = -1)$.

Finally, there may be a conflict between the sibling configuration of the parents and those of their children. The degree to which the configuration of children duplicates that of a parent is expressed by formula (7).

$$d_k = 1 - \frac{n_d}{n-1} \tag{7}$$

In formula (7), d_k expresses the conflict between a parent's and his children's sibling configurations; n_d is the number of those (dual) sibling relationships of a parent that have (one or more) duplicates among his children, whereas n is the number of children that constituted the parent's sibling configuration. In a family like b(sbb)/sbb/(b)s(b), the father would find two of his sibling relationships repeated among his children: b(b) and b(b). Hence for him $d_{k_b} = 1 - 2/(4 - 1) = 1 - 2/3 = 0.33$. The mother would find a duplicate among her children for one of her two sibling relationships: s(b). Her d_{k_b} equals 0.50.

Formula (8) could serve as an alternative to formula (7):

$$d_k = 1 - \frac{2n_d'}{n(n-1)} \qquad (8)$$

In formula (8), $n(n-1)/2$ is the number of all dual relationships that can exist among n children of a parental sibling configuration; n_d' is the number of all those dual relationships in the sibling configuration of the parent that have found a duplicate in any of the dual relationships extant among their children. Whereas n_d in formula (7) includes only the relationships of a parent to each of his siblings, n_d' in formula (8) also applies to the dual relationships of the parent's siblings among each other. According to formula (8), the example given above would render a d_{k_b} of 0.17 and a d_{k_s} of 0.33. Formula (7), however, is simpler and no less meaningful.

The number of children that the parents have had themselves has not been included in either formula. If the parents b(s) and (b)s have five children, say, b(s)/bsbbs/(b)s, their d_k values could be the same as when they have only two children, say b(s)/bs/(b)s. If the number of children should be explicitly included, formula (7) would have to be rewritten like this (formula 9):

$$d_k = 1 - \sqrt{\frac{n_d}{n-1}} \; \sqrt{\frac{2n_d'}{n'(n'-1)}} \qquad (9)$$

In formula (9), n' is the number of children a parent has and n_d' is the number of all those dual relationships prevailing among his children that have one or more duplicates in the parent's own sibling configuration. According to this, our example of b(sbb)/sbb/(b)s(b) would render $d_{k_b} = 0.18$ and $d_{k_s} = 0.29$. The example b(s)/bsbbs/(b)s, on the other hand, would yield $d_{k_b} = 0.37$ and $d_{k_s} = 0.37$, and the example b(s)/bs(b)s, in turn, $d_{k_b} = 0$ and $d_{k_s} = 0$.

In most instances, especially when the number of children that constituted the respective parents' sibling configurations was not very different from the number of their own children, formula (7) will do. After all, the probability of duplication of a parental sibling relationship among that parent's own children increases with the number of children. In this sense, the number of children is included anyway.

For a marriage as a whole, the degree of conflict, d_{k_m}, that exists between the configuration of children and the sibling constellations of the parents can be represented by formula (10):

$$d_{k_m} = \frac{d_{k_b} + d_{k_s}}{2} \tag{10}$$

For b(sbb)/sbb/(b)s(b), the coefficient $d_{k_m} = 0.24$; for b(s)/bsbbs/(b)s, $d_{k_m} = 0.37$; for b(s)/bs/(b)s, $d_{k_m} = 0$.

Formula (11) represents a combined rank and sex conflict coefficient:

$$d_{s_m, r_m} = \frac{d_{s_m} + |d_{r_m}|}{2} \tag{11}$$

This coefficient, which, incidentally, might be called an index aggregate, can also reach a maximum of 1. If it is 0, there is neither a rank nor a sex conflict between the two partners.

When computing d_{s_m} or d_{r_m} (as well as d_{n_m} and d_{k_m}), instead of simply adding the coefficients d_{s_b} and d_{s_s} or d_{r_b} and d_{r_s}, respectively, one could add their squares and find the square root of their sums, in order to obtain d_{s_m} and d_{r_m}. The same could be done with d_{s_m} and d_{r_m} when computing d_{s_m, r_m} (see also Erzigkeit 1970). Transforming scales in this way may be advantageous; the distribution of the empirical values of these coefficients may thereby become more continuous. The transformations introduce nothing new, to be sure. Occasionally they may seem to render more precision of the measurement of conflict than they actually can. All the coefficients mentioned at best produce measures of rank-order levels (according to Stevens 1951).

If the number discrepancy conflict (d_n) and the conflict with the configuration of one's own children should be incorporated in a total index d_t of conflicts that may exist in a marriage, formula (12) may be adopted:

$$d_t = d_{s_m, r_m, n_m, k_m} = \frac{d_{s_m} + |d_{r_m}| + d_{n_m} + d_{k_m}}{4} \qquad (12)$$

The maximal value of d_t is also 1, but the maximum can only be reached asymptotically.

The minimal value is 0. An example of $d_t = 0$ would be b(s)/bs/(b)s.

Relationships or friendships between persons of the same sex can be treated in a similar manner. The formulas for d_r and d_n (formulas 3, 4, 5, 6) remain unchanged regardless of whether the computations include all of a person's siblings or merely his same-sex siblings. In the latter case, the assumption would be that same-sex siblings matter more for same-sex friendships, just as opposite-sex siblings were considered more important for heterosexual partnerships and marriages. In formulas (1) and (2), n_s would be the number of opposite-sex siblings rather than same-sex siblings. Formulas (7) and (8) do not apply in this case. Hence d_t, when computed for a same-sex friendship, would read like this (formula 13):

$$d_t = \frac{d_{s_m} + |d_{r_m}| + d_{n_m}}{3} \qquad (13)$$

In formulas (11, 12, 13), the denominator is obviously equal to the number of coefficients that are being pooled.

In order to characterize something like the vitality or psychological health of a family, one may, among other things, compute the procreativity index. This index (p_e) reflects a couple's implicit desire for children in relation to their parents' implicit desire for children. Another index, p_g, does the same in relation to the couple's siblings' implicit or latent desire for children.

For any given spouse, p_e is the quotient of twice the number of children that constituted his own sibling configuration including himself, that is, $2n$, and the number n_e of the siblings of both his parents taken together, including the parents themselves: $p_e = 2n/n_e$. If $p_e < 1$, the spouse and his siblings are the product of parents whose manifest desire for children was weaker than that of their own parents. If $p_e > 1$, the spouse and his siblings are the product of parents who had a stronger manifest desire for children than their parents did. The relationship $p_e < 1$ would indicate that the spouse's original psychological milieu was less favorable and healthy than was the original psychological milieu of his parents, and vice versa if the equation is $p_e > 1$. In the first instance, the family could be considered on the decline, genealogically speaking, and in the second instance it could be viewed as being on the rise. All of this would only hold true provided other things were equal.

A couple's combined or total procreativity index would be $p_{e_m} = (p_{e_b} + p_{e_s})/2$, that is, half the sum of the procreativity indices of the husband (p_{e_b}) and of the wife (p_{e_s}). For example, if the husband's parents came from a three-child family (father) and a four-child family (mother), and he himself has only one sibling, then $p_{e_b} = 4/7 = 0.57$; if the siblings of the wife's parents including her parents themselves amounted to nine persons and she herself was an only child, her $p_{e_s} = 2/9 = 0.22$. Hence $p_{e_m} = (0.57 + 0.22)/2 = 0.39$. The spouses are the product of a declining family. A value of $p_{e_m} = 1$ would indicate an equally strong manifest desire for children among the couple's parents and their grandparents.

In a similar fashion, the manifest desire for children of the couple in question can be compared to that of the couple's parents. The number of the couple's children is doubled and then divided by the sum of the couple's siblings, including the spouses themselves. If the couple mentioned above has two children, the procreativity index of the milieu of the children (p_{e_k}) is $p_{e_k} = 4/3 = 1.34$. This suggests that these children are the product of a family on the rise. The couple's manifest desire for children is stronger than was that of their parents. A value of $p_{e_k} = 1$ would indicate that the couple's manifest desire for children is equal to that of their parents.

Spouses can be compared with each other according to similar criteria. One can estimate which spouse came from the more favorable family milieu and which one had to go farther out of his way as compared to his original experiences at home in arriving at the actual number of children of their own.

Analogous comparisons are also feasible between the manifest desire for children expressed by a couple and by the couple's siblings. We recommend computing a coefficient p_g for each spouse which includes the number of children the spouse has himself and the average number of children that all of the spouse's siblings had, including the spouse's own children. The values of p_g may be larger or smaller than 1, indicating, respectively, that the spouse had a larger or a smaller manifest desire for children than his siblings had on the average. The spouses can also be compared with each other by the degree to which the number of their own children surpasses or falls below their respective siblings' average number of children.

Measures of Loss

We have distinguished between permanent, temporary, and partial losses of family members (see p. 40ff). In this coming chapter we will deal for the most part with permanent losses suffered in the family, but we will also sketch how temporary losses as well as substitutions for a lost person (of the type of the person lost) can be quantitatively treated.

The following formulas attempt to articulate and integrate algebraically the rule by which losses of persons tend to exert their psychological effects (see p. 43ff). Substantively, they introduce nothing new.

$$l = \sum_{i=1}^{n_1} l_i \tag{14}$$

$$l_i = \left(\log \frac{1}{k}\right)^{-1} = -\frac{1}{\log k} \tag{15}$$

$$k = \frac{a_i t}{a_o a \sqrt{a (\bar{n} - 1)}} \tag{16}$$

In these formulas (formulas 14, 15, 16), l represents the combined or total loss that a person has suffered in his family; l_i stands for any individual loss of n_1 losses; k is a measure of the severity of an individual loss. Among the variables that determine k, there is a_i, the age of the person lost, a_o, the age of the oldest person in the core family before the loss occurred. The fraction a_i/a_o could be called the age coefficient. The length of time that the lost person lived with the person in question is t; the age of the person in question is a. The unit of all these variables is years, and always in relation to the year in which the loss occurred. The number of people constituting the family, i.e. parents, children, the person lost, and the person in question, is indicated by $\bar{n}$.

In order to also consider how a given loss changed the balance of sexes in the family, l may be multiplied by the reciprocal value of c, where c represents the coefficient of the sex-balance change in the family (formulas 17 and 18):

$$c = 1 - (s_b - s_a) \tag{17}$$

$$s = \frac{n_{s|}}{\bar{n}} \tag{18}$$

In formula (17), s_a stands for s after the loss has occurred, and s_b stands for s before the loss. In formula (18), s is the coefficient of sex balance, $n_{s|}$ is the number of persons in a family who are of the same sex as the lost person, and $\bar{n}$ is again the number of people who belong to the family. Perfect balance would render s = 0.50. The empirical values of c have a maximum of 1. The larger c is, the smaller the relative psychological effect of the loss. Hence, formula (14) should be expanded to read like formula (19);

$$l = \sum_{i=1}^{n_{|}} \frac{l_i}{c_i} \tag{19}$$

Let us illustrate this with an example. Suppose the older sister of a sister lost her mother when she herself was four years old. At that time her mother was 30, her father was 33, and her sister was 2 years old. Hence,

$$k = \frac{30 \cdot 4}{33 \cdot 4 \cdot \sqrt{4} \cdot 3} = 0.15 \tag{20}$$

Therefore, $-\log k = 0.82$ and $l_1 = 1.22$.

The coefficient of sex-balance change in this family would be $c = 1 - (3/4 - 2/3) = 0.92$. According to formula (19), $l_1 = 1.33$.

If the child had lost her father instead, c would be $c = 1 - (1/4 - 0/3) = 0.75$ and l_1 would be proportionately larger ($l_1 = 1.64$, if we ignore the fact that this situation would also change k).

If, after the loss of her mother, this girl should also lose her little sister, say, five years later, and only after her father, now 38 years old, remarried a woman a little younger than his first wife, and her sister was now 7, she herself 9, and her

new half-brother 3 years old, the following values would enter into k:

$$k = \frac{7 \cdot 7}{38 \cdot 9 \cdot \sqrt{9 \cdot 4}} = 1/82 \qquad (21)$$

$-\log k = 1.91$ and $l_2 = 0.52$; c would be $1 - (3/5 - 2/4) = 0.90$. According to Formula (19), $l_2 = 0.58$. The combined or total loss that the girl has suffered would be $l - l_1 + l_2 = 1.33 + 0.58 = 1.91$.

If a family is composed of merely two persons, a mother and daughter, for instance, a person from the outside would have to substitute for the mother if she should die or disap-pear. Before the substitution occurs, the loss index of the let us say 4-year-old child would be $k = 1/2$; $-\log k = 0.30$, and $l_i = 3.33$. Since $c = 1 - (2/2 - 1/1) = 1$, l_i would be 3.33 by formula (19) as well. This makes sense, since the loss of the mother would not change the balance of sexes in the family. There was no man in the family beforehand and there is none now. If this child had been only 1 year old at the time of the loss, we would obtain a value for $k = 1$, $-\log k = 0$, and $l_i = \infty$. If she had been even younger than 1 year old or had lost her mother at birth, we would still consider the age of the bereaved as being one year ($a = 1$).

The last variable that should be included in the loss index is the length of time that has elapsed since the loss occurred. The longer the time lapse, the smaller the remaining psy-chological effect of the loss should be. Hence, formula (19) should be further expanded to read as follows (formula 22):

$$l = \frac{1}{\log a_p} \sum_{i=1}^{n_i} \frac{l_i}{c_i} \qquad (22)$$

In formula (22), a_p would be the present age (in years) of the person in question, that is, the bereaved person.

If a parent is lost, an event that has more weight in the loss index than does the loss of a sibling, a substitute parent will often enter the family after a while. In the overall population of families there is a 60% probability that the father who was lost in a person's childhood or early youth will be replaced by a substitute father within five years. A mother who was lost by death or divorce during a person's childhood or early youth is replaced by a foster mother, a grandmother, an aunt, an adoptive mother, or a stepmother with a likelihood of almost 100% during the first five years after the loss has occurred and quite often much sooner (Toman & Preiser 1973).

Hence, in all estimates of loss effects we have to consider whether a substitute person of the same sex and about the same age as the person lost has been added to the family. This can be done in the following manner: Compute l_1 for the time t_1 at which the given loss occurred. Then compute l_2 for the time t_2, which is the time when a substitute person (of the same sex and about the same age as the lost person) has moved into the family. This computation must be done as if the original person had lived until t_2 and was lost at that time. The combined or total loss effect after another person has been substituted for the lost family member at the time t_2 is $l = l_1 - l_2$. The time difference between t_2 and t_1 should be rounded out to full years. Even if a substitute person came into the family just a few days after the family member departed, the difference would be considered as one year ($t_2 - t_1 = 1$). In this way, l_1 will always be larger than l_2. For reasons discussed earlier in this book (p. 47f), this would be psychologically meaningful. Only if the substitute person entered the family on the very day the original person died would l_1 be equal to l_2 and the effect of the loss would be $l = 0$. This is practically impossible for the most part. The substitute person is not sufficiently like the lost person. The bereaved could accept him or her only after a period of mourning had gone by (see p. 45).

Temporary losses of family members, such as the absence of the father for several years at a time (due to war or captivity, a prison sentence, an expedition, etc.) are computed in the same way. The loss index l_1 is calculated for the time t_1, the point in time when the separation began, l_2 for the time t_2, when the separation ended. However, these calculations are computed as if the family member did not return at this point in time, but has just disappeared. The subtraction $l_1 - l_2$ renders the measure of the effect of a temporary loss.

The losses of family members affecting the partners of a marriage or a similar enduring relationship can best be quantified as the sum of the loss indices of the husband (l_b) and of the wife (l_s). For the amount of loss psychologically effective in a marriage we could say:

$$l_m = l_b + l_s \qquad (23)$$

Formulas (14) to (23) are applicable with regard to losses affecting persons of the same sex, although l_i in formulas (19) and (22) ought to be multiplied by c rather than by the reciprocal of c. Better still, one should resort to formula (14).

In contrast to the measures of (d_s, d_r, d_n, and d_k), among those persons who have suffered any loss of a family member at all during their childhood or early youth, the loss index according to formula (19) shows a range of $l_i = 0.2$ to $l_i = 3.5$ for individual losses, a range of $l = 0.2$ to $l = 5$ for the combined or total losses suffered by a person. The median for both individual and combined losses is $Md_l = 0.9$. The distribution of loss measures slopes toward the left but it can be changed into a normal distribution by a simple scale transformation.

K. Eberhard has proposed and used a simplified loss index (formula 24). As in formulas (14, 15, 16, 22), a stands for the age of the person in question at the time he suffered the loss, a_p is the person's current age, and n is the number of family members; l_1 represents the person's first or earliest loss. The combined or total loss effect is equal to the product of the value of the first loss and the total number of losses that were suffered (Eberhard & Kohlmetz 1973).

$$l_1 = \frac{1}{a \cdot a_p(\bar{n}-1)} \tag{24}$$

Losses of siblings can complicate the calculations of the conflict coefficients d_s, d_r, d_n, and d_k. If a 16-year-old girl had an older brother and a younger sister, but lost the older brother when she herself was 12 years old, how should d_s or d_r be computed? On the basis of the sibling configuration before the loss or after the loss?

A simple way would be to compute the coefficients on the basis of the sibling configuration that was effective earlier in a person's life and/or for a longer period of time (see p. 195f). If two different sibling configurations have been effective for an equal length of time, the one that became effective earlier should be used. If the earlier sibling configuration was only effective for half as long as the later one, or even less than that, the later one should be used. If in doubt, try to decide intuitively or to interpolate between the two by computing the conflict coefficients for both (or all) alternatives, and taking the mean value. The individual coefficients that are derived in this way could be weighted according to the time that each of them had been effective.

On the basis of the double-alternative rule differentiating between earlier-later and longer-shorter, we can determine for the example given above which of the sibling configurations should be considered more effective: the one before or the one after the sibling loss. The 16-year-old girl should be considered the younger sister of a brother and an older sister of a sister sooner than merely the older sister of a sister.

If we want to assign a weight to the different sibling configurations in order to arrive at reasonable mean values, and if we learn that the girl's younger sister is four years her junior, we can proceed in the following manner: We determine how long each of a person's sibling positions has lasted. Our client was the younger sister of a brother, (b)s, for 4 years, she was the middle sister of an older brother and a younger sister, (b)s(s), for 8 years (from 5 to 12), and the oldest sister of a sister, s(s), for another 4 years (from 13 to 16). We can now compute the d_s values for each of these three positions. For (b)s, $d_s = 0$; for (b)s(s), $d_s = 1/2$; and for s(s), $d_s = 1$. Assigning (b)s a weight of 4/16, (b)s(s) a weight of 8/16, and s(s) a weight of 4/16 of the client's life time so far, we get $0 + 4/16 + 4/16 = 1/2$. This value must be divided by 3, since we have pooled three coefficients. Therefore, the interpolated value of d_s will be $d_s = 1/6$ Our 16-year-old client would have a slight sex conflict in her relationship with young men.

The coefficients d_r, d_n, and d_k can be calculated analogously to d_s. In practice, however, we recommend testing whether a decision for one of the alternatives could be reached beforehand on the basis of the double-alternative rule, and the remaining alternatives omitted. If not, we might even have to weight the different transitional sibling configurations that the person has held while growing up, even if there was no sibling loss at all. I am not sure whether the conflict coefficients are sufficiently valid to justify such extra work in clinical-psychological practice. If a computer program is available, however, calculations such as these are a mere trifle.

A Total Index and Discussion

Finally, mention should be made of an index aggregate that integrates the conflicts that lovers, spouses, or friends create for each other, as well as the losses of family members they have suffered, into a single measure. It should be pointed out, though, that this total index has not been suf- ficiently tested in empirical contexts. The psychological difficulties or the lack of such difficulties in a marriage or a friendship are indicated by P_m (formula 25):

$$P_m = (1+d_t)^{1+l_m} = \left(1 + \frac{d_{s_m} + |d_{r_m}| + d_{n_m} + d_{k_m}}{4}\right)^{1+l_m} \tag{25}$$

In formula (25), the value P_m expresses the overall expectation or chances of marriage or a friendship to last and succeed. The larger that value, the poorer the prognosis will be, on average. The smaller the P_m values, the better the prognosis. All symbols contained in formula (25) have been explained before. The theoretical range of this total stress indicator of a marriage extends from 1 to ∞, in practice from 1.1 to 20.

Even the conflicts and losses that the parents of the couple in question have suffered could be included in this psychological stress indicator for the couple's relationship with one another. Since the couple's parents, in turn, have been exposed to influences emanating from their own parents, it seems feasible to compute something like a genealogical stress indicator by weighting and then adding the P_m values of several generations, that is, those of the couple's parents, grandparents, and even their great-grandparents. Assuming that the childhood experiences of a couple's parents exert a smaller influence on the couple in question than did the couple's own childhood experiences, and assuming that the influence of the grandparents' childhood experiences is smaller still, the P_m values of previous family generations could be weighted by the reciprocal of the square of the number of P_m values calculated per each such family generation. Since a given couple has two pairs of parents, the sum of their P_m values (which shall be called P_{m_1}) would have to be divided by 4. Since each set of parents, in turn, has two sets of parents, which is the same as saying the couple has four sets of grandparents, the sum of their P_m values (P_{m_2}) would have to be divided by 16, etc. This computation program is symbolized by formula (26) yielding a couple's genealogical stress indicator P_{mt}.

$$P_{mt} = P_m + \frac{P_{m1}}{4} + \frac{P_{m2}}{16} + \frac{P_{m3}}{64} + \text{etc} \qquad (26)$$

Conflict indices and loss indices reflect the objective and enduring characteristics of the social environment in which a person has grown up and which may have influenced him (or her). This is also true of the complex indices or index aggregates described above. One could assume on the average that the social environment reflected by the index would have exerted the effects that were anticipated theoretically. In those instances where this does not seem to be the case, our appraisal on the basis of objective data of the person's, the couple's, or the family's social environment may still help us to understand the situation better. As observers, we should know what kind of an environment the persons in question responded to, regardless of whether they did so in an expected or an unexpected way. Those important enduring and objective data or details about the social environments in which the persons in question have grown up are contained in the indices suggested above including the total stress index.

Occasionally I have heard the objection that the quantifications of conflicts and losses suggested above will never do full justice to the individual conditions of those conflicts and losses and to their subjective experiences. I do not deny this, and I have already discussed this issue (p. 41). But what are we to do when dealing with 20 or 100 persons who have suffered early losses of family members if we want to compare them with persons who have not suffered such losses? It is all done in the hope of possibly arriving at a few universal statements about the facts of losses—statements that would be worth memorizing and might be applicable in psychological and psychotherapeutic practice. The suggested quantifications, most of which have been tested empirically, would be useful in this.

The expert will have noticed that the various conflict measures do not represent continuous scales. The empirical values are scattered somewhat irregularly and discretely along the scale range. For this reason these values will rarely be used to characterize individual cases. They may be helpful, though, when grouping larger numbers of cases on nominal or ordinal scales that could not be grouped by other means, at least not in as simple a manner. Index aggregates such as d_{s_m, r_m} or d_t yield empirical values that are more continuous anyway. This is also true of the super index aggregate P_m, although we must admit that the large number of variables that enter this aggregate put its practical utility in question. The best scales, relatively speaking, are provided by the loss indices. They furnish an almost unlimited number of empirical loss-effect measures within the range (of 0 to 5) that will cover the vast majority of cases.

15. Related Theories and Other Investigations

Related Theories

The theory of family constellations that has emerged from a large array of empirical data and some straight reasoning has favorable relations to a few other theories. Before all others, the fathers of depth psychology and psychoanalysis should probably be mentioned.

A child's interactions and conflicts with his parents are central to Freud's theory of motivational development (Freud 1916/17, 1920, 1923, 1926, 1933). The child passes through a phase of dependence, a phase of power struggles, and a phase in which he learns to respond sex-specifically to family members and other persons and to psychologically identify his own sex. Early childhood ends with the development of tender interactive relationships between the child and his opposite-sex parent, with a partial resolution of the conflicts arising between the child and his same-sex parent, and with the child's identification with that parent. One might argue that the theory of family constellations is an articulation of the consequences of this development under different types of a child's social environment.

Adler sketched the part that siblings play in a person's psychological development. He was the first to try to characterize sibling positions, but he was not systematic about it (Adler 1920, 1929, 1931, 1933; see also Ansbacher & Ansbacher 1956).

From these beginnings by Freud and Adler, the theory described above defined the basic types of sibling positions with the help of simple rules of combination. It also considered the parents' sibling positions to clarify the relations an individual person has toward his parents, it formulated theorems of human compatibility and developed the rules governing the effects that could result from early losses in the family. Following these precise descriptions of the presumably most relevant and pervasive aspects of a person's social environment, empirical evidence and proofs could be more easily searched for and more clearly differentiated than ever before. These evidences and proofs have for the most part already been reported (p. 40ff, 95ff). The remainder is the subject of this chapter.

Jung advanced the thesis, possibly prematurely, that a person and his parents may not only have conflicts with each other on the basis of their individual experiences, but also by virtue of differential archetypal response codes, that is, of inherited instinctive preferences or, if you like, species experiences (Jung 1912, 1916, 1923, 1939), and these conflicts could complicate a person's psychological development. A child may have an inborn unconscious wish for a strong father, but his father may be soft and weak in reality. An analysis of the sibling positions of parents and their children, however, will often provide better explanations of such family conflicts than recourse to species experience or archetype can afford. In the example given above, the father could be the younger brother of three sisters, and the child could be the oldest of several boys. Supposedly inborn or instinctive preferences are often revealed as being learned roles that have not come to a person through his ancestors and the distant past, but here and now through the social contexts to which he was exposed while growing up.

There is also a good relationship between the theory of family constellations and the concepts advanced by Lorenz (1943, 1963), Tinbergen (1951), and other ethologists. Their concept of "imprinting" implies that an individual becomes more vehemently conditioned to certain objects (mostly individuals of his own race or species) or certain situational aspects, the earlier and the more exclusively and enduringly those objects or aspects have "lived with" the individual in question. Attachments to objects other than the original ones depend on their similarity to these original ones. The human baby, however, is different from the young of practically all animals in that its family is maintained, though with occasional structural changes, over much longer periods of time, comparatively speaking. Animal siblings have practically no chronological rank order, as do human siblings. Higher rank within a litter is associated with the greater size, strength, and intelligence of the individual animal. With the human young, the first-born is an average of three years older than his younger sibling, and that automatically implies that he (or she) is taller, stronger, and in effect more intelligent at first than is the second-born.

The theory of family constellation also has a little in common with the theory of games (von Neumann and Morgenstern 1947), or at least I have been told that it does. In the theory of family constellations, the concept of utility has a place and a part, particularly if one considers the choices of persons the game, and the "compatibility" of partners the value or profit of the game. One could conceive of a pay-off matrix that included the various degrees of conflict. Usually, however, it is both partners in a relationship such as marriage or friendship who win. The degree of preference for maintaining a relationship may be considered the safest indicator for the numerous little profits that the partners make in the course of their relationship with each other. Hence, one might also view such enduring relationships between two (or more) persons as coalitions. Their gains would have to be compared with the gains that other coalitions could extract from the bank or, more appropriately in our context, from life and fellow human beings. The safest total indicator of these gains would be those coalitions that the off-spring of the original coalitions is able to enter. More concretely: The ultimate gains of a marriage are the abilities of its children to enter marriages of their own. Other things being equal, couples can be said to have won when they are happier with each other than other couples are and when they are able to pass on more happiness to others, and to greater numbers of others.

Other monographs or books dealing with siblings and family relations in the field of family research have come out since my book "Family Constellation" was first published in 1962. Dechêne (1967) studied the correlations between the neurotic disturbances of preadolescents and their sibling positions. Lucille Forer (1969) offered a phenomenological survey of the roles that persons of different sibling positions look for and attain in life. Both authors draw on the theory of family constellations that I have presented. König (1964) reviews cultural periods and historical personalities from the point of view of typical sibling positions and their influences. Sutton-Smith and Rosenberg (1970) wrote a detailed survey of psychological studies (including their own) of children in different sibling positions. They tested behavior and attitudes in extrafamilial contexts (such as kindergarten) and in the psychological laboratory. The variables under investigation were masculinity-femininity, the need for dependency and affiliation, anxiety, achievement behavior, and attitudes vis-à-vis authorities. They also described changes in their subjects' extrafamilial behavior and in their sibling relationships within relatively short observation intervals. The authors tried to explain observed behaviors and behavior changes with the help of principles of operant conditioning, imitative or model learning, and counteractive learning.

The observations and results of these studies have been more frequently arranged according to authors and psychological dimensions than according to types of sibling positions. For this reason, they impress the clinician and practioner as being somewhat too complicated and partly contradictory. On the whole, however, these observations and studies have confirmed our own observations and descriptions; we have expanded these to include adults and adult life situations and have ordered them according to basic types of sibling positions and partner relationships.

Other Studies

In addition to our critical experiments testing the duplication theorem (p. 95ff, 146f), our studies of loss effects (p. 46f, 105f), and other studies we have already reported, there are various other research projects that were conducted by members of our research team. In addition to these, there are numerous studies that explore the effects of sibling positions and other characteristics of family constellations, as well as those of losses of family members. The most important of these studies will be briefly reported or at least mentioned in the following sections.

Studies of the effects of sibling role conflicts

The duplication theorem would suggest that, other things being equal, parents of children who need psychological counseling or treatment would have more rank and/or sex conflicts of their sibling roles than can be expected by chance. This was confirmed through samples from three different child guidance clinics in Greater Boston (Toman & Gray 1961). In a student and faculty counselling center of a university, however, the clientele showed no significant deviations from chance in these respects (Levinger & Sonnheim 1965). The possible reasons for this and a source of error were discussed (Toman 1965b). Baxter (1965) found a correlation between the rank conflicts of sibling roles among the parents of college students and a psychological index of intramarital conflict. Sex conflicts of sibling roles, on the other hand, showed no significant correlation with this psychological conflict index. With a sample group of junior executives, Kemper (1966) was able to demonstrate that they judged their own marriages more favorably if they had no rank conflict with the sibling roles of their wives. Their judgments of their own marriages were particularly favorable in those cases where they were oldest brothers of sisters themselves and their wives youngest sisters of brothers.

The effects of the complementarity or non complementarity of parental sibling positions upon their children have been demonstrated in the following ways (see Toman 1960a, 1966): The leaders of youth groups, more often than the nonleading members of those same groups, had parents whose sibling roles were complementary (Bernhöft 1967). Only children of parents with complementary sibling roles scored higher on a psychological dominance scale than only children of parents with noncomplementary sibling roles did (Oswald 1963). Achievement motivation as measured by a projective test was higher among the adolescents whose parents had rank and/or sex conflicts of sibling roles than it was among all the other adolescents in the sample studied (Lompa 1967).

Youngsters of parents with incompatible sibling roles had slightly better school grades (Zielinski 1966), showed more resistance to the group pressure of the class (Langenmayr 1966) and, according to an attitude test by Toman (1955), had poorer relationships with their own siblings (Borkholder 1966). Incompatible sibling roles of parents were twice as frequent as would be expected by chance among those 6-year-old children whose admission to the first grade of elementary school was postponed by a year (Bauer 1967). Depressed inpatients in a psychiatric hospital had parents with noncomplementary sibling positions more often than chance (Kort 1967).

Complementarity of sibling roles was also found

relevant in (same-sex) friendships. In addition to the studies already quoted (Kassel 1962, Schott 1966, Toman 1972b, Toman, Gasch, Schmidt 1972), Toman (1959b, c), Gray (1960) and von Hintzenstern (1968) should be mentioned. Friendships between persons of the same sex tend to last longer when the sibling roles of the friends are complementary. More friends than would be expected by chance have sibling roles that are complementary to the person's own sibling position. Male friends, however, demonstrated this trend more clearly than did female friends.

It was also observed that more often than by chance men who came from monosexual sibling configurations chose wives whose sibling positions were similar to, or identical with, those of the men's own mothers. This was particularly true of oldest brothers (Toman 1964). Spouses between whom the age difference was unusually large showed more incidents of sibling role conflict than average spouses (Toman 1963a). This could be taken to mean that the large age difference compensated for the lacking complementarity of the sibling roles of such partners.

Parental preferences for a particular child among their own children also seemed to depend on complementarity aspects of the sibling roles of the parent and the child. From the reports of the children it became apparent that parents who had sons only or daughters only responded relatively more favorably to the child whose sibling rank was complementary to the parent's own sibling rank. If the parents had both sons and daughters, they tended to prefer among their children a child of the opposite sex whose sibling rank was complementary to their own. If children of the same sex were preferred, in a significant number of instances it was the ones who had the same sibling rank as their parents did. One may assume that this was an identification relationship between the parent and his child (Toman 1969). It could also be shown that the greater the similarity of their sibling positions, the more the parent and his same-sex child resembled each other in behavior characteristics such as attitude toward a test situation, understanding of educational measures taken by the parents, and emotional response to certain situations, (U. Gasch 1967, Kurz 1969, Erzigkeit 1970). Incomplete statistics of case records suggest that the problem child in a family is frequently that child who has either an identification conflict with the same-sex parent or an interaction conflict with the opposite-sex parent, or both (Toman 1969, 1973b). Even school performance and teacher evaluation was proven to be dependent, among other things, on the compatibility of the sibling roles of the student and the teacher (Freyn 1974).

Studies on the effects of loss

The research projects of Toman (1962), Toman and Preiser (1973), and Zielinski (1966) on the effects of early losses of family members have already been reported (see p. 45f). I may add that an increased incidence of losses of significant persons was observed in various samples of delinquents by Toman, Preiser, Gasch, Plattig (1967), B. Gasch (1964), Hiese (1964), and Becher (1967). Neurotic children and youngsters had also suffered more losses of family members than would be expected by chance (Toman & Gray 1962, Toman, Preiser, Gasch, & Plattig 1967). Bauer (1967) found more losses among the 6-year-old children whose admission to first grade had been postponed by a year, Gösswein (1968) and Toman, Preiser, Gasch, & Plattig (1967) found more losses among unwed mothers and divorced couples, Kort (1967) among depressive inpatients, Lösel, Dillig, Wüstendörfer and Linz (1974) as well as von Hintzenstern (1975) among adolescent criminals than was expected by chance (see also Shannon 1968).

A sample group of foster-mothers working for the international organization of Children's Villages (SOS-Kinderdorf) and caring for an average of nine children of both sexes and different ages all of whom had come from broken homes revealed that those foster-mothers had suffered more early losses of family members themselves than was to be expected by chance (Toman 1959b, c). The foster-mothers in the sample group who had not yet been given a "family" of nine children or who felt they did not even want one were the ones who had suffered the gravest and earliest losses of family members. For curiosity's sake, I should mention that the original families of these foster-mothers comprised an average of nine children and that there were about twice as many girls among them as there were boys. Surprisingly, the ratio of adult women to adult men working in the Children's Villages was about 2 : 1. Among the children themselves, who lived in the Children's Villages, however, there happened to be significantly more boys than girls.

Early studies on the psychological effects of loss were conducted by Hoenig (1929), Anna Freud and Dorothy Burlingham (1943), and Bowlby (1951). Bowlby found correlations between delinquency, crime, and psycho-pathology on the one hand and losses of family members on the other. Separated or incomplete families seemed to increase the probability of their children becoming delinquents or neurotics. Glueck and Glueck (1943, 1959, 1970) as well as Hartmann (1970) confirmed that trend. An early survey of the literature was given by Bergler (1955).

Schraml (1954) observed that the temporary separation of children from their mothers during their early years of life tended to retard their emotional and social development. Earle and Earle (1961) later observed that children of that type developed sociopathic personalities. Gardner (1956) reported adverse effects of temporary absences of their fathers early in their lives upon the children's sense of their own value, Lynn and Sawrey (1959) reported similar effects in Norway upon the children's emotional and social responses, and Gabower (1959) reported the same effects on the children of American Navy men. Stephens (1961) reconstructed from the reports of social workers about fatherless families that boys tended to be more spoiled and their mothers more jealous of their sons' girl friends than they were in intact families. More than half of the parents of such incomplete families had grown up in incomplete families themselves.

Comparing children living in children's homes without contacts with their parents with children who spend their evenings and weekends with their parents, Klackenberg (1956) and Heinicke (1956) found the former more aggressive. The difference was not as marked, though, as Spitz (1945) had reported. Rouman (1955) confirmed this difference and others with children whose mothers worked during the day. These children seemed to be more aggressive, more introverted, more nervous, and poorer in their performance in school than children from the control group.

Spitz (1945) and Spitz and Kaethe Wolf (1946) noticed an intensive emotional reaction among the children who suffered temporary or permanent losses of their mothers during the second half of their first year of life. The authors called the response "anaclitic depression." O'Kelly (1957) observed that young female thieves who had been temporarily separated from their mothers in their early childhood were given to confabulations and appeared both less objective and less self-critical than young female thieves who had suffered no such early separations from their mothers. Andry (1957) reported that delinquent boys had better relationships with their mothers than with their fathers; 75% of the boys had been temporarily separated from their parents. Monahan (1960) confirmed this and found, in addition, that there were fewer traumatic effects, the later in the youngsters' lives those separations or losses occurred. Naess (1962) demonstrated an increased frequency of early separations from their mothers among adolescent delinquents. The ones who had committed graver offenses had suffered such early separations even more often. Badami (1962) also reported a higher rate of unwed mothers.

Wolff (1961) showed that children who consulted counseling centers frequently had lost a parent early in their lives. Archibald, Bell, Miller, and Tuddenham (1962) found more and earlier losses of persons among psychiatric patients than among a control group; Brill and Liston (1966) found more losses of parents due to separation or divorce among psychiatric patients of all kinds than in the general population. Brown (1961) reported losses of a parent among 41% of all patients with psychotic depressions (the loss of the mother appeared always to have such pathogenic effects whenever it occurred, whereas the loss of the father only when it occurred between five and 14 years of age); Bruhn (1962) found losses of one or both parents among 42% of a sample of suicides. Similar effects of losses were observed among psychiatric patients in England (Birtchnell 1970, 1971, 1972).

Studies on the effects of sibling positions

Researchers have tested the effects that the sibling position alone of a person exerts on his behavior, on his attitudes, and on his personality development more often than they have the more complex effects of different degrees of complementarity of sibling roles and of losses of family members. Differences in behavior trends, attitudes, and personality characteristics as a function of the sibling positions of the persons being studied could be demonstrated in practically all instances.

Oldest siblings and only children were found to be leaders of (male) youth groups (Bernhöft 1967) and the elected class leaders in school (Oswald 1963) more frequently than would be expected by chance. Oldest brothers and only children were also over-represented among a sample of distinguished persons (those whom *Time Magazine* had selected for their cover stories over a period of twelve years). Middle brothers were significantly infrequent among them. Disregarding only children for the moment, distinguished persons came from predominantly or exclusively male sibling configurations. Among the women, who constituted less than 10% of the sample, the only statistically significant over-representation was that of oldest sisters (Toman & Toman 1970).

Keller (1964) found that male adolescents who came from monosexual sibling configurations displayed more physical aggression than the rest of their sample, and those with greater numbers of siblings showed less verbal aggression. Oldest brothers showed relatively extreme reactions to frustration, whereas middle siblings showed relatively mild ones, when measured by Rosenzweig's picture frustration test (Wellhöfer 1964). The aspiration level (tested by a series of simple arithmetical computations) was higher among oldest siblings and only children and more variable among youngest siblings than among the rest. When called upon to predict their own achievements, oldest siblings and only children increased their estimates more often and by a greater degree and lowered it less often than did youngest siblings (Müller 1965). In a projective test (TAT) achievement motivation was higher than average among oldest siblings and only children (Lompa 1967). In responding to one of Sodhi's tests, (1963), middle siblings yielded most to group pressure, and only children and persons with only one sibling yielded least, relatively speaking. Persons with siblings of the opposite sex were more susceptible than average to such pressures (Langenmayr 1966; see also Toman 1972a).

Only children showed more positive attitudes toward parents and more negative attitudes toward siblings in general and toward their classmates than did children of other sibling positions (Borkholder 1966). Oldest siblings had more concrete professional plans than youngest siblings. The latter appeared to be more influenced than others by persons they knew in these professions. Youngest siblings and only children knew less about the professions they aspired to than others did. Only children favored independent work and self-employment and were more disinclined toward social work jobs than other adolescents

(Schiller 1966). In self-evaluations based on Osgood's semantic differential (Osgood 1957), oldest siblings scored highest in the dimension "power." They were followed by only children, youngest siblings, and middle siblings. The dimensions "activity" and "evaluation" revealed no clear differences between different sibling positions (Gerstner 1967). Oldest sisters of brothers were found more frequently than by chance among those mothers who had "well-behaved" sons. Those mothers who had "difficult" children were often youngest sisters of sisters (Skiba 1968).

Among a sample of juvenile delinquents, only children committed the gravest offenses as measured by the length of their sentences. They were followed by youngest siblings, middle siblings, and, finally by oldest siblings (Gasch 1964). Among the juvenile delinquents who had been sent to a home for delinquents, the oldest siblings were the ones who committed the worst delinquent acts, the youngest siblings the mildest ones, comparatively speaking (Becher 1967). Since these delinquents were younger than the sample of juvenile delinquents above, the different effects may be due to the differences in age. Male juvenile delinquents who were apprehended for homosexual offenses had only or predominantly sisters among their siblings more often than by chance. The (male) juvenile delinquents who committed heterosexual offenses (such as rape, sexual assault of minors, etc.) often came from monosexual sibling configurations, that is, from families of boys only (Toman, Preiser, Gasch, & Plattig 1967, Gasch 1964). This seems to run counter to our theoretical expectations. If one considers, however, that these youngsters became conspicuous and were arraigned for offenses in those areas of conduct where they lacked pertinent experiences in their original families, the finding is plausible.

Many researchers have been studying selected aspects of family constellations for general effects for over several decades. The first to be mentioned here is Adler, who observed some sibling roles in the course of his psychotherapeutic work and who described the oldest, second-oldest, the youngest, and the brother of sisters (Adler 1929, 1931, 1933, Ansbacher & Ansbacher 1956).

Age ranks among siblings (sometimes regarding the siblings' sexes as well) and their psychological effects were explored by Goodenough and Leahy (1927), Stagner and Katzoff (1936), Krout (1939), Damrin (1949), Sears (1950), and very elaborately and systematically by Koch (1955a, b, 1956a, b, c, d, e, 1958, 1960), and also by Hillinger (1958), Schoonover (1959), Vuyk (1959, 1961), Hodges and Balow (1961), and Stark (1962). The subjects studied were mostly children in kindergartens and in schools. Rosenow (1930) and McArthur (1956) described the position of the first-born and compared it with other sibling roles, Fischer (1952) did so with the position of the second-born, Koch (1958) and Maxwell and Pilliner (1960) that of the youngest, and Guilford and Worcester (1930) and Hooker (1931) that of the only child.

Behavior problems within the family as well as without and their relations to sibling positions were studied by Levy (1931), Wile and Jones (1937), Koch (1956d, e), Morgenstern (1956), and Katzenstein (1957). Handschin-Ninck (1956) analyzed the characters of oldest and youngest siblings in fairy tales. West (1960) examined the age rank of scientists and the numbers of their siblings and concluded that they had often been isolated during their childhood. Schachter (1963), Altus (1965a, b), and Warren (1966) found more first-borns and only children among college students, Cobb and French (1966) among medical students, whereas Bayer (1966) could only confirm the greater incidence of only children and the significant under-representation of middle siblings among college students. Rosenberg and Sutton-Smith (1966) reported that first-borns achieved better grades in languages, especially when they came from two-child families; de Lint (1967) found that later-borns scored higher on certain intelligence tests (such as WAIS), whereas Belmont and Marolla (1973) reported progressively lower intelligence scores (as tested by Raven-Matrices) with later-borns. Since this test is ordinarily conducted as a power-test with no time limit, differential motivation could have played a part. Even a socioeconomic class effect has not been altogether ruled out, although the authors tried to do so.

Schachter (1964) noticed that first-born adolescents mentioned fewer names and identical names more frequently than did later-born adolescents in a sociometric test. First-borns and only children supported a lecturer more willingly than later-borns (Weiss 1966). First-borns displayed a better verbal understanding, second-borns a better comprehension of gestures and actions (Rosenberg, Sutton-Smith, & Griffiths 1965). In sociometric tests first-borns were chosen more frequently and their own choices were more frequently reciprocated than those of later-borns (Alexander 1966). First-borns scored higher in tests of achievement motivation and autonomy and lower on test anxiety than second-borns (Sampson & Hancock 1967, Oberlander & Jenkin 1967). First-born males and only children (also male) kept promises and secrets better than later-borns (Wuebben 1967). First-borns enjoyed being subjects in research or test studies, but disliked social science experiments more than later-borns did (Dohrenwend, Feldstein, Plosky, & Schmeidler 1967). Wilson, Patterson, and Lysons (1966) reported no such preferences among female subjects (in Australia).

Rosenfeld (1966) found no difference in affiliation need among first-borns and later-borns, whereas Sinha (1967) reported that first-borns were more concerned with the experiment, later-borns with personal contact and affiliation. Moran (1967) observed a greater need for recognition by others among first-borns than among later-borns and that more among female than among male subjects. Hall (1965) found that only children are more likely than others to break their engagements, and that male only children are more likely to get a divorce than would be expected by chance. Murdoch (1966) reported that first-born males marry sooner than later-borns, and that first-born females "want to marry" sooner than later-borns. This coincides with Schachter's theory that the older child is more dependent on the family and the family tradition than is the younger child (Schachter 1959). This seems to be contradicted by the study of pregnant unmarried women (Wohlford & Jones 1967), among whom the first-borns displayed less insecurity and anxiety about their condition than did other women in the sample. Regardless of sibling position, age correlated negatively with insecurity and anxiety.

These findings agree for the most part with my descriptions of sibling positions and with our empirical tests. Minor deviations and occasional contradictions seem to be related to the methods of study, to the relative isolation of the questions that were asked, and to the fact that it was more often children and pre-adolescents than adolescents and adults who were studied. They also seem to be related to the fact that the observation periods were relatively short and that the studies and tests focused on rather circumscribed and specific behavior and personality characteristics. It is conceivable, moreover, that different cultures such as that of Central Europe, North America, Australia, or India (where the studies reported were conducted) perceive and evaluate sibling positions in somewhat different ways. In rapidly growing populations, families are bound to have larger numbers of children. Hence, only children are more likely to be in a minority there than they are in slowly growing populations.

The effects of numbers of children were also studied. Chopra (1966) and Nisbet and Entwistle (1967) reported that the size of the family was negatively correlated with the intelligence of the child under study. However, there was no correlation between sibling rank and intelligence. Cicirelli (1967) could not confirm the negative correlation mentioned, but found higher intelligence quotients and creativity scores among those children who were very close to their siblings in age. Green, Eastman, and Adams (1966) observed a lower incidence of parapsychological phenomena, the smaller the family was to which the subject belonged.

Family constellation characteristics and mental disturbances

In another group of studies, the relationships between mental disturbances and disorders on the one hand and characteristics of   family constellation on the other were investigated.

Berman (1933) found more first-borns than persons with other sibling positions among patients suffering from psychotic depressions; Schooler (1961, 1963) found more youngest than oldest siblings among schizophrenics; Solomon and Nuttall (1967) found more oldest siblings among schizophrenics; Caudill (1963), in Japan, found more oldest sons and youngest daughters among psychotic patients than were to be expected by chance. Patterson and Zeigler (1941), Grosz and Miller (1958), and Burton and Bird (1963), however, reported a lack of clear relationships between schizophrenia and age rank among siblings, or between sex distribution among siblings or size of family. Esman, Kohn, and Nyman (1959) obtained similar findings with regard to schizophrenic children.

Some of these studies must be considered less than satisfactory on methodological grounds. The research questions, the control groups, and the numbers of cases leave something to be desired. Esman, Kohn, and Nyman draw their conclusion on the basis of the study of a total of 11 cases.

Hau and Rueppell (1966) observed that first-borns among psychosomatic patients suffered from circulatory rather than digestive and intestinal disorders; L. Müller (1967) discovered that schizophrenic patients of both sexes remained hospitalized for longer periods of time when they had sisters very close to them in age; Eisenman (1966) learned that first-borns spoke more in group-therapy sessions, but were also more anxious, than later-borns.

Martensen-Larsen (1956, 1957a, 1963) found that alcoholics (in Scandinavia) were youngest brothers, and mostly of older sisters, more often than chance. Their wives were usually older than they themselves. Losses of parents, particularly of fathers, played a part. Among the grandparents of alcoholics, matches of two oldest siblings were unusually frequent, while matches of youngest siblings were rare. Female alcoholics were often surrounded by next-older and next-younger sisters, as were their mothers and even their grandmothers. If they had lost a parent, it was always the father. In an American sample of alcoholics, Smart (1963) noticed that they came from relatively large families. Youngest siblings were no more frequent than other sibling positions.

Shield and Grigg (1944) reported a connection between criminality and extreme sibling positions. Mukherjee and Kundu (1961) found a large number of middle siblings among male (Indian) prisoners, and Berg (1967) found an overrepresentation of first- or early-borns among problem boys. O'Kelly observed that sexually delinquent girls often had unstable mothers and disturbed relations with their fathers, but during their childhood they had had relatively calm relations with their mothers. Young female thieves had often lost their mothers.

Among neurotic outpatients, the ones who complained about pain more frequently and persistently than others were the ones who had above average numbers of siblings (Gonda 1962). Only children were more frequently found among mentally disturbed (American) soldiers than among healthy soldiers. If the mentally disturbed soldiers came from families of five or more children, they were oldest or youngest siblings significantly more often than by chance. Patients with good prognoses, married patients, and married soldiers had more siblings, on the average, than patients with poor prognoses, unmarried patients, or unmarried healthy soldiers. Married patients who were cured had younger brothers more often than by chance (Vogel & Lauterbach 1963).

In a literature study of different ethnic contexts Fox (1962) found that the intensity of heterosexual attraction among adolescents who had grown up together was negatively correlated with the intensity of their prepuberty heterosexual contacts. Fox felt that this confirmed Westermarck's and Freud's thesis that propinquity or closeness of relatives shows an inverse relationship to the degree of incestuous behavior. This is supposedly why father-daughter incest is relatively more frequent than mother-son incest.

Davies (1963) reported that more than 25% of a sample of feebleminded children came from incomplete families, that the mothers of these children were older at the time of their births than average mothers were, and that the children themselves were frequently youngest siblings. Relations between their mothers and the mother's parents were often disturbed (Clarke & Davies 1963).

Homosexuals of both sexes came from monosexual sibling configurations more often than by chance. This even held true of the sibling configurations of their fathers and grandfathers. Only children and youngest siblings were overrepresented among male homosexuals, oldest sisters and youngest sisters among female homosexuals. The latter had lost their fathers more often than they had their mothers (Martensen-Larsen 1957b). Gundlach and Riess (1967) found that more lesbian women were only children and oldest siblings than would be expected by chance.

Gray (1960) used projective tests of the effects of sibling positions. An elaborate but more complicated projective test of family relations has been devised by Howells and Lickorish (1967). Wasilewski-Flierl (1973) has standardized this test for Germany. The reader should keep in mind, however, that the very advantage of family constellation data is their objectivity, their high reliability, and the fact that, given careful collection and thoughtful interpretation, these data tend to be more informative than projective tests, or other psychological tests and more informative than many combinations of both.

Discussion

The reported studies of effects of family constellations have, for the most part, selected certain aspects without regard to their relation to other aspects. The results are not always impressive, but all of them seem to confirm that characteristics of family constellations do influence and differentiate behavior modes, social attitudes, and personality traits. Bowlby may have provided the most comprehensive study, comparatively speaking, but he failed in part to ask what caused those disruptions and neglects in the families studied, which, in turn, determine the psychopathology and delinquency of the children. Only Martensen-Larsen went beyond sibling positions and the immediate effects of losses of family members. He included the parents and even the grandparents in his studies.

In our own research, family constellations were viewed as systems that are influenced by the preceding generation and interact with the subsequent generation. This systems approach has proven so useful that it should probably be given preference over any segment approach and any research on isolated aspects. System approaches have also proven successful in related fields, especially in sociological studies of the family and marriage. Terman (1938), Landis and Landis (1948), Hollingshead (1950), Parsons (1951), Parsons and Bales (1955), Winch and McGinnis (1953), Winch (1963), Bossard and Böll (1956), Burgess, Locke, and Thomes (1963), Kirkpatrick (1963), Goode (1964), Nimkoff (1963), Williamson (1966), as well as König (1946, 1965), Schelsky (1954), Wurzbacher (1958, 1960, 1968), and Rosenmayr and Köckeis (1965) merit mention. In the area of family pathology and family therapy, Bowen (1960) and Ackerman (1961) should be remembered. U. Moser offers an expanded psychoanalytic approach (1965).

I am certain that this book is not the final word regarding research on family life and on the construction of a theory of family constellations. Many additional studies are needed in order to clarify issues. Systematic documentation in psychotherapy, education, guidance, and social work is expected to be the most valuable source of data. Workers in those fields already probe into family life and family relations, and they could easily add a little rigor and system to the methods of their work and to their evaluations. As a matter of fact, they ought to document their work in any case in order to keep an account of what they have done as psychotherapists, educators, or social workers. Without such documentation, the traces of one's own activities vanish rapidly and constantly into the infinite past. Only implicit and vague memory images may be retained, and these are neither sufficient for research or teaching nor even for continued practical work. With explicit records of family data, however, which are probably among the simplest and most relevant data of clinical psychology, one can keep a hold on one's cases. One can look them up, feed them into a computer, and sort them, count them, and have any number of interrelationships tested within seconds.

This work of documentation can be entrusted to psychotherapy, education, guidance, and social work for a special reason: These disciplines deal with the real and serious psychological problems of their clients. The psychotherapist, educator, and social worker keeps in touch with real life, with fate and family histories. Those researchers, on the other hand, who go into the laboratory or into the field with isolated theoretical questions, usually ask their clients what is of interest to the researcher, but not what moves the client. For this reason they often reap much more ephemeral and unstable data, which have little meaning for their clients. The special kind of fleeting contact with a client that such research is able to establish enters as a considerable source of error. This even applies for the recording of past events that are thought to be impervious to distortions due to forms of inquiry or biases of the interviewer. The clients' recollection can be swayed by such influences.

The objective data of family constellations that we have

used and recommended, however, seem to be stable and reliable in almost any kind of examination. Moreover, clients usually like to report them. Many of them enjoy the fact that someone is interested in them and in their families. Incidentally, this is precisely what is requested of the researcher. He must indeed be interested in the client and in his family. Otherwise the client may become suspicious, reluctant, or leave.

16.   Securing Data on
         Family Constellations

The following guide is recommended for use in research requiring data about family constellations. The order in which the data are collected is irrelevant. In fact, the client should be given as much freedom as he wants in telling about himself and his family. The researcher must be careful in seeing that none of the data is omitted. In order to achieve a complete record, a little more than the usual attention may be needed, but after a little practice this becomes routine. A few data collections with the help of this guide will soon render it redundant and superfluous.

Guide for Securing Data

The person questioned and, if married, the person's spouse, should give information about the following data:

1.   Date and place of interview. Name of the investigator.
— All further references concern the person interviewed.

2.   First name and surname (maiden name, pseudonym), sex, date (or at least year) and place of birth. Current address, previous residences, current profession, previous professions (including time periods expressed in calendar years), marital status (single, married, widowed, separated, divorced, remarried), duration of marriage in calendar years (e.g. 1968-1970, or 1960-present), duration of previous marriages (expressed in calendar years).

3.   The following data should be secured about a person's children (including any deceased children): First name, sex, year of birth, year of death— stepchildren can be indicated by (st). Marital status of a child, duration of marriage in calendar years, duration of previous marriages in calendar years; if marriage was terminated by death of spouse, indicate deceased by (+). Number of children that each child has had, or at least total number of children that all the children have had. Indicate deceased children by (+), or at least give the number of deceased children.

4.   The following data should be secured about a person's siblings (including half-, step- and deceased siblings): First name, sex, year of birth, year of death;—half-siblings can be indicated by (h), step-siblings by (st). Marital status, duration of marriage in calendar years, duration of previous marriages in calendar years; if marriage was terminated by death of spouse, indicate deceased by (+). Number of children that each sibling has had, or at least total number of children that all siblings have had. Indicate deceased children by (+), or at least give number of deceased children.

5.   The following data should be secured about a person's father and mother: First and surname (maiden name, pseudonym), (approximate) year and place of birth, current residence, current or latest profession, previous professions, duration of marriage in calendar years, duration of previous marriages in calendar years, death years of parents. These data should also be secured for stepparents. The parents' siblings

should be recorded as in paragraph 4. If that is not possible, their age relations to the respective parents should at least be noted; whether he or she is (has been) married and has had at least one child should also be noted. If possible, give the total number of children that all of each parent's siblings have had.

6. The following data should be secured about a person's four grandparents: (approximate) year and place of birth, (approximate) death year, approximate duration of their marriage in calendar years. Grandparents who were married to other spouses before or after should be designated by (x).

7. Schools attended by the person being interviewed as full-time student, including length of attendance in calendar years. Evening schools or once-a-week schools may be omitted. At least indicate the number of schools that the person has attended.

8. Hospitalizations that the person being interviewed has experienced (indicating times in calendar years). Number of hospitalizations, longest hospitalization (in weeks). Total time spent in hospitals before the person's 16th birthday (in weeks).

9. Number of (different) residences while the person was still living with his parents; age of the person when he left the parental household; number of residences occupied since then. Current residence of parents, siblings, children, including the approximate geographic distances in miles.

10. A few further suggestions: An unmarried couple living together should be considered as if they were married. A missing person should be considered as if he were dead. If a person has had step- or foster-parents, the data asked about parents should also be secured about them. In that case, indicate in calendar years when the person has lived with his natural parents and when with his step- or foster parents.

Finally, as a reminder: all these data should also be secured of a person's present spouse and of previous spouses, if any.

Should a person express uncertainty about any of these data, he or she should be encouraged to guess as best he can. The interviewer himself may also try to make the best estimate, if objective accuracy is not possible. Every opportunity to check the given information should be utilized. The person being interviewed should be assured of strict confidentiality.

Epilogue

A note of caution is in order. When talking to or interviewing friends, colleagues, or relatives the reader should proceed with tact and sensitivity. It is even more important that he or she should not make any great pronouncements about his psychological analyses of the family relations of the individuals concerned. He should guard against exuberant or shaking predictions. For the most part, people are grateful for a chance to talk about themselves and their families, but they become annoyed if they recognize a surreptitious purpose behind the interviewer's interest. If the reader wants to prove something to somebody by his knowledge of the rules and principles of family constellation effects, if he uses it in order to win a person's favor or in order to intimidate the person, perhaps to vindicate himself in some way, he should not be surpised to find little gratitude in return.

Whoever among the readers has begun to worry about himself and about his current personal relationships should feel assured that he needs neither to get a divorce nor to break up his friendships, that he will not have to sue his parents or change his profession, his philosophy of life, or his children, and that he need not return to his first love just because my books seem to imply it. The reader should be aware that he has always acted by the rules and principles governing family constellations and family relationships, indeed long before this book brought them to his attention. Before he (or she) begins to wonder what he should do differently in the future, he owes himself (or herself) an attempt to explain why he (or she) has done things so far the way he (she) did. If he can explain some of it on the basis of the principles of family constellation effects, he is in a better position than if he were to literally adopt the implications and recommendations in this book as they seem to fit on the surface. If he had been bothered all along, however, by problems and conflicts with himself and with others, and if he is unhappy about this situation, this book can probably offer him a few clues to better understanding his own life situation.

If a reader feels he cannot escape the fate of his family constellation and he resigns himself to it, he is mistaken. The principles of family constellation effects are but one portion of those principles that govern human behavior in general. Some family constellations may be quite pronounced, but even then their effects are not absolutely compelling. The reader may be assured, though, that knowledge of these principles would not reduce or destroy his freedom, but rather enhance it. With his knowledge he can play a better game of life than without it. He may be able to transform his personal relationships a little, enter new relationships with greater caution, and move away in small steps from what he feels is his fate. He is free to do that. Should he, however, try to move away in giant steps or even do the very opposite of what he has been used to in his original family, he may fail. If he knows the principles, he also knows the limits of his freedom. This, in itself, *is* greater freedom.

BIBLIOGRAPHY

Ackerman, N. W. et al. (Ed.). *Exploring base for family therapy.* Family Service Association of America, 1961.

Adler, A. *Praxis und Theorie der Individualpsychologie.* Munich: Bergmann, 1920.

_____. *Understanding human nature* (1929). New York: Greenberg. 1946.

_____. *What life should mean to you.* New York: Allen and Unwin, 1931.

_____. *Der Sinn des Lebens.* Vienna, Leipzig: Passer, 1933.

Alexander, C. N. Ordinal position and sociometric status. *Sociometry,* 1966, *29,* 41-51.

Altus, W. D. Birth order and academic primogeniture. *J. Pers. and Soc. Psychol.,* 1965a, *2,* 872-876.

_____. Birth order and its sequelae. *Science,* 1965b, *151,* 44-49.

Andry, R. G. Faulty paternal and maternal child relationships, affection and delinquency. *Brit. J. Delinqu.,* 1957, *8,* 34-48.

Ansbacher, H. L. and Ansbacher, Rowena R. *The individual psychology of Alfred Adler.* New York: Basic Books, 1956.

Archibald, H. C., Bell, Dorothy, Miller, Christine, and Tuddenham, R. D. Bereavement in childhood and adult psychiatric disturbance. *Psychosom. Med.,* 1962, *24,* 343-351.

311

Badami, H. D. A psychological study of some factors of juvenile delinquency. *Educ. Psychol. Rev.*, *Baroda*, 1962, *2*, 101-106.

Bauer, Jutta. Die Milieuabhängigkeit der Schulreife unter besonderer Berücksichtigung der Theorie der Familienkonstellation. Unpubl. dissertation, Univ. Erlangen-Nürnberg, 1967.

Baxter, J. C. Parental complementarity and parental conflict. *J. Indiv. Psychol.*, 1965, *2*, 149-153.

Bayer, A. E. Birth order and college attendance. *J. Marriage and Family*, 1966, *28*, 480-484.

Becher, Sigrun-Heide. Der Einfluß der Familienkonstellation auf die Verwahrlosung Jugendlicher. Unpubl. dissertation, Univ. Erlangen-Nürnberg, 1967.

Belmont, Lillian and Marolla, Francis A. Birth order, family size and intelligence. *Science*, 1973, *182*, 1096-1101.

Berg, I. et al. Birth order and family size of approved school boys. *Brit. J. Psychiat.*, 1967, *113*, 793-800.

Bergler, R. *Kinder aus gestörten und unvollständigen Familien.* Weinheim and Berlin: Beltz, 1955.

Berman, H. H. Order of birth in manic-depressive reactions. *Psychiat. Quart.*, *1933*, 7, 430-435.

Bernhöft, G. Untersuchung eines möglichen Zusammenhangs zwischen Familienkonstellation und der Übernahme von Führerrollen in Jugendgruppen. Unpubl. dissertation, Univ. Erlangen-Nürnberg, 1967.

Birtchnell, J. Early parent death and mental illness. *Brit. J. Psychiat.*, 1970, *116*, 281 ff.

———. Early parent death in relation to sibship size and composition in psychiatric patients and general population controls. *Acta Psychiat. Scand.*, 1971, *47*, 50 ff.

———. Early parent death in psychiatric diagnosis. *Soc. Psychiat.*, 1972, 7, 202 ff.

Borkholder, Ursula. Familienkonstallation und der multiple Einstellungstest von Toman. Unpubl. dissertation, Univ. Erlangen-Nürnberg, 1966.

Bossard, J. H. S. and Böll, Eleanor S. *The large family system: An original study in the sociology of family behavior.* Philadelphia: University of Pennsylvania Press, 1956.

Bowen, M. Family concept of schizophrenia. In: *Etiology of schizophrenia* (Ed.: Jackson, D. D.). New York: Basic Books, 1960.

Bowlby, J. *Maternal care and mental health.* London: World Health Organization, 1951.

Brandenburg, H. H. Umwelt und Verwahrlosung. Unpubl. dissertation, Univ. Erlangen-Nürnberg, 1956.

Brill, N. Q. and Liston, E. H. Parental loss in adults with emotional disorders. *Arch. Gen. Psychiat.*, 1960, *14*, 307-314.

Brown, F. Depression and childhood bereavement. *J. Ment. Sci.*, 1961, *107*, 754-777.

Bruhn, J. G. Broken homes among attempted suicides and psychiatric out-patients. *J. Ment. Sci.*, 1962, *108*, 772-779.

Burgess, E. W., Locke, J. H., and Thomes, Mary M. *The family from institution to companionship.* 3rd ed. New York: American Book Co., 1963.

———— and Wallin, P. Predicting adjustment in marriage from adjustment in engagement. *Amer. J. Sociol.*, 1944, *49*, 524-530.

Burton, A. and Bird, J. W. Family constellation and schizophrenia. *J. Psychol.*, 1963, *55*, 329-336.

Caudill, W. *Social background and sibling rank among Japanese psychiatric patients.* Conf. Modernization of Japan, January, 1963.

Chopra, Sukhendra L. Family size and sibling position as related to intelligence test scores and academic achievement. *J. Soc. Psychol.*, 1966, *70*, 133-137.

Cicirelli, V. G. Sibling constellation, creativity, IQ, and academic achievement. *Child Develop.*, 1967, *38*, 481-490.

Clarke, Cecily M. and Davis, D. R. The families of mentally retarded children. *Developm. Med. Child Neurol.*, 1963, *5*, 270-286.

Cobb, S. and French, J. R., Jr. Birth order among medical students. *J.A.M.A.*, 1966, *195*, 312-313.

Damrin, Dora E. Family size and sibling age, sex, and positions as related to certain aspects of adjustment. *J. Soc. Psychol.*, 1949, *29*, 93-109.

Davies, Ch. G. The families of severely mentally retarded children: family composition and health. *Calif. J. Educ. Res.*, 1963, *14*, 121-130.

Dechêne, Ch. H. *Geschwisterkonstellation und psychische Fehlentwicklung.* Munich: Barth, 1967.

Dohrenwend, Barbara S., Feldstein, Sol, Plosky, Joyce, and Schmeidler, Gertrude R. Factors interacting with birth order in self-selection among volunteer subjects. *J. Soc. Psychol.*, 1967, *72*, 125-128.

Earle, A. M. and Earle, B. V. Early maternal deprivation and later psychiatric illness. *Amer. J. Orthopsychiat.*, 1961, *31*, 181-186.

Eberhard, K. and Kohlmetz, G. *Verwahrlosung und Gesellschaft.* Göttingen: Vandenhoek und Ruprecht, 1973.

Eisenman, R. Birth order, anxiety, and verbalizations in group psychotherapy. *J. Consult. Psychol.*, 1966, *30*, 521-526.

Erzigkeit, H. Über den Zusammenhang faktoriell aufgefaßter Persönlichkeitsdispositionen mit Identifikation, beschrieben durch den Ähnlichkeitsvergleich des semantischen Differentials. Unpubl. dissertation, Univ. Erlangen-Nürnberg, 1970.

Esman, A., Kohn, M., and Nyman, L. Parents of schizophrenic children: II. The family of the "schizophrenic" child. *Amer. J. Orthopsychiat.*, 1959, *29*, 455-459.

Fischer, A. E. Sibling relationships with special reference to the problems of the second child. *J. Pediat.*, 1952, *40*, 254-259.

Forer, Lucille, K. *Birth order and life roles.* Springfield, Ill.: Charles C. Thomas, 1969.

Fox, J. R. Sibling incest. *Brit. J. Sociol.*, 1962, *13*, 128-150.

Freud, Anna and Burlingham, Dorothy T. *War and children.* New York: Medical War Books, 1943.

Freud, S. Mourning and melancholia (1916). *The standard edition of the complete psychological works of Sigmund Freud*, vol. 14. London: Hogarth Press, 1953-1966.

_____. A general introduction to psychoanalysis (1916/17). *Stand. ed.*, vol. 15, 16.

_____. Beyond the pleasure principle (1920). *Stand ed.*, vol. 18.

_____. The ego and the id (1923). *Stand ed.*, vol. 19.

_____. The problem of anxiety (1926). *Stand. ed.*, vol. 20.

_____. New introductory lectures to psychoanalysis (1933). *Stand. ed.*, vol. 22.

_____. An outline of psychoanalysis (1938). *Stand. ed.*, vol. 23.

Freyn, W. Lehrer-Schülerverhältnis und Schulerfolg. Unpubl. dissertation, Univ. Erlangen-Nürnberg, 1974.

Gabower, Genevieve. *Behavior problems of children in navy officers'*

families: as related to social conditions of navy family life.
Washington, D.C.: Catholic Univ. of America Press, 1959.

Gardner, G. E. Separation of the parents and the emotional life of the child. *Ment. Hyg.*, 1956, *40*, 53-64.

Gasch, B. Die Familienkonstellationen von jugendlichen Strafgefangenen. Unpubl. dissertation, Univ. Erlangen-Nürnberg, 1964.

Gasch, Ulrike: Über den Zusammenhang von Identifikation und Familienkonstellation. Unpubl. dissertation, Univ. Erlangen-Nürnberg, 1967.

Gerstner, Uta: Die Abhängigkeit der Beurteilung von Menschen auf dem "semantischen Differential" von der Familienkonstellation. Unpubl. dissertation, Univ. Erlangen-Nürnberg, 1967.

Glueck, S. and Glueck, Eleanor. *Unravelling juvenile delinquency.* New York: Commonwealth Fund, 1950.

_____. *Predicting delinquency and crime.* Cambridge, Mass., Harvard University Press, 1959.

_____. *Towards a typology of juvenile offenders.* New York and London: Grune and Stratton, 1970.

Gösswein, Christel. Familienkonstellationen von unverheirateten jungen Müttern. Unpubl. dissertation, Univ. Erlangen-Nürnberg, 1968.

Gonda, Th. A. The relation between complaints of persistent pain and family size. *J. Neurol. Neurosurg. Psychiat.*, 1962, *25*, 277-281.

Goode, W. J. *The family.* New York: Prentice-Hall, 1964.

Goodenough, F. C. and Leahy, A. M. The effect of certain family relationships upon the development of personality. *Ped. Sem.*, 1927, *34*, 45-71.

Gray, B. An investigation of the family constellation as a basic determinant of personality development. Unpubl. dissertation, Brandeis Univ., 1960.

Green, C. E., Eastman, M. E., and Adams, S. T. Birth order, family size and extra-sensory perception. *Brit. J. Soc. and Clin. Psychol.*, 1966, *5*, 150-152.

Grosz, H. J. and Miller, I. Sibling patterns in schizophrenia. *Science*, 1958, *128*, 30 p.

Guilford, R. B. and Worcester, D. A. A comparative study of the only and non-only child. *J. Genet. Psychol.*, 1930, *38*, 411-426.

Gundlach, R. H. and Riess, B. F. Birth order and sex of siblings in a sample of lesbians and nonlesbians. *Psychol. Rep.*, 1967, *20*, 61-62.

Hall, Everette. Ordinal position and success in engagement and marriage. *J. Indiv. Psychol.*, 1965, *21*, 154-158.

Handschin-Ninck, Marianne. Ältester und Jüngster in Märchen. *Prax. Kinderpsychol. Kinderpsychiat.*, 1956, *7*, 167-173.

Hartmann, K. *Theoretische und empirische Beiträge zur Verwahrlosungsforschung.* Berlin: Springer, 1970.

Hau, T. F. and Rueppell, A. Zur Familienkonstellation bei psychosomatisch Erkrankten. *Zft. Psychother. med. Psychol.*, 1966, *16*, 211-219.

Heinicke, Ch. M. Some effects of separating two-year-old children from their parents: a comparative study. *Hum. Rel.*, 1956, *9*, 105-176.

Hiese, M. Übertragungsphänomene bei verwahrlosten männlichen Jugendlichen. Unpubl. dissertation, Univ. Erlangen-Nürnberg, 1964.

Hillinger, F. Introversion und Stellung in der Geschwisterreihe. *Zft. exp. angew. Psychol.*, 1958, *5*, 268-276.

v. Hintzenstern, Gisela. Schulfreundschaften und Familienkonstellation. Unpubl. dissertation, Univ. Erlangen-Nürnberg, 1975.

————. Psychologische Wirkungen von Verlusten bei Erziehungsberatungsfällen und männlichen Strafgefangenen. Unpubl. dissertation, Univ. Erlangen-Nürnberg, 1974.

Hodges, A. and Balow, B. Learning disability in relation to family constellation. *J. Educ. Res.*, 1961, *55*, 41-42.

Hoenig, Charlotte. Die Stiefelternfamilie. *Zft. Kinderforsch.*, 1929, *35*, 187-331.

Hollingshead, A. B. Cultural factors in the selection of marriage mates. *Amer. Sociol. Rev.*, 1950, *15*, 619-627.

Hooker, H. F. The study of the only child at school. *J. Genet. Psychol.*, 1931, *39*, 122-236.

Howells, J. G. and Lickorish, J. R. *Family relations indicator (Manual).* Edinburgh, London: Oliver and Boyd, 1967.

Hull, C. L. *Principles of behavior.* New York: Appleton, 1943.

Jung, C. G. *Wandlungen und Symbole der Libido.* Leipzig, Vienna: Deuticke, 1912.

————. *The psychology of the unconscious.* New York: Moffat Yard, 1916.

————. *Psychological types.* New York: Harcourt, Brace 1923.

————. *The integration of personality.* New York, Toronto: Farrar Rinehart, 1939.

Kassel, H. Geschwisterkonstellation und gegengeschlechtliche Freundschaften. Unpubl. thesis, Univ. Erlangen-Nürnberg, 1962.

Katzenstein, Betti. Einfluß von Geschlecht, Lebensepoche und Stellung in der Geschwisterreihe auf das Aufsuchen einer psychologischen Beratungsstelle in Brasilien. *Zft. Kinderpsychiatrie*, 1957, *24*, 42-48.

Keller, R. Determinanten der Familienkonstellation in ihren Beziehungen zu aggressiven Verhaltensweisen. Unpubl. dissertation, Univ. Erlangen-Nürnberg, 1964.

Kemper, T. D. Mate selection and marital satisfaction according to sibling type of husband and wife. *J. Marriage Family Living*, 1966, *28*, 346-349.

Kirkpatrick, C. *The family as process and institution*. 2nd ed. New York: Ronald Press, 1963.

Klackenberg, G. Studies in maternal deprivation in infants' homes. *Acta paediatr. Stockholm.* 1956, *45*, 1-12.

Koch, Helen L. Some personality correlates of sex, sibling position, and sex of sibling among five- and six-year-old children. *Genet. Psychol. Monogr.*, 1955a, *52*, 3-50.

_____. The relation of certain family constellation characteristics and the attitudes of children towards adults. *Child Developm.*, 1955b, *26*, 13-40.

_____. Children's work attitudes and sibling characteristics. *Child Developm.*, 1956a, *27*, 289-310.

_____. Children's attitudes toward their peers as related to certain characteristics of their siblings. *Psychol. Monogr.*, 1956b, *70*, (19), No. 426.

_____. Some emotional attitudes of the young child in relation to characteristics of his siblings. *Child Developm.*, 1956c., *27*, 393-426.

_____. Sibling influence on children's speech. *J. Speech. Dis*, 1956d, *21*, 322-328.

_____. Sissiness and tomboyishness in relation to sibling characteristics. *J. Genet. Psychol.*, 1956e, *88*, 231-244.

_____. Der Einfluß der Geschwister auf die Persönlichkeitsentwicklung jüngerer Knaben. *Jb. Psychol. Psychother.* 1958, *5*, 211-225.

_____. The relation of certain formal attributes of siblings to attitudes held toward each other and toward their parents. *Monogr. Soc. Res. Child Developm.*, 1960, *25*, (4), No. 78.

König, K. *Brüder und Schwestern*. Stuttgart: Klotz, 1964.

König, R. *Materialien zur Soziologie der Familie*. Bern: Francke, 1946.

———. *Soziologische Orientierungen*. Cologne: Kiepenheuer und Witsch, 1965.

Kort, Helga. Familienkonstellationen von einer Gruppe endogener Depressionen. Unpubl. dissertation, Univ. Erlangen-Nürnberg, 1967.

Krout, M. H. Typical behavior patterns in 26 ordinal positions. *J. Genet. Psychol.*, 1939, *55*, 3-30.

Kurz, Charlotte. Über die Identifikation zwischen Eltern und Kindern auf Grund ihrer Familienkonstellation und ihre Auswirkungen auf die Erziehbarkeit. Unpubl. dissertation, Univ. Erlangen-Nürnberg, 1969.

Landis, J. T. and Landis, M. G. *Building a successful marriage*. New York: Prentice-Hall, 1948.

Langenmayr, A. Der Einfluß der Familienkonstellation auf die Urteilsbildung im sozialen Kraftfeld. Unpubl.dissertation, Univ. Erlangen-Nürnberg, 1966.

Lasko, J. K. Parent behavior toward first and second children. *Genet. Psychol. Monogr.*, 1954, *49*, 97-137.

Levinger, G. and Sonnheim, M. Complementarity in marital adjustment: reconsidering Toman's family constellation hypothesis. *J. Indiv. Psychol.*, 1965, *21*, 137-145.

Levy, J. A quantitative study of behavior problems in relation to family constellation. *Amer. J. Psychiat.*, 1931, *10*, 637-654.

de Lint, J. Note on birth order and intelligence test performance. *J. Psychol.*, 1967, *66*, 15-17.

Locke, H. J. *Predicting adjustment in marriage. A comparison of a divorced and a happily married group*. New York: Henry Holt, 1951.

Löhr, G. Widererkennen von Geschwistern an Hand von spontan selbstverfaßten Charakterbildern bei Jugendlichen. Unpubl. dissertation, Univ. Erlangen-Nürnberg, 1966.

Lösel, F. Eine Delinquenzbelastungsskala für männliche Jugendliche. Research report, Sonderforschungsbereich 22, Univ. Erlangen-Nürnberg, 1973.

——— Dillig, P., Wüstendörfer, W., and Linz, P. Über Zusammenhänge zwischen Merkmalen der sozialen Umwelt und der Kriminalitätsbelastung jugendlicher Straftäter. Research report, Sonderforschungsbereich 22, Univ. Erlangen-Nürnberg, 1974.

Lompa, N. Der Einfluß von Familienkonstellationen auf die Leistungsmotivation mit ihren Grundrichtungen "Hoffnung auf Erfolg" und

"Furcht vor Mißerfolg." Unpubl. dissertation, Univ. Erlangen-Nürnberg, 1967.

Lorenz, K. Die angeborenen Formen möglicher Erfahrung. *Zft. Tierpsychol.*, 1943, 5, Heft 2.

_____. *Zur Naturgeschichte der Aggression: Das sogenannte Böse.* Vienna: Borotha-Schoeler, 1963.

Lynn, D. B. and Sawrey, W. F. The effects of father-absence on Norwegian boys and girls. *J. Abn. Soc. Psychol.*, 1959, *59*, 258-262.

Martensen-Larsen, O. Family constellation analysis and male alcoholism. *Acta. Psychiat. Neurol. Scand. Supp.*, 1956, 106, 241-247.

_____. The family constellation analysis and alcoholism. *Acta Genet. Statist. Medica*, 1957 a, 7, 441-444.

_____. The family constellation and homosexualism. *Acta Genet. Statist. Medica*, 1957 b, 7, 445-446.

_____. Kann der Unterschied in der Familienkonstellation der Alkoholiker, Epileptiker und Schizophrenen psychodynamische Ursachen enthüllen? *Acta Psychiat. Scand.*, 1963, *39*, Supp. 169, 193-196.

Maxwell, J. and Pilliner, A. E. G. The intellectual resemblance between sibs. *Ann. Hum. Genet.* 1960, *24*, 23-32.

McArthur, Ch. Personalities of first and second children. *Psychiatry*, 1956, *19*, 47-54.

McNemar, Q. Special review of Newman, Freeman and Holzinger's "Twins: A study of heredity and environment." *Psychol. Bull.*, 1938, *35*, 237-249.

Monahan, T. P. Broken homes by age of delinquent children. *J. Soc. Psychol.*, 1960, *51*, 387-397.

Moran, G. Ordinal position and approval motivation. *J. Consult. Psychol.*, 1967, *31*, 319-320.

Morgenstern, J. J. Socio-economic factors in stuttering. *J. Speech Hear. Dis.*, 1956, *21*, 25-33.

Moser, T. *Jugendkriminalität und Gesellschaftsstruktur.* Frankfurt: Suhrkamp, 1970.

Moser, U. *Die Psychologie der Partnerwahl.* 2nd ed. Bern, Stuttgart: Huber, 1965.

Müller, G. Spezifische Daten der Familienkonstellation als determinierende Faktoren bei der Bildung des Anspruchsniveaus. Unpub. dissertation, Univ. Erlangen-Nürnberg, 1965.

Müller, L. Family structure and conditions of hospitalization for schizophrenia. *Community Ment. Health J.*, 1967, *3*, 125-132.

Mukherjee, K. and Kundu, S. A study of birth order and family positions of the criminals. *Indian J. Psychol.*, 1961, *36*, 127-132.

Murdoch, P. H. Birth order and age at marriage. *Brit. J. Soc. Clin. Psychol.*, 1966, *5*, 24-29.

Naess, Siri. Mother separation and delinquency: further evidence. *Brit. J. Criminol,* 1962, *2*, 361-374.

Neumann, J. von, and Morgenstern, O. *Theory of games and economic behavior.* Princeton: Princeton University Press, 1947.

Newman, H. H., Freeman, F. N., and Holzinger, K. H. *Twins: A study of heredity and environment.* Chicago: University of Chicago Press, 1937.

Nimkoff, M. F. *Comparative family system.* Boston: Houghton Mifflin, 1963.

Nisbet, J. D. and Entwistle, N. J. Intelligence and family size, 1949-1965. *Brit. J. Educ. Psychol.*, 1967, *37*, 188-193.

Oberlander, M. and Jenkin, Noel. Birth order and academic achievement. *J. Indiv. Psychol.*, 1967, *23*, 103-109.

O'Kelly, Elisabeth. Some observations on relationships between delinquent girls and their parents. *Brit. J. Med. Psychol.*, 1955, *28*, 59-66.

————. An investigation by means of Object Relation Test into some of the effects of early separation from the mother on the personal relationships of adolescent delinquent girls. *J. Ment. Sci.*, 1957, *103*, 381-391.

Osgood, C. E., Suci, G. J., and Tannenbaum, P. H. *The measurement of meaning.* Urbana: University of Illinois Press, 1957.

Oswald, W. D. Untersuchung der Abhängigkeit dominanten Verhaltens von speziellen prägenden Faktoren der kindlichen Umwelt. Unpubl. dissertation, Univ. Erlangen-Nürnberg, 1963.

Parsons, T. *The social system.* Glencoe, Ill.: The Free Press, 1951.

———— and Bales, R. F. *Family, socialization and interaction process.* New York: The Free Press and Collier-Macmillan, 1955.

Patterson, R. M., and Zeigler, T. W. Ordinal position and schizophrenia. *J. Psychiat.*, 1941, *98*, 455-458.

Rosenberg, B. G., and Sutton-Smith, B. Sibling association, family size, and cognitive abilities. *J. Genet. Psychol.*, 1966, *109*, 271-279.

———— Sutton-Smith, B., and Griffiths, Judith. Sibling differences in empathic style. *Percept. Mot. Skills*, 1965, *21*, 811-814.

Rosenfeld, H. Relationships of ordinal position to affiliation and achievement motives: Direction and generality. *J. Personality*, 1966, *34*, 467-479.

Rosenmayr, J., and Köckeis, Eva. *Umwelt und Familie alter Menschen.* Neuwied, Berlin: Luchterhand, 1965.

Rosenow, C. The incidence of first-born among problem children. *J. Genet. Psychol.*, 1930, *37*, 145-151.

Rouman, J. School children's problems as related to parental factors. *Understanding the Child*, 1955, *24*, 50-53.

Sampson, E. E., and Hancock, Francena T. An examination of the relationship between ordinal position, personality, and conformity: An extension, replication, and partial verification. *J. Personal. Soc. Psychol.*, 1967, *5*, 398-407.

Schachter, S. *The psychology of affiliation.* Stanford, Calif.: Stanford University Press, 1959.

_____. Birth order, eminence and higher education. *Amer. Sociol. Rev.*, 1963, *28*, 757-767.

_____. Birth order and sociometric choice. *J. Abn. Soc. Psychol.*, 1964, *68*, 453-456.

Schelsky, H. *Die Wandlungen der Deutschen Familie in der Gegenwart.* Stuttgart: Enke, 1954.

Schiller, Dagmar. Untersuchung eines möglichen Zusammenhangs zwischen der Geschwisterposition und verschiedenen Daten zur Berufswahl. Unpubl. dissertation, Univ. Erlangen-Nürnberg, 1966.

Schooler, C. Birth order and schizophrenia. *Arch. Gen. Psychiat.* 1961, *4*, 91-97.

_____. *Birth order and hospitalization for schizophrenia.* National Institute of Mental Health Report, 1963.

Schoonover, Sarah M. The relationships of intelligence and achievement to birth order, sex of sibling and age interval. *J. Educ. Psychol.*, 1959, *50*, 143-146.

Schott, F. Untersuchungen über Freundschaften männlicher Studenten, besonders vom Aspekt der Theorie der Familienkonstellation her betrachtet. Unpubl. dissertation, Univ. Erlangen-Nürnberg, 1966.

Schraml, W. Zum Problem der frühen Mutter-Kind-Trennung. *Prax. Kinderpsychol. Kinderpsychiat.*, 1954, *3*, 234-249.

Sears, R. R. Ordinal position in the family as a psychological variable. *Amer. Sociol. Rev.*, 1950, *15*, 397-401.

322 Bibliography

Shannon, L. W. Scaling juvenile delinquency. *J. Res. in Crime and Delinquency*, 1968, 5, 52-63.

Shield, J. A., and A. E. Grigg. Extreme ordinal position and criminal behavior. *J. Crim. Law and Criminol.*, 1944, 35, 169-173.

Sinha, J. B. Birth order and sex differences in n-Achievement and n-Affiliation. *J. Psychol. Res.*, 1967, 11, 22-27.

Skiba, Antje. Versuch der Erfassung von Erziehungsstilen von Müttern schulpflichtiger Kinder auf Grund der systematischen Retrospektion Unpubl. dissertation, Univ. Erlangen-Nürnberg, 1968.

Skodak, M., and Skeels, H. M. A final follow-up of one hundred adopted children. *J. genet. Psychol.*, 1949, 75, 3-19.

Smart, R. G. Alcoholism, birth order and family size. *J. Abn. Soc. Psychol.*, 1963, 66, 17-23.

Sodhi, K. S. Sozialpsychologie. In: Rohracher und Meili: *Lehrbuch der experimentellen Psychologie*. Bern, Stuttgart: Huber, 1963.

Solomon, L., and Nuttall, R. Sibling order, premorbid adjustment and remission in schizophrenia. *J. Nerv. Ment. Dis.*, 1967, 144, 37-46.

Spitz, R. A. Hospitalism. An inquiry into the genesis of psychiatric conditions in early childhood. *Psychoanalytic Study of the Child*. Vol. 1. New York: Internat. Universities Press, 1945.

———— and Wolf, Käthe. Anaclitic depression. An enquiry into the genesis of psychiatric conditions in early childhood. *Psychoanalytic Study of the Child*. Vol. 2. New York: Internat. Universities Press, 1946.

Stagner, R., and Katzoff, E. T. Personality as related to birth order and family size. *J. Appl. Psychol.*, 1936, 20, 340-346.

Stark, S. Symptom und Geschwisterposition im Spiegel einer Verhaltensbeobachtung. *Prax. Kinderpsychol. Kinderpsychiat.*, 1962, 11, 177-187.

Stephens, W. N. Judgments by social workers on boys and mothers in fatherless families. *J. Genet. Psychol.*, 1961, 99, 59-64.

Stevens, S. S. Mathematics, measurement and psychophysics. In S. S. Stevens (ed.): *Handbook of experimental psychology*. New York: Wiley, 1951.

Sullivan, H. S. *The interpersonal theory of psychiatry*. New York: Norton, 1953.

Sutton-Smith, B., and Rosenberg, B. G. *The sibling*. New York: Holt, Rinehart and Winston, 1970.

Terman, L. M. *Psychological factors in marital happiness.* New York: McGraw-Hill, 1938.

Tinbergen, N. *The study of instincts.* London: Oxford University Press, 1951.

Toman, W. The multiple attitude test: A diagnostic device. *J. Abn. Soc. Psychol.,* 1955, *51,* 163-170.

———. Repetition and repetition compulsion. *Int. J. Psychoanalysis,* 1956, *37,* 347-350.

———. A general formula for the quantitative treatment of human motivation. *J. Abn. Soc. Psychol.,* 1959a, *58,* 91-99.

———. Die Familienkonstellation und ihre psychologische Bedeutung. *Psychol. Rundschau,* 1959b, *10,* 1-15.

———. Family constellation as a basic personality determinant. *J. Indiv. Psychol.,* 1959c, *15,* 199-211.

———. Family constellation as a character and marriage determinant. *Int. J. Psychoanalysis,* 1959d., *40,* 316-319.

———. On the periodicity of motivation. *Nebraska Symposium on Motivation.* Jones, M. R. ed. Lincoln: University of Nebraska Press, 1960a, 80-95.

———. Haupttypen der Familienkonstellation. *Psychol. Rundschau,* 1960b, *11,* 273-284.

———. *Introduction to psychoanalytic theory of motivation.* London, New York: Pergamon Press, 1960c.

———. *Family constellation: Theory and practice of a psychological game.* New York: Springer, 1962a, 2nd rev. ed. 1969.

———. Family constellations of divorced and married couples. *J. Indiv. Psychol.,* 1962b, *18,* 48-51.

———. Large age differences among spouses and their family constellations. *Psychol. Rep.,* 1963a, *13,* 386.

———. Die prägenden Wirkungen der Geschwisterkonstellation auf den Charakter. *Zft. Psychother. mediz. Psychol.,* 1963b, *13,* 113-117.

———. Hauptmerkmale der psychologischen Umwelt des Menschen und ihre Aufschlüsselung. *Conference Report of the International Association of Correctional Medicine,* Vienna, 1963c, 159-172.

———. Choices of marriage partners by men coming from monosexual sibling configurations. *Brit. J. Medical Psychol.* 1964, *37,* 43-46.

———. *Familienkonstellationen.* Munich: Beck, 1965a. 2nd revised ed. 1974.

_____. Complementarity in marital adjustment: Comment. *J. Indiv. Psychol.*, 1965b, *21*, 146ff.

_____. *Familienkonstellationen. Schule und Psychologie*, 1966, *13*, 33-39.

_____. *Motivation, Persönlichkeit, Umwelt*. Göttingen: Hogrefe 1968.

_____. *Family constellation: Its effects on personality and social behavior*. 2nd rev. ed. New York: Springer, 1969.

_____. The 'duplication theorem' of social relationships as tested in the general population. *Psychol. Review*, 1971, *78*, 380-390.

_____. Geschwisterkonstellation und Leistungsmotivation. *Schule und Psychologie*, 1972a, *19*, 65-72.

_____. *Complementarity of sibling roles in individual friendship systems*. 20th Internat. Congress of Psychology. Tokyo, 1972b, Proceedings p. 440, Science Council of Japan, University of Tokyo Press, 1974.

_____. *Einführung in die allgemeine Psychologie*. 2 Bde. Freiburg i. Br.: Rombach, 1973a.

_____. On the extent of sibling influence. *Conference of the Society for the Study of Behavioral Development*. Ann Arbor, Mich., 1973b.

_____, and Gray, B. Family constellations of "normal" and "disturbed" marriages: An empirical study. *J. Indiv. Psychol.*, 1961, *17*, 93-95.

_____, Preiser, S., Gasch, B., and Plattig, Gerda. Die Wirkungen von Familienkonstellationen auf die Person, ihre sozialen Beziehungen und die nachfolgende Generation. Research project (1962-66), Deutsche Forschungsgemeinschaft, Bad Godesberg, 1967.

_____, Gasch, Ulrike, and Schmidt, R. Individuelle Freundschafts-systeme. Research project (1968-71), Deutsche Forschungsgemein-schaft, Bad Godesberg, 1972.

_____, and Preiser, S. *Familienkonstellationen und ihre Störungen*. Stuttgart: Enke 1973.

_____, and Toman, Eleonore. Sibling positions of a sample of distinguished persons. *Percept. Mot. Skills*, 1970, *31*, 825-826.

Vogel, W., and Lauterbach, C. G. Sibling patterns and social adjustment among normal and psychiatrically disturbed soldiers. *J. Consult. Psychol.*, 1963, *27*, 236-242.

Vuyk, Rita. *Das Kind in der Zweikinderfamilie*. Bern, Stuttgart: Huber, 1959.

_____. Eltern vergleichen ihre beiden Kinder. *Schweiz. Z. Psychol.*, 1961, *20*, 224-237.

Warren, J. R. Birth order and social behavior. *Psychol. Bull.*, 1966, *65*, 38-49.

Wasilewski-Flierl, Helga. Das Relationsgefüge der Familie unter dem Einfluß familiärer Störvariablen. Unpubl. dissertation, Univ. Erlangen-Nürnberg, 1973.

Weiss, R. L. Some determinants of emitted reinforcing behavior: Listener reinforcement and birth order. *J. Personal. Soc. Psychol.*, 1966, *3*, 489-492.

Wellhöfer, P. Untersuchung der Aggressionsrichtung und der Reaktionstypen auf alltägliche Frustrationen und deren Abhängigkeit von Daten der Familienkonstellation mit dem Rosenzweig P-F-Test. Unpubl. dissertation, Univ. Erlangen-Nürnberg, 1964.

West, S. S. Sibling configuration of scientists. *Amer. J. Sociol.*, 1960, *66*, 268-274.

Wile, I. S., and Jones, A. B. Ordinal position and the behavior disorders of young children. *J. Genet. Psychol.*, 1937, *51*, 61-93.

Williamson, R. C. *Marriage and family relations.* New York: Wiley, 1966.

Wilson, P. R., Patterson, J. R., and Lysons, A. M. Sex, birth order and volunteering behavior. *Austral. J. Psychol.*, 1966, *18*, 158-159.

Winch, R. F. *The modern family,* rev. ed. New York: Henry Holt, 1953.

Wohlford, P., and Jones, M. R. Ordinal position, age, anxiety, and defensiveness in unwed mothers. *Proc. 75th Ann. Conv. Amer. Psychol. Ass.*, 1967, *2*, 177-178.

Wolff, Sulammith. Social and family background of pre-school children with behavior disorders attending a child guidance clinic. *J. Child Psychol. Psychiat.*, 1961, *2*, 260-268.

Wuebben, P. L. Honesty of subjects and birth order. *J. Personal. Soc. Psychol.*, 1967, *5*, 350-352.

Wurzbacher, G. *Leitbilder des gegenwärtigen deutschen Familienlebens.* Stuttgart: Enke, 1958.

_____. Leistungen und Leistungsbehinderungen des Familie in der modernen Gesellschaft. In: *Schriften der Gesellschaft für sozialen Fortschritt,* vol. 12, 89-103. Berlin: Duncker und Humblot, 1960.

_____ (hsg). *Die Familie als Sozialisationsfaktor.* Stuttgart: Enke, 1968.

Zielinski, W. Schulleistung, Intelligenz und Familienkonstellation. Unpubl. dissertation, Univ. Erlangen-Nürnberg, 1966.

AUTHOR INDEX

SUBJECT INDEX